I0824886

EVIDENCE
OF THE
EXTRAORDINARY

EVIDENCE

OF THE

EXTRAORDINARY

DISCOVERIES FROM THE SERIES *THE PROOF IS OUT THERE*®

MIGUEL SANCHO

ATRIA BOOKS

New York Amsterdam/Antwerp London
Toronto Sydney/Melbourne New Delhi

An Imprint of Simon & Schuster, LLC
1230 Avenue of the Americas
New York, NY 10020

First Atria Books hardcover edition May 2026

ATRIA BOOKS and colophon are registered trademarks of Simon & Schuster, LLC

Interior design by Jill Putorti

Manufactured in the United States of America

1 3 5 7 9 10 8 6 4 2

Library of Congress Cataloging-in-Publication Data has been applied for.

ISBN 978-1-6680-8545-5
ISBN 978-1-6680-8547-9 (ebook)

To Lydia and Sebastian,

The most extraordinary beings I've ever encountered

CONTENTS

EVIDENCE
OF THE
EXTRAORDINARY

INTRODUCTION

It feels like I know you.

You're somewhere between five and seven feet tall, roughly one hundred to four hundred pounds, and you've been blessed with a custom-tailored unit of the most impressive and complicated machine in the universe, the human brain. Better yet, you're among the subset of *Homo sapiens* endowed with a sense of wonder so commanding that, for a moment at least, you've forsaken the temptations of countless high-dopamine stimuli to dip your nose into a book. A book about the unexplained, no less. You're curious, you enjoy a good mystery, and part of you *really* enjoys mysteries that can't be solved.

I knew we had something in common.

This book has been written for you. It's supposed to be fun. It is not supposed to be work. You can pick and choose which chapters to read, and you don't need to read them in order. You can agree or disagree with its findings, sneer at what it's left out, or belittle what it regards as important. The only thing you can't do is get bored. It's my job to make sure that doesn't happen.

At its core, this book is about anomalous phenomena that have been documented on video, still photography, or audio recordings. But on its deepest level it is about the human desire for answers, for adventure, and for meaning. And on its most superficial level—which also might be the most fun—it's about a TV show. Let me tell you about it.

The Proof Is Out There® series has been running on the HISTORY® network since 2021, and I'm the guy who, much to my own surprise, wound up running it. In each episode we scour the world for compelling videos of unexplained or anomalous phenomena; then with the aid of some of the world's top experts, we try to figure out what these videos have actually captured. Most of the time we solve the puzzle—a UFO turns out to be a drone; a Bigfoot turns out to be a bear. But sometimes we get stumped—not just our producers, not just the eyewitnesses, but the experts too. In short, there are some things we simply can't explain, things that provoke profound thoughts about our universe, our natural history, and our reality. As our team painstakingly forges our way to completing our one hundredth episode, we find we've worked with a treasure trove of amazing encounters, compelling images, and fascinating ideas. In short, the surprises, revelations, and laughs we've encountered along the way could fill a book. Now it's time to do just that.

A little bit about me: I've been a TV journalist for thirty years, most of those at national news networks, making a living telling tough stories about crime, fraud, politics, and war. Then I wrote a book about rare diseases and breakthrough medical treatments, based on my family's experience with our son, Sebastian. Absolutely none of this had anything to do with "the paranormal." On paper I might be the last person on earth who should be writing a book like this.

Since I started producing this show, however, the situation has changed. After five years neck-deep in the world of the unexplained,

I find that I've arrived at a peculiar place—a position of agonizing and exhilarating equipoise in the no-man's-land between two warring camps that have been locking horns for centuries: the Skeptics and the Believers.

The Skeptics reject any claims of extraterrestrial visitation, cryptozoological sightings, miracles, you name it. They're the proud "serious people" who see themselves defending the fortress of the scientific method against the barbarians at the gates: the hoaxers, the charlatans, and the pitiably misguided suckers who are little more than slaves to their own confirmation bias.

The Believers insist there is ample proof that UFOs, among other things, do exist, and claim it requires the willful blindness of an ostrich or the malevolence of a serpent to argue otherwise. Many base their beliefs not only on official reports, testimonies, empirical data, and yes, video, but on what they describe as intense, incontrovertible personal experiences that have influenced their lives profoundly.

For the first decades of my career, anyone hoping to pay a mortgage working in journalism was unofficially required to side with the Skeptics. Believers, frequently derided as newsroom "kooks," might not get fired, but they certainly did not get promoted. Then something happened. On December 16, 2017, the *New York Times* published its first story on the now-famous Pentagon UFO videos—known as "GIMBAL," "FLIR," and "GOFAST." They depicted what were classified as "Unidentified Anomalous Phenomena" (the military's current euphemism for UFOs) recorded years earlier by US Navy aviators stationed on the USS *Nimitz* and the USS *Theodore Roosevelt*. The videos—which allegedly recorded an object in the shape of a Tic Tac and another described as "a sphere encased in a cube"—were backed up by testimony from the aviators themselves, and later officially verified by the Pentagon.

Of course, none of that inhibited the Skeptics from having their say about those UAPs, which they've dismissed alternately as software malfunctions, Chinese military probes, or weather balloons. And in 2024, the Pentagon said it had in fact been able to explain one of the incidents. It didn't matter. Almost overnight, it became OK to talk about UFOs in polite company. Lengthy articles on the topic popped up in *Popular Mechanics* and the *Washington Post*. It took them till 2021 to do it, but even *60 Minutes* covered the story without derision. Decades after the "flying saucer" craze of the 1950s had been written off as a quaint Cold War relic, the twenty-first-century UFO renaissance was born, and it shows no sign of abating. The Pentagon has formed a dedicated task force to investigate UAPs, the All-domain Anomaly Resolution Office or AARO. And in the spring of 2022, Congress held the first of a series of historic UFO hearings, during which several new UAP videos have been released. The government has evolved past denying the issue to publicly acknowledging its national security implications. And for every anomalous military-grade video that gets debunked, a fresh one gets leaked: in 2025, yet another Tic Tac video, shot in the same area off the California coast as the original *Nimitz* UAP, handed the Believers another clip of ammunition.

Intrigued, I embraced the opportunity and the challenge: launching the show was an embarkation. A journey had begun—a journey that would lead us into the rogue fields of UFOlogy, cryptozoology, secret archaeology, miracle hunting, and anomalies of physics, to name a few. And as I learned, there was no shortage of compelling footage. In fact, it's become my sincere belief that of the world's 6.92 billion smartphones, at any given moment at least 2 million of them are recording video of something anomalous, at least according to the excited person holding the camera. That's how we've found stories everywhere from the bottom of the sea to the fringes of the known universe, from the Mesozoic era to the distant future. Along the way, we did what journalists are supposed to do—we listened, we gathered data, we kicked the tires on every theory we were presented, and above all, we considered whether what we thought we knew about our world might be incomplete, or in some cases, completely wrong.

The first thing one realizes when one opens one's mind to this kind of stuff is that there is actually quite a bit to know—events, places, dates, controversies, and above all people whose work and experiences form the current foundation of these bodies of knowledge. This book is designed, primarily, to give the reader an accessible and concise introduction to these curious fields, to deliver in the course of a six-hour read a fluency in the lingua franca of the unexplained that it's taken me five years to acquire. If you want to participate in an informed conversation about Bigfoot, for instance, you really need to know something about the famous Patterson-Gimlin film, anatomy professor Jeff Meldrum's theory of the midtarsal break, and the audio recordings known as the Sierra Sounds. If you want to discuss psychic powers, you really should have some familiarity with the CIA's Project Stargate, the debunking of Uri Geller, and the work of the Princeton Engineering Anomalies Research lab (PEAR).

I am at all times a journalist or documentarian, and not *the* expert here. But I am absolutely confident in this: this book will give you solid grounding in the realms of the unexplained in a hurry. And if you make it to the end, you will be well prepared to become the life of any cocktail party. Is there really any higher goal to be achieved in this world?

In a sense the book will also be a travelog, chronicling my journey into this world and my encounters with some of its most well-known figures. For as the show has endured and grown, I've become personally familiar with many of its most famous characters. I've spent several days on Skinwalker Ranch; I've gone "Bigfooting" with the man behind some of the most famous Sasquatch footage ever; I've sipped bourbon with Lue Elizondo, the original Pentagon UFO whistleblower.

These people have shown me that the world of the unexplained contains multitudes—it is a realm of journalistic inquiry; it touches on a broad swath of scientific disciplines; it is sometimes a matter of national security and defense; it can bear resemblance to the realms of spirituality and religion; and it engages numerous fields of philosophy from epistemology to metaphysics.

It is also a world hideously polluted by fakery and fraud. Seeking profit, attention, or simply their own amusement, an army of hoaxers forms a halo of flies around any truth-seeking endeavor in this space. That's why, using a high-tech arsenal of forensic analysis, we make it our business to expose them.

But a hiccup remains, and it's taken some time for me to digest this: even with our most sophisticated tools of dissection and analysis, *not everything can be explained*. Even those of us who nod our heads in agreement when we're told to "follow the science" find that in many cases "the science" leads into a dark forest where we have no bearing and no answers. At the end of our journey, we find that there is so much left to be discovered and understood, it is not only permissible but perhaps necessary to view the world of the unexplained as an ongoing theater of wonder and yes, even enchantment.

This book is a road map for that world.

Chapter 1

HOW DO YOU KNOW?

A BIGFOOT BELIEVER

Claudia Ackley was terrified. The tremolo in her voice, the intermittent stutter from the back of her throat—Jamie Lee Curtis in the last reel of *Halloween* never conveyed fear so convincingly. It had been years since the encounter, and she was calling from the safety of her home, yet the simple act of retelling had transported her back to the tension and helplessness of those shocking moments.

Her account, in brief, was this: on the evening of March 17, 2017, Ackley was hiking in California's San Bernardino Mountains with her two daughters. The girls were the first to spot what Ackley would later describe to a local news outlet as "a Neanderthal man with a lot of hair" perched in a tree about thirty feet above the ground. The creature was huge, roughly eight hundred pounds by her estimate, and despite the cuddly depictions of Sasquatch in films like *Harry and the Hendersons*, Ackley did not view this thing as benevolent. "All I'm thinking is, 'Please don't go near us, because I have my children,' " she said.

Claudia called 911. The cops dismissed her story, suggesting she'd likely seen a bear. Outraged, Claudia not only stuck by her account; she filed a lawsuit against the California Department of Fish and Wildlife for refusing to acknowledge the existence of Bigfoot and taking proper measures to protect it from the public and vice versa.

She was speaking to me in 2022 because she'd recorded several seconds of the encounter on home video. Like almost all Bigfoot sightings, the footage was mediocre, and what was actually recorded open for debate. That was fine by me—my job was to get people like Claudia to share her video and her story, put everything in front of a team of experts, and if possible determine what we were really seeing.

Claudia was willing to share her video, but she refused to go on-camera. She told me she'd spoken to the media already; she felt that the play-by-play of her experience had been covered enough. Plus, as she was already making clear, recounting those events—regardless of what she had or hadn't seen—upset her profoundly. If she was going to put herself through that, she wanted to do it in a different forum. Specifically, she wanted me to produce a show built around a group therapy session with a trauma expert treating people like her who had suffered emotionally and psychologically from their Bigfoot experience, and paid a staggering social cost to boot as friends, family, and colleagues dismissed, ridiculed, or shunned them when they tried to share what had happened.

I thought the idea might have potential. I told her I'd bounce it off the network and get back to her. She never returned my follow-up calls. In 2023 Claudia died of a heart attack at the age of fifty-one. Her lawsuit, to no one's surprise, was dead on arrival.

Despite our brief and attenuated communication, I think of Claudia semi-regularly, not because I believed her, but because *I believed she believed herself*. In a space crowded with hoaxers and publicity hounds, Claudia stood out as one of those committed, unwavering individuals who had attained a genuine and rare intellectual state when it comes to the realm of the anomalous. A state of absolute certainty.

In our everyday lives, whether we consciously work through our thought processes or not, we all arrive at this state of certainty, or at least "reasonable certainty," every time we take a deliberate action. How? Just as there are varying degrees of certainty, there are a variety of ways of achieving it—of determining what we believe to be true.

It is the business of our show to make the most confident statements we can about claims of anomalous phenomena. To maximize our own certainly before putting something on air, we employ many of these diverse "truth-finding" methods that professionals and laypeople alike have been using for centuries. A big part of being confident in what you're saying is knowing how you know. A big part of being inquisitive is thinking about thinking. We want what we say to be taken seriously, and assuming you do too, it's worth reviewing the handful of methods by which people arrive at certainty. They are not all created equal.

I KANT BELIEVE IT (. . . BUT SHOULD I?)

The eighteenth-century philosopher Immanuel Kant used the term "pure reason" to describe a kind of truth we attain using nothing but a set of givens and the rules of logic. These are things we can conclude without having to see, hear, or feel anything. This "a priori knowledge" is knowable *prior* to any observation, with no support from real-world data.

Simple examples are everywhere. You can believe me when I

say "my cat is a mammal" without observing my cat; all you have to do is accept the initial claims that I do indeed have a cat, and that all cats, definitionally, are mammals. If you accept as a given my statement "I have three children," you don't need to meet and physically count them to believe I have more than two children. The truth of the statement proceeds not from observation, but from the a priori truth that three is greater than two. All of mathematics is constructed this way, from elementary school geometry up through multivariable calculus and beyond.

"But," you might say, *"this book is about experiences and documented phenomena, the validity and interpretation of empirical evidence. Why mention a priori knowledge at all?"*

Two reasons:

One, as we shall see, there are quite a few people walking our planet right now firmly convinced of things that simply don't make sense. I'm not necessarily saying their belief systems are silly. I'm saying that *even within their own belief systems*, and even if we accept their own postulates no matter how absurd they might sound, their ensuing reasoning is illogical.

Take, for example, the popular online theory that a mysterious aircraft spotted over Wichita, Kansas, in 2016 was a secret prototype of the Navy's Avenger II aircraft, a project that was canceled in 1991.

Even if we accept that the Avenger program was never canceled, and that its development continued secretly under the Pentagon's "black budget," the logic of the theory falls apart because of an inherent contradiction: the military would never conduct a test flight of a secret aircraft in a location *where it could be observed by the public.*

And two, there is also the matter of those who make a fetish of formal logic, who don't accept the fact that strict provability is *not* the sole valid evidence of truth. These are the folks who reject the humility demanded by Hamlet's great line:

> *There are more things in heaven and earth, Horatio, than are dreamt of in our philosophy.*

(That Shakespeare guy sure could write!)

As we weigh the credibility of people's accounts—anomalous or otherwise, mind you—we must constantly ask ourselves, Does this claim make any sense? And, conversely, are our critiques of extraordinary claims grounded in *logic* or are they grounded in *prejudice*? Are we being honestly skeptical of the anomalous claim, or are we merely expressing bias against a challenge to presumptions we hold dear?

Once we confirm the foundations of everyone's abstract reasoning, it's time to step into the material world and evaluate the observable evidence.

ARE YOU EXPERIENCED?

Is there anything more real than what we experience with our five senses? The color of my floor tiles, the touch of these keys on fingers, the sound of the airplane passing overhead. If I didn't trust the veracity of these sensory inputs, reality would become quite impossible to navigate, would it not?

I'm reasonably certain the laws of physics will apply when I throw my son a football, whether or not I've studied them; I'm reasonably certain the recipient of my last email will get it soon, whether or not I know much about how the internet works (and I don't); and I'm reasonably certain the drivers in the opposite lane of traffic will not cross into mine and hit me head-on, whether or not I know if they recently chased three Hindu Kush gummies with a couple of BuzzBallz. Why? The short answer is past experience. Nothing anomalous has happened when I've done these things before, so I shouldn't expect them to happen the next time.

The trouble, as pointed out by great thinkers from Plato to the creators of the *Matrix* movies, is that our senses are not as reliable as we'd like. Not only do we often perceive our dreams as real while we're in the middle of them, but even in waking life basic perceptions turn out to be maddeningly subjective.

Anyone who wasn't living in a cave in 2015 will recall the online phenomenon known simply as "The Dress," which had the internet aflame with debate over whether a dress shown in a viral photo was white and gold, or blue and black, underscoring the sometimes-drastic differences in human color perception. That was superseded by the famous "Yanny/Laurel" phenomenon of 2018, in which the same recording was perceived by different people as the sound of two entirely different words.

This curious notion that we might all be living, to some extent, in our own individual realities has contributed to the popularity of the term "my truth." It can pose quite a challenge to those of us, like the team on *The Proof Is Out There*® series, charged with evaluating the testimony of the people who report strange phenomena. *My truth* can be so intense, so impactful, so transcendent, that for those who live through alleged anomalous events, *my truth* is not just real, but more real than even their daily reality thereafter. People can go on to reorient their whole lives around that *my truth* experience as *my truth* becomes something larger, an epiphany as powerful as Paul's on the Damascus road.

Claudia Ackley was one such person, and while it's easy—

perhaps convenient—to dismiss her as a kook, as we will soon see, many such people have been equally transformed whom we'd otherwise regard as credible, trustworthy, and responsible. These people include commercial and military pilots, Pentagon intelligence officers, and covert operatives. They speak fluently and precisely in the language of science and national security, usually with the earnest and honest mien of a Boy Scout. These are your upright citizens, who would perform well on any witness stand; the kind of guys you wouldn't mind marrying your daughter, either as groom or officiant.

But where does that leave the rest of us, the ordinary folks who weren't there, who haven't been to the mountaintop, whose perceived experiences have been consistently ordinary? On *The Proof Is Out There®* series, we listen to these wondrous accounts with respect, even hospitality. But we need more.

THE SCIENTIFIC METHOD

There are very few conveniences of the modern world for which we do not owe the scientific method a debt of thanks. The computer I'm typing on, the refrigerator from which I just retrieved my third lime La Croix of the morning, the toilet I'll be flushing shortly—none of these would exist were it not for people today and generations preceding implementing its procedures and adhering to its standards. If math is sense, science is progress.

There are various versions of the scientific method, and many important thinkers have disputed it as vulnerable to bias or mythmaking, but the basics haven't changed much at least since Francis Bacon was making the case for empiricism back in the seventeenth century: the formulation of hypotheses based on prior study of a given topic; the performance of repeatable experiments that generate observable evidence to test the hypothesis; and the analysis of the data that leads to conclusions that either confirm, modify, or disprove it. Above all, the scientific method relies on the principle of *falsifiability*, the foundational criterion that any given hypothesis must be able to be disproved through experimentation. The term came about in the 1930s in the work of philosopher and scientist Karl Popper, though it was applied long before there was a name for it.

In my short time on this planet, I've noticed that science is, strangely, a polarizing force. When they're not casually taking science for granted, people seem to actively hate it or love it. From *Frankenstein* to *Jurassic Park* to *The Social Network*, Hollywood movies traditionally demonize scientists as ego-driven misfits compelled to achieve greatness and fame through their brilliant discoveries, numb to the human wreckage their great breakthrough might leave in its wake. Those humorless geeks—they're all head, no heart.

On the other hand, there are those who don't just respect science; they worship it, and are eager to inflict severe sanctions on anyone who questions or deviates from its orthodoxies.

The science fetishists forget or willfully ignore two key points. First: in the early phases of any emerging area of research, data will be limited, and inevitably the first generation of hypotheses will be weak. Second: scientific progress itself would never happen without the pesky questioning of perceived verities and the promotion of "radical" theories that seem risible at first, only to be recategorized as "groundbreaking" after they're proved.

Sometimes that takes a while, and the innovative genius who first proposes the new theory suffers immensely for his trouble.

Among serious scientists who devote energy to "wacky" ideas like UFOs, the tragic tale of Ignaz Semmelweis has become the epitomic example.

The story goes like this: In the 1840s Semmelweis was a physician and scientist who was working in the respected Vienna General Hospital's obstetrical clinic, where pregnant women had their babies delivered in either one ward staffed by midwives, or another staffed by doctors. A strange and disturbing pattern had emerged: women who delivered in the doctors' wards were dying at three times the rate of those treated by midwives.

Semmelweis noticed that many of those same doctors were also performing postmortem examinations on corpses and hypothesized that the doctors were carrying what he called "cadaverous particles" from the morgue to the obstetric clinic. He proposed a simple solution: the doctors should wash their hands between conducting autopsies and delivering babies. When this "radical" suggestion was adopted, maternal mortality plummeted on the doctors' ward.

Nevertheless, Semmelweis' theory was widely ridiculed and ignored. He became increasingly bitter, lost his job, was committed to a lunatic asylum, and died after a vicious beatdown by the guards. More than twenty years passed before Louis Pasteur redeemed Semmelweis' name and work by presenting an adequately articulated germ theory of disease that we now all accept as not only true but obvious. How many people died unnecessarily in the interim is unknown. We do know Semmelweis himself was one of them.

Of course, not every crackpot idea is a paradigm-shifting breakthrough. Most are simply crackpot ideas. Similarly, most sightings of allegedly "anomalous" phenomena aren't truly anomalous; they are misidentified or under-identified prosaic events that, when subjected to proper scrutiny, can be properly demystified.

In mathematical probability, the likelihood of a truly anomalous event is represented as ϵ, epsilon, a nearly infinitesimal (though existent) value.

It pops up in equations like this:

$$P[|Xn-X\infty|>\epsilon]\to 0$$

Epsilon can be understood as the mathematical representation of the great astronomer Carl Sagan's famous dictum "extraordinary claims require extraordinary evidence." And as I delved into this field, I was surprised to discover that it's a phrase many current scientists actively despise. Physicist Kevin Knuth is one of many who argue that Sagan's decree contributes to a widespread problem: our epsilons are too small. We're writing the improbable almost entirely out of the equation, handcuffing us to an extreme posture of skepticism that reality does not warrant. How rare are anomalous events anyway? Even as I was in the course of working on this chapter, three historically unprecedented events have unfurled before us: Hurricane Helene wiped out a good chunk of western North Carolina; Freddie Freeman hit a walk-off grand slam to win Game 1 of the 2024 World Series for the Dodgers; and Donald Trump pulled off the most improbable political comeback since the founding of the American republic. And those are just the three that come most easily to mind.

"Black Swan" events do happen, often enough that we need to account for them. As *The Black Swan* author himself, Nassim Nicholas Taleb, has noted, every farm-raised turkey could logically conclude, based on past experience, that the turkey farmer is dedicated single-mindedly to the care and growth of the turkey population—right up till early November. The turkeys would assign a very small epsilon to the probability of their mass slaughter at the hands of their benevolent master as Thanksgiving approaches. And they'd be mistaken.

Perhaps we are looking at the world upside down—instead of expecting an "equilibrium state" of normality to be interrupted by singular anomalous events, we should approach existence as a series of anomalous events spaced out by stretches of normality. In any event, the scientific method remains the most solid means of generating truth, but it is obligated to make space, amicably and humbly, for what remains to be discovered.

LEGAL TRUTH, JOURNALISTIC TRUTH, AND "THE PROOF METHOD"

The justice system, when it works, is a marvel of truth finding. Adversarial parties present evidence from diverse sources, construct logical arguments around it, and then a jury deliberates and delivers a verdict that carries the force of law. And yet, courts acknowledge their own fallibility, and have institutionalized that acknowledgment through the appeals process. We journalists don't have the same evidentiary standards or the authority of the courts, but we aspire to truth nonetheless. We aim to tell factually accurate, narratively compelling stories, using sources as varied as official documents, published research, computer-assisted data analysis, individual testimonies provided through on the record interviews, the firsthand observations of the journalists themselves, and audio/video recordings and photos. When it's done well, journalism performs a crucial function—taking important information that was either suppressed or unnoticed and giving it merited public attention. When it's done badly, which is often, journalism is little more than gossip. As Paul Newman noted in my favorite journalism movie, *Absence of Malice*, "You don't write the truth. You write what people say."

To deliver something better than "what people say," we're supposed to have standards such as independent, contemporaneous attestation from multiple sources. You can get closer to the truth that way, right? But for us TV journalists, there's no source as trustworthy, nor any catnip more stimulating, than video evidence. It's irresistibly compelling in a visual medium, and it's potent ammunition in the fight for truth. A twofer!

Video evidence has become so closely associated with our common understanding of truth, we often don't believe something really happened *unless* it was captured on video. This parallels a development in criminal law sometimes known as "the CSI effect" regarding DNA evidence. Harking back to my early days in journalism, O.J. Simpson was found not guilty, the verdict derived in part from the jury's suspicions about DNA evidence, which was new and not widely understood at the time. Fast-forward thirty years, with popular TV shows like *CSI* leading the charge, and the culture has done a 180. Now prosecutors often tell me that if they *don't* have rock-solid DNA evidence tying defendants to the crime, the jury will perform intellectual acrobatics to keep reasonable doubt aloft, whether that doubt is reasonable or not.

But our faith in video, however fervent, can be misguided. We're well aware that CGI and deep fakes are all over the internet, an issue that will get worse, perhaps exponentially, as AI elevates the capabilities of digital manipulation to dizzying heights. The bad actors are bad enough. But even when no one is intentionally trying to deceive us, our own eyes often can, and do. Optical illusions such as the parallax effect, natural illusions like fata morgana mirages, and technical illusions such as the artifacting that occurs with cheap consumer security cameras in low light lead us to think something is there that's not there. Misinformation gets all the headlines; in my world the real boogeyman is misidentification.

That's because the explosion of video and audio evidence has profoundly transformed the field of the unexplained. The same dominant cultural mindset that applies to criminal investigations applies to paranormal investigations (although the preferred term these days is "metanormal"). If it wasn't caught on-camera, it didn't happen; if it was, it did.

That's why video authentication is key to our process on *The Proof Is Out There®* series. One of the first calls I made when I was creating the show and trying to assemble our all-star roster of experts was to Michael Primeau, a mustachioed, chain-smoking, and implacable video forensics analyst who works out of Michigan for the company his father started in the late 1980s, now known as Primeau Forensics. Most of their clientele are prosecutors or defendants in criminal cases who need video or audio recordings authenticated and analyzed, often with sworn testimony in court. They've worked on high-profile cases including the Trayvon Martin case and the Alec Baldwin shooting. I figured if Michael is good enough to withstand a Daubert challenge—a motion made at trial to exclude testimony from an unqualified expert witness—he'd be good enough for us. The bigger question was whether a guy devoted to weighty legal matters would have any interest in the weird world of the anomalous. It turns out that he does: "The show gives me a unique opportunity that many experts won't have," he said, "which is to apply methodology to a different set of source data, which stretches my capabilities and comfort zones. I'm exposed to things that I can't explain, so it has enlarged my world."

Primeau's specialty is determining whether or not a given video was digitally manipulated. That weeds out most of the CGI hoaxes, but the question remains—assuming something really is there, what is it? Most of our other experts have expertise in various fields—aviation, anatomy, physics, and so on—to help us nail down an answer. You'll meet many of them as we proceed.

In the chapters that follow, you'll see how we've applied "The Proof Method"—if you can call it that—to evidence of every popular type of anomaly that has captivated the public's attention. Our format draws inspiration from the judicial system. In essence we consider each piece a bench trial where evidence is presented to the audience, with eyewitnesses and experts "testifying" in favor of its anomalous bona fides; and others making the case for how it can be explained. At the end, our "judge," host Tony Harris, renders our verdict. We actually call it that. We've purloined the term to underscore our efforts to weigh all the facts and arguments.

We are not in the business of making leaps—of logic, judgment, or faith. Our journey is a plodder's path. At every cautious step we take our bearings, test the ground beneath our feet, look behind at where we've come from, try to correct our prior missteps, and look ahead at what's coming up over the horizon.

Are you ready to join us?

Chapter 2

SIGNS AND WONDERS

AN ANGEL IN THE CLOUDS

Cory Hearon knew where he was going, yet he was lost. Behind the wheel of his Ford F-350, he was en route to his job as a yard foreman at Wolfe Mechanical in Camden, South Carolina, on a sunny morning in October 2016. Nothing unusual distinguished this commute, but Cory was accompanied by a familiar companion: the lingering feeling that something wasn't right. At age thirty, Cory's life was progressing with the expected allotment of joys and sorrows—he'd describe himself as generally content and he had people who loved him—but it seemed as if the days were simply playing out, one after the next, with no sense of purpose or direction.

Then something caught his eye. Up in the sky, suspended in the cobalt blue, a humanoid shape with wings, a translucent robe, a faceless, marshmallowy head, and what appeared to be hands folded in prayer. Was it . . . peering down on him? It sure looked like it. Of course it was a cloud, but it looked so unmistakably like an angel that Cory was transfixed.

He knew it was often the case that clouds resemble something familiar or meaningful at first glance, only to shape-shift into amorphous blobs as the wind remolds them. But this one didn't move. It simply hung there like a Christmas tree ornament, for five minutes, then eight, then ten. Dumfounded, Cory took out his phone and began live streaming on Facebook. "I know nobody would believe me unless I got this on-camera," he narrates. "You can almost see a face. . . . Isn't that amazing? I'm seeing an angel. I don't know if anybody sees anything different. . . ."

Within a week the video had been viewed more than 7 million times, generating 126,000 comments and landing Cory on the *Today* show. And soon the story was about more than the cloud angel. It was about how Cory felt he'd been touched by the divine, and inspired to recommit himself to the Christian faith in which he'd been raised. As the song goes, he was once lost. Now, thanks to whatever he'd seen in that sunny South Carolina sky, he was found.

THE M-WORD

Miracles abound in every major religion, yet *The Proof Is Out There®* series doesn't cover many them often—maybe three every season—so why start here with a beefy chapter about alleged acts of God? Quite simply because God is the original anomaly, the original supernatural force, the original explanation for the unexplained. And in today's smartphone-saturated world, some of the most popular shared videos are those that purport to document God's works in various forms of miracles.

I have a complicated relationship with the M-word. It irks me that people toss it around casually to characterize any event that is both fortuitous and improbable. I'd prefer we stick to a stricter definition—an occurrence that's both fortuitous and *impossible*, according to our latest science.

But maybe I'm missing the point. Maybe, as Samuel L. Jackson's Jules Winnfield opined in *Pulp Fiction*, what matters is not whether a given event was an "according to Hoyle" miracle, but whether the experiencer genuinely "felt the touch of God."

If the polls are accurate, the general public is with Jules on this one. Miracles maintain a firm grip on the public consciousness, at least in the United States. A recent Pew study is one of several that have consistently shown a whopping majority of Americans—in this poll it was 80 percent—say they believe miracles "probably or definitely" happen. In a data-driven age where everything seems either known or immanently knowable, why this persistent attachment to a concept any sapient species should probably dismiss as magical thinking?

THE HOLE IN PASCAL'S HEART

The more we can explain empirically, the less we should depend on "superstition." Still, even though the cosmos, evolution, and the human body have been demystified, billions of people persist in their belief in an almighty deity that created everything, knows everything, and can intervene in our everyday lives whenever He chooses to do so. We can dismiss these billions offhand as fools, but as we shall see, there's video evidence suggesting such a dismissal would be both hasty and arrogant.

Indeed, long before video cameras were invented, most of the world's smartest people were people of faith. For the better part of the past two thousand years, academically gifted individuals became clergymen of one sort or another—it's what bookish types did. (Followers of Abrahamic monotheistic religions are in fact often referred to as "People of the Book.") Nor were these Believers uniformly opposed to the bold men of science to whom we owe what we call progress—on the contrary, some of them were scientific pioneers themselves, personally responsible for a portion of that same progress.

Blaise Pascal is just such a figure. A seventeenth-century polymath who made substantial contributions to mathematics and physics, the French whiz kid was also a devout Catholic who spent his later years writing almost exclusively on matters of faith. This pivot was accelerated by two major events. The first, which he called his "Night of Fire," was an intense experience of religious ecstasy that occurred in 1654, some say after a near-death experience involving an accident with a horse carriage. The second, in 1656, was Pascal's close encounter with a miracle. Specifically, his ten-year-old niece, Marguerite Périer, who'd suffered for years with a disfiguring eye tumor, was allegedly cured when she touched a sacred relic—a Holy Thorn from Christ's crown—to her eye. The miracle became a famous event throughout France.

Pascal's faith went from mild to superspicy thanks to these intensely personal experiences—"his truth." But for those who hadn't lived through such transformative events, he reached back into his mathematician's bag of tricks and, using some rudimentary principles of probability, formulated a game theory argument for religious piety that became his biggest claim to fame: Pascal's Wager. As shown in the following table, based on the logic of expected returns, Pascal makes a convincing case in his *Pensées* that, whether or not you feel the stirrings of the divine in your soul, it's in your best interest to have faith—or at least to fake it till you make it.

	You bet that He exists	You bet that He does not exist
God exists	+ ∞ (infinite gain)	- ∞ (infinite loss)
God does not exist	- x (finite loss)	+ x (finite gain)

As the table makes clear, even if the odds of God existing are slim, the expected return from betting on Him far exceeds what one can expect from betting against Him.

This argument appeals to a primitive instinct—pain avoidance. But Pascal didn't think such a blunt sales pitch was necessary, because God, in his view, was a product that sells itself. He believed that humans are driven by more than mere self-interest—they are born with a built-in demand for spiritual fulfillment. He made this point in perhaps his second-most famous concept, the "God-shaped vacuum," which is articulated later in the *Pensées*:

> *There is a God-shaped vacuum in the heart of every man which cannot be filled by any created thing, but only by God the Creator, made known through Jesus Christ.*

It is this God-shaped vacuum, now commonly referred to as the "God-shaped hole," that explains why, in the face of overwhelming empirical evidence, people have persisted in their devotion to religious practice. Clearly it fills some basic human need.

The sociobiologist E. O. Wilson had a Darwinian explanation for this. In his great book *On Human Nature*, he argued that societies in which a measure of altruism is established as a cultural norm have a reproductive advantage over those that don't. A tribe in which people care for each other, at least to some degree, will endure and expand over generations better than one in which it's every man for himself. Religion usually inculcates and reinforces some sense of altruism, regardless of how misguided its cosmology may be, so people drawn to it by some genetic predisposition—hearts with "God-shaped holes"—will reproduce more than those who don't, passing on that predisposition until the God-shaped hole becomes a standard feature of the species.

I once had the opportunity to bounce Wilson's argument off the great philosopher and atheist Daniel Dennett. He replied that the God-shaped hole may have been a reproductive advantage at some point in our evolution, but it is now a trait that has slipped into obsolescence. He compared it to the sweet tooth—it was once very helpful for primitive *Homo sapiens* to crave the taste of sugar, as it quickly provides the glucose necessary for survival. But now, with sources of sustenance in abundance, it is not only unnecessary, but often disadvantageous.

The social utility of organized religion in today's world is a thorny issue to ponder. On the one hand, as the great atheist Christopher Hitchens once said, it would be hard to denounce it as bad news if there were a sudden and widespread outbreak of secularism throughout the Middle East. On the other, there is a compelling mental experiment formulated by Stephen Fry: imagine yourself alone at night, in a city you've never visited before, walking down a street, when you see a group of large men coming straight for you in the opposite direction. Would you feel more or less endangered if you knew they were coming from a prayer meeting?

I've seen up close how the power of faith can sustain families through periods of crisis, especially the death or illness of a loved one. Faith can provide solace, strength, peace, the power to push through. The need for spiritual fulfillment is tied to our survival instinct.

But that need is not necessarily met by religion. Importantly, as I will argue throughout these chapters, many of the most fervent Believers in anomalies and the theories behind them aren't only reporting what they've witnessed; they're filling this God-shaped hole with belief systems that aren't religious per se, but perform the same function. UFOlogy often veers into theology; Bigfoot researchers often invoke Native American spiritual traditions. Ghost sightings are, definitionally, spiritual phenomena. As we approach all these accounts, we must constantly confront the question—are these strange events truly anomalous, or are they merely being used to fill someone's God-shaped hole?

THE WORDS OF THE LORD

As we take up the question of miracles, a quick disclaimer—while I have a healthy respect and passing layman's knowledge of most world religions, the lion's share of this chapter will focus on Christianity. For one thing, almost all of the alleged miracles we've investigated are within the Christian tradition. Secondly, it's the religion in which I was raised—Roman Catholicism to be precise—so it's the only one I feel even remotely comfortable writing about.

Let us stipulate that every religion includes in its sacred texts and traditions events that the faithful consider wondrous, and non-Believers might consider absurd or ridiculous. This encompasses everything from burning bushes; prophets ascending to heaven; lotus petals sprouting from footprints of the great teacher. But Christianity is distinguished by its self-identification as a historical religion. The Gospels assert that certain events happened at specific times and places. The preamble to the Gospel of Luke, in particular, unabashedly declares itself a serious journalistic enterprise. The author has spoken to multiple "eyewitnesses," achieved a "perfect understanding" of what events transpired, and will be providing the reader "certainty of those things." As such it is entirely reasonable that practicing Christians interpret the scripture's descriptions of miracles not as allegories or compelling but fictional "literary truths," but as documented instances of divine intervention in the physical world.

If Christian fundamentalists are vulnerable to the critique that they take things too seriously and too far, a similar critique can be leveled at those extreme atheists who insist not only that God doesn't exist, but that Jesus too is a myth. Let's dispense with that misconception quickly, for as the biblical scholar John Dominic Crossan puts it, as much as we know anything about the ancient world, we know Jesus lived and was crucified. All four Gospels say so, but even if we want to dismiss them as theological propaganda, two other independent, contemporaneous, non-Christian historians of the first century note his emergence, ministry, and execution. The Jewish historian Josephus and the Roman historian Tacitus, neither of whom had any interest in promoting the seditious new Jesus cult, each separately remark upon the phenomenon of Jesus and his followers. While there will forever be debate about what deeds and words included in the New Testament Jesus actually did and said, we know for a fact they were disruptive enough to get Him crucified. Make no mistake: whether or not Jesus was the son of God, Christians' claims to be a historical religion have some basis in the historical record. They're not just making the whole thing up.

And yet Christianity's sacred texts aren't so easy to take literally, even if one is predisposed to do so. There are four of them, and they often contradict each other. This was a new religion, violently opposed by both the Jewish faith from which it sprouted and the Roman polytheism that was the official religion of an occupying hegemonic power. One might assume its early adherents would have had the good sense to get their own story straight. But no, we have four separate accounts, four separate sets of miracles performed in different orders. Four different Jesuses really, ranging from a traditional Jewish messiah (in Mark) to a Divine-with-a-capital-*D* savior in John.

These four made it into the canon (whereas many others didn't) because they were each being used throughout early Chrisitan communities and therefore each had a constituency. And it has long been argued that the life of Jesus is so important and complex that it defies the constraints of a singular linear narrative. Like a great city or a building, it can only be comprehended from a variety of viewpoints and perspectives. Fair enough, but did Jesus' miracles really happen?

Crossan argues no—they are presented by the evangelists as morally instructive and inspiring stories. Jesus spoke in parables about God; why wouldn't the Gospel writers have spoken in parables about Jesus? Evangelical scholar Ben Witherington argues yes—many of the miracle stories are so fantastic—starting off with a real doozy, the Virgin Birth—that an upstart religion trying to convert Skeptics would not have promoted such wild tales for fear of alienating potential converts . . . *unless they'd really happened.* The stories are too crazy *not* to be true. (Thomas Jefferson, it is worth nothing, didn't think the miracles mattered at all. His Jefferson's Bible stripped out all the miracles and supernatural events, and presented the words and teachings of Jesus as compelling—one might say "self-evident"—messages on how to live, unabetted by anything he considered superstition.)

It should be noted that some recent respected contemporary scholarship comes close to endorsing the thesis that miracles have occurred—bona fide supernatural events, not just touching allegories and metaphors. In his 2023 book *They Flew*, Yale professor of history and religious studies Carlos Eire examined medieval accounts of the miraculous, especially levitation. The most famous case is that of Saint Joseph of Cupertino, who allegedly levitated all the way up to the ceiling of his convent, a feat witnessed by enough people that he eventually came under suspicion for witchcraft and was transferred to another Franciscan friary for observation.

While many Skeptics consider the accounts of Saint Joseph's levitation highly exaggerated, Eire is not as dismissive. "Levitation cannot be discounted," he told us, "because of the testimonies that we have. It can't be proved conclusively, but the testimonies, I think, speak for themselves. The testimonies are a fact." (Professor Eire is no sucker, mind you. He came on our show to debunk a modern-day "levitator" as a dancer performing an act of aerial legerdemain with a piece of rope.)

Given that miracles play a high-profile role in its teachings, one might think the Catholic Church would be eager to endorse claims they continue to occur in the present day. In theory, a regular pipeline of miracles would help both recruitment and retention. The Church has not closed the book on such claims—a prerequisite for the canonization of a new saint is the performance of at least two confirmed miracles. But, to its credit in my view, the Vatican is highly reluctant to ratify alleged instances of Marian apparitions, stigmata, or faith healing, even if they draw widespread acclaim and come with video documentation. The process requires a meticulous, arduous, years-long investigation, one that the Church often refuses even to initiate. But times may be changing—in 2023, the Vatican announced the launch of the Pontifical International Marian Academy (PAMI), described as a scientific institution of the Holy See, which plans to investigate mystical phenomena around the world including weeping statues of the Virgin Mary, stigmata, and ghost sightings.

THE MIRACLE HUNTER

We have neither years to investigate nor close enough ties to the Vatican to get one of its official PAMI experts to help out with our own investigations. As I assembled our experts for the show's first season, I knew I needed someone who had both street cred and interest in participating. That's how I found Michael O'Neill, "the Miracle Hunter." He's both a devout Catholic and a trained mechanical engineer. In his books, blog, and radio show, O'Neill explores and opines upon miracles new and old, merging the principles of his faith with the rigor of his scientific training.

O'Neill nestled into his niche thanks to two influential women—his mother and, of all people, Condoleezza Rice. His mom, for reasons he never knew, had a lifelong fascination and devotion to Our Lady of Guadalupe, whose story traces back to a miraculous apparition of the Virgin Mary to an indigenous Aztec named Juan Diego in 1531, and is credited with the conversion of the region to Christianity. Though he doesn't have a drop of Mexican blood, O'Neill was raised to have reverence for this tradition, and with a hungry curiosity about what miracles really had happened.

Then, as he was graduating from Stanford with his engineering degree, Dr. Rice, university provost at the time, offered him some advice that he took to heart: "Become an expert in something." So O'Neill decided to apply his professional skills to his childhood passion. "In the Venn diagram of things, I like what lies in the intersection of science and the supernatural," he told me. "So I set up my website and did it kind of secretly at first. I was an engineer by day, miracle hunter at night. I wanted to provide resources for people, especially Catholics, so they could know what can be believed."

It was a clandestine operation at first—O'Neill didn't tell his girlfriend, his mother, or his friends what he was doing until he was "discovered" by the *New York Times* and the *Washington Post.* He has since gone pro. Blaise Pascal would be proud.

TEARS OF GLASS

O'Neill's work is not only inspiring; at his best he functions like a *Consumer Reports* for alleged miracles, gently but firmly alerting his audience to the abundant charlatans out there eager to take advantage of the faithful. There's a demand for miraculous phenomena among people of all faiths, and no shortage of fraudsters happy to supply them, even if it means putting people close to them at risk.

One such case we investigated few years ago involved a teenage girl named Hasna Masalmani from the Bekaa valley of Lebanon, whose father announced to the world that his daughter had been touched by God in a most peculiar way. She could cry tears, not of liquid, but of solid crystal, which her dad would pluck from her eyelid on-camera. In the footage we reviewed, Hasna reclines in peaceful repose, calmly excreting the glass tears from her eyes, exhibiting no sign of the intense irritation—make that agony—your average person would likely feel if anything that large and sharp were to get lodged between their eyeball and lid. The alleged divine connection here was through Imam ʿAlī, the cousin of the Prophet Muhammad. In the family's narrative, the spirit of ʿAlī came to the girl in her room and told her to give the glass shards she cried to the sick. As the story spread, people came from all over the country to witness the phenomenon firsthand. Doctors examined the shards and confirmed they were real, but didn't specify what material they were composed of.

O'Neill was suspicious of the claims, not only because there was no tradition in either Sunni or Shiite Islam of such a miracle, but because there was a prosaic, if bizarre, explanation. It turns out there is ample space between the eyeball and eyelids where small objects can be placed. Skeptical investigator Joe Nickell had managed to replicate Hasna's tears simply by procuring some quartz crystals of similar size, pinching a pouch of flesh under his own eye, and inserting the "tears" himself. Our team of medical and biological experts came to the same conclusion: the Lebanese miracle was a shameless hoax, perpetrated with what I'd consider an act of child abuse.

OUR LADY OF CLEARWATER

As I stated previously, most debunkings uncover misidentification and misinterpretations rather than deliberate premeditated frauds, though I submit there is an important subclass of "deliberate misidentifications," many of which trace back to Pascal's "God-shaped hole." Many people aren't just open-minded about anomalous events; they *want* to believe. How else to explain the multitudes—half a million in total—who lined up outside the offices of Seminole Financial Corporation in Clearwater, Florida, during the 1996 holiday season? Starting on December 17, large, colorful swirls appeared in the office's two-story glass window, and you didn't need to squint to recognize a familiar figure. It was the Virgin Mary. Within hours a customer had called a local TV station and the word spread like wildfire. In the weeks that followed, more than six hundred thousand pilgrims flocked to the site, dubbing the image "Our Lady of Clearwater," and praising the Christmas miracle. Photographer Chris Lauber was there and remembers the moment vividly. "I just stood there and was like, 'Wow, this is amazing,'" he told us. "And it wasn't one of these kinds of things where, oh gee you need to look at it a half hour before sunset and don't blink because it'll be gone. It was so readily apparent."

This case resonated with O'Neill, since it evoked his mother's devotion to Our Lady of Guadalupe. Still, we knew that of the countless reported Marian apparitions over the centuries, the Church has only confirmed sixteen as legitimate. And the Vatican never thought much of the Clearwater Madonna. It declined to investigate or give even a vague hint of endorsement. The *St. Petersburg Times* quoted a spokesman of the local archdiocese saying, "People should exercise a great deal of heavy skepticism."

Which is exactly what we did, bringing in physicist Matthew Szydagis to review the images and documents from the case. He first tackled one of the explanations put forth at the time, which was that light entering the glass was being refracted at slightly different angles, causing the prismatic or rainbow-like images—an effect known as tonal internal refraction. But that theory didn't withstand scrutiny since the natural light would obviously change throughout the day with the movement of the sun and varying cloud cover—yet Our Lady of Clearwater retained her shape and size all day, for weeks. So Szydagis ended up focusing on the biggest clue on-site—broken sprinkler heads in the building's fire alarm system. He believed they may have malfunctioned at some point, causing interior water damage. "I think we're seeing a scientifically explainable process here where we have a protective layer on the glass or maybe we have metal oxides in the glass itself and we might have damage to the protective layer from heat and moisture that also warps the glass underneath," he concluded, echoing the sentiments of a local chemist who'd been brought on to investigate at the time. "This creates an effect that's similar sometimes to the rainbow patterns you see on an oil slick on top of water."

That was enough to convince us too, and we declared Our Lady of Clearwater a result of corrosion of the glass coating. Still, one has to ask—if this is a natural occurrence, then why has nothing like it been seen before or since? "It's weird," mused one of the building's architects to the *Tampa Bay Times*, "and I've been designing buildings for 40 years."

THE BLOOD OF SAINT JANUARIUS

Do official, Vatican-sanctioned miracles hold up any better under scrutiny? O'Neill suggested we investigate a story from a sector of the miracle space I find highly dubious in general—supernatural occurrences relating to relics. At a church in Naples, Italy, alleged blood samples of the fourth-century martyr Saint Januarius are preserved in two sealed ampules. Under normal conditions, that blood is coagulated and immobile, but three times a year the bishop brings it before a crowd and—often, but not always—it liquefies on its own, a miracle interpreted by the Neapolitans as a good omen.

This event happens in front of onlookers armed with smartphones, so we have video to work with.

Spectroscopic analysis has confirmed on two separate occasions that the vials contain hemoglobin, so there's grounds to believe that there's real blood in there. So what could account for its change of state? One of the proposed scientific explanations is that when the ampules are brought forth from their chamber and placed near candles in the church, the heat "melts" the coagulated blood into liquid. But our own medical expert Dr. Ed Hope didn't think the heat differential from candles would be strong enough to account for the transition.

A more compelling theory was put forth by Italian chemistry professor Luigi Garlaschelli. It involves a chemical property known as *thixotropy*. With thixotropic substances, the more stress you apply, the less viscous the material becomes. In simple terms, the more you stir or shake such a substance, the easier it is to pour. Garlaschelli's team went so far as creating fake blood using only compounds that were available in the fourteenth century, when the legend first took root, like calcium carbonate and ferric chloride. It demonstrated many of the same properties as the substance in the ampules alleged to be the martyr's blood.

Miracle debunked? Not quite, says O'Neill, because known thixotropic gels typically hold their thixotropic properties for no longer than ten years. The blood of Saint Januarius has been liquefying for centuries. Have some unscrupulous priests been refilling the ampules with fake thixotropic "blood" to perpetuate the legend? To eliminate that possibility, the Church would have to permit independent analysis of the blood. But that's not happening, says Dr. Hope. "The Church won't let anyone open the vial to find out what's in there. That's kind of understandable, because they don't want to disturb whatever's going on. But it's also a bit of a convenience." Says O'Neill: "As long as no scientific investigation is allowed on the actual liquid, we may never know." Is this a true miracle, or is there some trickery at play? On the show we were noncommittal, concluding that this was a "possible miracle." I personally think that was a bit generous.

MYRNA'S STIGMATA

With Our Lady of Clearwater, the Church was explicitly dismissive. With the blood of Saint Januarius, it's been explicitly supportive. But sometimes it remains officially noncommittal, preferring to send subtle signals that a given phenomenon might be the real deal without making any formal declaration. That's what happened with the strange case of stigmata that happened repeatedly on the outskirts of Damascus, Syria, in the early 2000s. This type of phenomenon—the alleged appearance of wounds on bodies of devout Christians that correspond to the crucifixion wounds of Jesus Christ—has been happening for centuries, going back to Saint Francis of Assisi. But the video from this case was the first we deemed worthy of our attention.

In the clips, we see forty-year-old Myrna Nazzour lying in bed as blood pours out in a cross shape across her forehead; similar cuts appear on her hands and feet. Myrna states that this has been happening to her since age nineteen, and it's happening for a reason: "I was chosen by God to convey a message to others. The message of Jesus and the Virgin Mary is the unity of the Church." She claims the wounds disappear after three hours.

Myrna's stigmata had been witnessed in 2004 by a team of European doctors and medical engineers. None could provide a solid explanation for what they observed. Other Skeptics have argued that among some religious fanatics the intensity of their faith can trigger the spontaneous rupturing of blood vessels, just as there have been cases where psychosomatic symptoms of pregnancy present in women who believe they're pregnant but aren't.

I personally was eager to debunk this case, especially since stigmata stunts have been perpetrated in the modern era in ways I consider truly reprehensible. There is no more troubling case than that of Padre Pio, the Italian friar canonized by the Church in 2002. In the 1910s and '20s, Pio was exhibiting weeping stigmata scars before masses of pilgrims. The Vatican grew worried that his growing cult was spinning out of control. Suspicious that the wounds were caused and maintained artificially, the Church dispatched a doctor to examine him. In 2007, Italian historian Sergio Luzzatto found documents indicating that Padre Pio had been secretly pouring carbolic acid on his hands and feet to create the stigmata. How this guy ever became a saint is, to my mind, a scandal. (Though, by the standards of the twentieth-century Catholic Church, a relatively small one. Sheesh.)

So what did our experts make of the Syrian caught-on-camera case? For starters, Dr. Ed Hope eliminated the psychosomatic explanation, since in his opinion the wounds were simply too large and the bleeding too profuse. There is a known medical condition, hematohidrosis, which causes blood to seep from sweat glands. But in those cases the blood comes from a diffuse area, not specific, cross-shaped lines. Dr. Hope's best guess is that Myrna was engaged in a practice common among professional wrestlers known as "blading," in which the wrestlers create fine nicks in their skin using concealed blades.

O'Neill disagrees. Myrna's stigmata did not occur at random, but only—she claimed—during Holy Week every four years when the Orthodox and Catholic Easters align. With that advance notice, medical observers and cameras were able to be in position to observe the whole process. They have seen no evidence of blading or any other hoaxing. While it's certainly possible those observers are all in on a massive hoax, O'Neill thinks that's unlikely. And he finds it significant that Myrna was granted an audience with Pope Francis. While the Vatican has made no official ruling about this case, the mere fact that the Pope agreed to meet with the stigmatic is a strong sign of support. "There's absolutely no chance that this is her inflicting the wounds on her own body," says O'Neill. "This seems to be an authentic case of stigmata."

TOUCHED BY ANGELS

Widening our aperture beyond Catholic tradition, what to make of the broader phenomenon of angel sightings? On these matters O'Neill advises caution. Take some specifics of the Cory Hearon incident with which I kicked off the chapter. Note that Cory's angel is in a wispy, ethereal, semi-corporeal form, but it's not emanating light. That doesn't quite align with tradition. The Hadith, a traditional collection of information about the prophet Muhammad, declares: "The angels were created from light." Christians and Jews often describe angels as glowing with light from within as a physical manifestation of the passion for God that is burning within angels. The angelic beings of Hinduism are considered to be minor gods called devas, which means "shining ones."

Just as often, in the Christian tradition angels are represented as fully embodied beings. The archangel Michael is typically depicted as muscular and martial, poised to decapitate Satan with his sword. Wispy, he ain't.

In short, the "angel cloud" report, on its face, deviates from traditional descriptions of angels. Then there's the matter of the impossible being made possible. While the Hearon citing can certainly be characterized as unusual, did anything really happen that contradicted the laws of physics? Yes, the cloud retained an angelic shape for minutes on end, but that could simply be attributed to a lack of wind. Our meteorologist Dr. Deanna Hence researched the weather conditions in Camden, South Carolina, at the time and concluded: "There was actually a pretty broad, high-pressure region over the eastern United States. Winds within a high-pressure region are often very calm and it's very typically very sunny, so that would actually set up the conditions to be calm enough that the cloud is able to hang around for a long period of time."

The angel cloud story also has an Achilles' heel that pops up in almost every kind of incident we investigate—the human brain's tendency to recognize familiar patterns in random objects and then to superimpose meaning upon that interpretation. The name for this—a word worth knowing in my business—is "pareidolia." The most common example is probably the recognition of a face in a common three-pronged electrical outlet. (A recent Apple iPhone 15 ad went to town with this, with a pair of outlets singing "Way Too Long" as they pined for bygone happy days when the iPhone required frequent charging.) When both the object and the pareidoliac interpretation are as prosaic as that, we say "wow" and then dismiss the matter as something cute or funny. When the interpretation has a spiritual meaning, the reaction can be profound, but it's just our minds playing tricks on us. Given all that, we declared the Hearon cloud angel a natural phenomenon.

Contrast that angelic sighting with the 2008 case of Chelsea Banton of Charlotte, North Carolina, who was hospitalized with severe pneumonia that traced back to congenital health issues. Chelsea was on a ventilator in the intensive care unit. Her situation was grim. Then a nurse called Chelsea's mother, Colleen, over to a nearby monitor displaying a security cam feed of the ICU door. On the monitor, Colleen was stunned to see a bright light, in the shape of an amorphous body with wings. Colleen photographed the image, which she said appeared repeatedly over the next five days, during which Chelsea experienced a remarkable convalescence. She made it out of the ICU and returned home for the holidays, and her story, like the Hearon angel, made national news.

Was it a real miracle? To investigate, we first had our forensic image analyst Michael Primeau do his thing with Colleen's photo. Since it was a picture of a video monitor there were inherent limitations in what he could conclude, but he was positive the photo did not merely capture the reflection on the monitor from a flash in Colleen's camera. The reason? The scan lines from the monitor are embedded within the angel image. "This was definitely something the camera was seeing," he declared.

But was the source of light something genuinely divine, or was there a mundane explanation? To help us figure that out, we were fortunate—OK, I'll say blessed—to have one of the world's premier theoretical physicists on hand. Prof. Michio Kaku has been with the show since its inception, largely because he believes it is the responsibility of any professional scientist to educate the public in layman's terms whenever possible. For that we are eternally grateful.

After studying the photo, Professor Kaku concluded that the image was likely some light reflecting off the hospital floor or the

ICU door window when it was opened in a given position at that time of day. "The bright light is probably sunlight reflected at that precise angle," he observed, "giving the impression that there was this angel that was in the room."

We were ready to dismiss the incident as exactly that kind of trick of the light, but one thing gave us pause—both the nurse and Chelsea's mom, Colleen, consistently stated that the image was *only* visible on the video monitor, not to the naked eye watching the hallway. Remember—the nurse initially called Colleen to the monitor, not to the hallway, to witness the "angel."

Even if the light has a natural explanation, to this day Chelsea's recovery does not. Sadly, while that recovery was real and impressive, it was not permanent. Chelsea passed away due to complications from her health issues seven years later at the age of twenty-one. But Collen is convinced her daughter's life was extended by an Act of God. Our verdict? Unexplained phenomenon.

"MIRACLE" SURVIVALS

Finally, we turn to a category of anomalous event to which the word "miracle" is applied most liberally: "I should have been dead" incidents where, against all odds, someone survives a life-threatening accident or disaster. As I mentioned earlier, our standard requires candidate survival miracles to be more than improbable and fortuitous. They have to be events in which "the impossible was made possible."

O'Neill goes further. In his view, any Act of God has to amplify and promote faith in some form. It can't just be a freak occurrence. "Miracles are not mysteries and marvels," he cautions. "I'm looking for something that works for the good, something that shows a loving God looking out for us."

Instances of caught-on-camera "miraculous" rescues or survival stories are some of the most breathtaking pieces of footage we've ever aired. I will admit that because they are generally so eye-catching, I'm predisposed to feature them on the show, even if we end up debunking them. But while jaw-dropping video might attract viewers, nothing lends these stories credibility more than eyewitnesses who aren't devout Believers but people of science, who are nevertheless positive they saw something miraculous.

Put Dr. Rocky Khosla into that camp.

On February 27, 2006, Dr. Khosla and his family were on their way to dinner in Pueblo, Colorado, when they hit a bad rainstorm. They approached a flooded underpass and were preparing to turn around when they noticed a red SUV ahead of them attempting to drive through the water. "I remember thinking, 'That's weird,'" Khosla told us. "I didn't know what the person was thinking when they drove that way."

That person was thirty-five-year-old Charlene Deherrera, hurrying to get home from her job at a beauty salon. In her haste, she made the unfortunate decision to try to ford the churning waters that, unbeknownst to her, were ten feet deep. (This is why you should never drive into a flooded road. It may look like the water is only inches deep because the surface of the water may appear flat, but there's no way of knowing how far down the road slopes.)

Within seconds Deherrera's car was engulfed. "As I looked, this car took off and started floating away real fast," Khosla recalled. "Way faster than I expected."

Serendipitously, a local news crew was passing by, and as the life-and-death situation unfolded, they started rolling. In the footage it's clear Deherrera's SUV has gone into the water with all its windows rolled up as you'd expect for Colorado in February. It's also clear that Dr. Khosla acts heroically. He dives into the water and attempts to smash the driver's side window with a piece of driftwood, but to no avail. "I was really hammering away with this piece of wood and making absolutely no progress," he said. Deherrera didn't have one of those glass-breaking hammers safety experts recommended for situations just like this, and to boot, she didn't know how to swim. As her SUV sinks and its interior fills with water, it seems inevitable she will perish in one of the worst ways possible—on the evening news.

But that's not what happens. Just as Deherrera looks done for, another man who has jumped in to help her, forty-three-year-old unemployed store manager Howard Absetz reaches into the water, somehow feels Deherrera grasp his hand, and pulls her up to the surface. Dr. Khosla was amazed: "The next thing I know, this person is popping out of there like a champagne cork!" EMTs arrive shortly thereafter, extend a ladder, and complete the stunning rescue.

The obvious explanation here is that somehow the driver's side window came down, allowing Deherrera to escape in the nick of time. Here's the thing though—as the video shows, *when the SUV was pulled from the water, all four windows were up and all four doors were closed and locked.* In the nineteen years that have elapsed since the incident, no one who was there that day has been able to explain what happened. Dr. Khosla—a physician, not a psychic or a Reiki practitioner—says he's still "mystified by the whole thing."

The clip has since become an internet classic and the incident is touted on several religious websites. But is it legit? To investigate, we first consulted another of our in-house physicists, Prof.

Hakeem Oluseyi. He was certain the SUV's power windows would have shorted out within seconds of the vehicle going into the water—and even if Deherrera, Khosla, Abetz, or anyone else had been able to lower them, nobody had the time or motivation to raise them back up.

Could the door have been opened? Professor Oluseyi noted that the water pressure pushing on the air-filled cab of the car would have created an immense force against the car's exterior. "So a person inside the car, when they try to open that door, they're working against that incredible force. And there is no person on earth strong enough to open such a car door." The pressure on both sides of the door would equalize once the car was completely filled with water, but the incident didn't take that long, none of the witnesses said the door opened, and remember, the SUV was retrieved with all doors closed and locked. Our man of science was stumped.

Our miracle expert Michael O'Neill agreed that there is no clear explanation for what happened, and he has no problem with people believing a divine presence opened (and then considerately closed) the window or the door to aid Deherrera's escape. He also noted that in the Bible, quite a number of divine acts involve water—the flood, the parting of the Red Sea, the salvation of Jonah, Jesus walking on water. Aquatic environments, he said, are traditionally ripe for God's interventions. But O'Neill was cautious about using the M-word, and it's not hard to see why. In the Church's view the event in question can't just be an instance of God making the impossible possible—it has to come with a message that accords with Church teaching, and it has to have a direct and profound impact on the faith lives of those involved. By these standards, the Pueblo SUV rescue does not qualify.

As we investigated the incident, I was also troubled by one

nettlesome problem—Charlene Deherrera never responded to our requests for an interview. There are always a handful of strong reasons why someone might not want to talk to a TV show, first among them a hesitancy to relive a traumatic moment. Still, the Skeptic in me suspects there's a piece of this story she doesn't want to reveal. We declared the incident "unexplained," but we didn't have the confidence to call this proof of God's existence.

Another amazing near-death story brought us a step closer. It took place on October 2, 2022, in Milford, Ohio. Eighty-seven-year-old Franciscan friar John Bok, a former physics teacher, was on his way to celebrate Sunday Mass at St. Andrew Catholic Church. As he steered his white Hyundai past a funeral home with an outward-facing security camera, a black SUV came barreling off-road from the left and was on course to T-bone Father Bok's car. According to police reports, the teen driving the SUV had suffered a seizure and passed out with his foot on the gas. If you know anything about the NHTSA statistics of SUV versus sedan collisions of this nature, you know Father Bok's chances of survival were slim.

Then, in a moment that requires slo-mo playback, the SUV smashes through some thin metal signposts and . . . *launches right over the Hyundai,* clearing it by inches, then lands bumper-first, in the funeral home parking lot. Meanwhile, Father Bok drives off without a scratch, or, he would later say, without even realizing anything had happened. (He is blind in his left eye and wears hearing aids, so his obliviousness to the event is explainable.) The SUV ended up rolling into a building—the teen's foot came off the accelerator after the Dukes of Hazzard jump and he was not injured—but the Milford police had no idea anything else had happened until officers checked the security cameras. Chief Jamey Mills told us, "I think it took all of us a processing period as we watched that to fully comprehend what had happened. This was an absolute miracle. It's unbelievable that no one was injured or killed." The cherry on top—October 2 is the Catholic Church's Feast Day of the Guardian Angels.

Michael O'Neill was ready to call this the real deal: "We can't definitively say that this is a guardian angel here, but we have a Catholic priest on his way to say Mass on the Feast Day of the Guardian Angels. Seems like a clear-cut case, in my opinion, of something that might be a miracle." Some might find this unsurprising, since he's usually hesitant to get behind "meme miracles" that haven't received some form of recognition from Rome.

Far more remarkable, however, was the judgment rendered by Professor Kaku, a guy who has spent his career pondering the many quirks and paradoxes with which the universe confronts and confuses normal folks like us. A theoretical physicist is not the kind of guy you'd expect to use the "M-word" on television. And yet, he did not hesitate: "This is a miracle made possible by the First Law of Thermodynamics, the Conservation of Energy. First, the black car comes in from the side at a certain energy. That energy, the kinetic energy of motion, is then converted to the energy of being thrust into the air because it hit that rail. So the energy of motion turns into a gravitational energy. . . . The white car had come in at just the right velocity to clear the trajectory of the black car." And of course, the precise positioning of the metal signpost was key. "The thing that prevented a tragedy from taking place was this bar. [It] had to be at the right angle. It had to be with the right strength. It had to be positioned just right so that it would thrust the black car into the space just missing the white car. So after everything's said and done, I think what we're looking at is a miracle."

When a world-famous physicist opens the door for miracles, it's a good sign that we should all be more humble and hesitant before we slam it shut. Indeed, the cases we deemed potential miracles on the show have inspired me to revisit a philosophical argument I first encountered long ago. Known as the Kalam Cosmological Argument (or KCA) for short, it's a medieval Islamic school of thought that "proves" the existence of God through the reasoning of causality. In a nutshell it goes like this:

1. Everything that begins to exist was caused to exist.
2. The universe began to exist.
3. Therefore, the universe has a cause—which we call the Creator, or God.

The KCA has enjoyed impressive longevity in academic circles and there are still plenty of modern theologians and philosophers who defend it. That gives us license to lean into a related line of thinking when the story warrants it. Remember Cory Hearon's cloud angel? Yes, we decided it was made by natural forces. But the cloud angel was also something that began; therefore, it was caused to exist. If the KCA is true, and the universe has a creator, couldn't that creator be manipulating natural forces to cause the cloud angel to appear just for Cory? It's not the place of a TV show to say.

Chapter 3

A BEGINNER'S GUIDE TO THE UFO RENAISSANCE

CAPTAIN DELGADO AND THE MEXICAN FEDEX UFO

On the evening of March 19, 2020, Capt. Erik Delgado was sitting comfortably in his happy place—behind the controls of a Boeing 767. Thirty-five thousand feet above northern Mexico, Captain Delgado had every reason to expect an uneventful flight. His FedEx cargo plane had departed Monterrey without incident, his crew was in good spirits, and aside from a spot of weather off to the west, the skies were clear. Air traffic into Memphis, the FedEx hub where he'd landed hundreds of times, was unremarkable. Checking the cockpit instruments, Delgado noted that neither the radar nor the Traffic Collision Avoidance System (TCAS) was signaling any cause for concern. Captain Delgado engaged the autopilot and pivoted his attention to his in-flight dinner—a burrito.

Then it happened.

According to Captain Delgado and his crew, a glowing orb descended from the sky, hit the plane with a rotating lighthouse-like beacon, then took a position off to the port side and tailed the plane for twenty minutes before veering off and disappearing.

The object had no wings, rotors, FAA-mandated safety lights, nor any discernible means of propulsion. Delgado says he felt an initial wave of terror that the object posed a flight safety risk but soon came to feel there was no danger emanating from the orb.

The moment merited documentation, so of course out came the smartphones. On the footage, the object is relatively unremarkable—a light in the sky, the image blurring, then resolving as the phone's camera struggles to find focus through the cockpit window—but you can clearly tell the crew is in a unanimous state of amazement. "Oh, man, that is phenomenal!" you can hear Delgado exclaim. "It's definitely a UFO," says another crewman.

"Guys, calm down. That's just the planet Venus," was *not* said.

By far the most intriguing moment in the video is not of the UFO itself. It's at about the forty-five-second mark, when the camera pans right to the radar and TCAS monitors on the 767's console. You can clearly see some clouds, but no other aircraft appears on the screen.

"I was flabbergasted," Delgado would tell us later. "It was just wonderment. I didn't sense any hostility, any malevolence. I guess now I can definitively say we are not alone."

The video is impressive to be sure, but is it the most compelling piece of UFO footage ever? Not by a long shot. It's getting this prominent position in this chapter because it had a profound impact on the show, and by proxy, my career.

The Proof Is Out There® series had just launched, we were in the initial stages of preproduction, and my biggest challenge was determining whether or not there was enough of a pipeline of legitimately unexplained videos out there to sustain a series for a single full season, possibly more. As I had had little exposure, interest, or credulity for this kind of content, my first instinct was: no, there is not.

After stumbling across Delgado's video on YouTube, I contacted a handful of experts on aviation and video forensic analysis. They confirmed Captain Delgado's video wasn't doctored, and the flight data he reported that night was correct. There was definitely something on the video and it definitely did not appear on radar or TCAS. So . . . what was it?

The expert analysis was helpful, but what moved me most powerfully was Delgado himself. He was not seeking publicity, as hoaxers always are. "I'm not the story," he insisted. "The footage is the story!" But that wasn't entirely true. Delgado was more than an average experiencer. He evinced three of the premier traits any TV producer is looking for in a subject. He was candid, he was credible, and he was committed to telling his story.

This came with some risk. As mentioned earlier, pilots reporting this kind of encounter, much less going public with it, have historically been grounded and/or sent for psychological evaluation. Nor should we ignore the degree to which speaking out can imperil one's domestic tranquility. After Captain Delgado's expressed initial interest in going on-camera with us, it became clear his wife did not share the same enthusiasm. For a while, it seemed like he was ghosting us. Then a couple of weeks later, with our scheduled interview a few days out, he texted to confirm his appearance.

A journalistic conundrum ensued. If this pilot, who'd been entrusted for decades with the care of millions of dollars of property and even more precious human life, was one of the *Believers*, if the video and the experts backed him up, and if he was in fact the latest in a long string of pilots who'd made similar, credible claims, who was I to dismiss him? Captain Delgado was no kook, and I could do nothing more than put his story on our new show, confess our own befuddlement, and declare that this thing was, definitionally, a genuine Unidentified Flying Object. Captain Delgado's story and his video became the lead piece in our premier episode.

Since then, I've learned Captain Delgado is far from a lone voice crying in the wilderness. There is a robust and devout UFO community out there, it's been there for decades, and it has grown into something of a modern UFO Renaissance, spurred by a potent amalgam of leaked videos and documents, outspoken whistleblowers, and the nitrous oxide of the internet. Now there is even an informal "caucus" of U.S. congressmen keeping the issue in the public light. This Renaissance shows no signs of sunsetting. So how did this happen, and what does it all mean?

THE UFO CANON AND THE ANALYSIS ALL-STARS

Be forewarned—this field is vast, diffuse, and fragmented. There is no "grand unified theory" that purports to make everything in the fact pattern fit. It encompasses the fields of cosmology, astronomy, physics, biology, aviation, national security, intelligence gathering, and engineering, to name a few. (This all has its utility—the amoeba-like nature of UFOlogy makes it harder to pin down and disprove conclusively. That's why it will never go away.)

There is, however, something of a "UFO Canon," a catalog of key events that all serious UFOlogists discuss with fluency, and many believe to the letter. They are more than answers to trivia questions. These are the seminal incidents that form the historical bedrock upon which the current UFO discourse is built. They are the totemic moments that shape and inform the interpretation of recent events, the lens through which this week's viral video must be viewed. Without a foundational understanding of this Canon, we couldn't make the show.

I did not create this Canon myself. As I compiled it, I consulted many of the respected "Analysis All-Stars" who are regulars on the show, including:

Lue Elizondo, Former Head of AATIP, the Pentagon's Advanced Aerospace Threat Identification Program

Perhaps more than anyone else, Luis "Lue" Elizondo will be remembered as the founding father of the modern UFO Renaissance. After joining the Army and working for years in military intelligence, Elizondo says he was recruited into a then-secret and now-famous group known as AAWSAP, the Advanced Aerospace Weapons System Applications Program, the earliest Pentagon UFO investigators. AAWSAP later evolved into AATIP, and (after Lue left) was eventually reconstituted as AARO, the All-domain Anomaly Resolution Office, which today is the official, public Pentagon UFO team. In truth, the only reason there is an AARO that holds public hearings now is because in 2017 Lue and others went public in the *New York Times* with a bombshell report that revealed the existence of AATIP, and leaked the game-changing Pentagon UFO videos. (More on those shortly.) Eight years later, Lue is still at the forefront of the movement, regarded by some as a hero, by others as a charlatan, especially those who give credence to the Pentagon's efforts to discredit him. The heat around him has taken its toll, but Lue remains on mission: "The only thing I wanted to accomplish was to tell the American people the truth, how their money was being spent, and how the government was suppressing a major national security issue. To be honest I never thought that eight years later I'd still be doing it. I figured someone else would have taken the baton by now."

Marc D'Antonio, MUFON Investigator

Long before it became socially acceptable to discuss UFOs in polite society, and way before our TV show existed, an organization known as MUFON—the Mutual UFO Network—was the place the Believers went to feel like they belonged. The organization has its own colorful and spotted history, but as the core tenets of UFOlogy have seeped into mainstream culture, it can take pride in being part of a movement that has made an impact and endured. This is in part because MUFON has maintained a team of in-house investigators who examine sightings with an impressive degree of scrutiny. Marc D'Antonio is foremost among them.

An astronomer and computer scientist by training, D'Antonio got into the field in a most unusual and personal way. He claims that when he was around nine years old he experienced what he calls a "missing time event." On a school field trip, he recalls getting off the bus with his bag lunch, then getting back on and, still carrying his uneaten sandwich, asking his friends when they were going to go to the pond, bereft of any recollection that they'd been there all day. When he came home, he experienced a series of seizures that subsided after his parents took him to the hospital. They never recurred, but the young Marc was left with a lingering feeling when he looked up into the night sky that something was up there. This motivated his decision, first to join MUFON at age eleven, then to study astronomy.

Fast-forward to 1996 and the story gets freakier. Marc claims that he was lying in bed when he heard a knocking on his roof. When he went out to check, he was hit with a bright light; then a being approached, holding what he calls a "glowing pen-like thing." The next thing he recalls was awaking in his bed with blood on his pillow. Eventually, he would be examined by a doctor, who removed what Marc calls an implant from his sinus cavity. In his telling the implant was sent to pathology for examination, after which he got a call from his doctor telling him it was not a malignant tumor, but the sample had subsequently been lost.

One can imagine that telling such a story would be a quick way to end a first date or a job interview, but as I was initially putting the show together I was desperate to find people with expertise for examining UFO videos. Marc's scientific background and decades with MUFON had cemented his reputation in the community. I knew I'd have some hard-core Skeptics on the team, so why not have a Believer? Plus, judging from his demeanor on the phone, I suspected he might be the nicest guy on earth. If it turned out he was a dud on-camera interested only in peddling "the Woo," I figured we'd simply cut him out of the show and find someone else.

To my surprise, Marc turned out to be a withering and relentlessly dismissive critic of most alleged UFO sightings. He will usually be the first to debunk a light in the sky as a misidentified meteor, satellite, or the planet Venus. Days prior to this writing, he and his MUFON colleagues debunked an attention-grabbing video that purported to show U.S. military contractors recovering an alien "egg." Yes, there have been a few cases where he's been unable to explain videos we show him—more on those later—but, to his credit, he's been able to put aside whatever biases "his truth" might imply, and stick to his scientific training. An example for us all.

Richard Hoffman, SCU Director

Richard Hoffman runs a relatively new and relatively serious organization called the Scientific Coalition for UAP Studies, or SCU. A UFO nerd since grade school, Hoffman rose through the ranks at

MUFON like D'Antonio but left his leadership role in 2017. (Like most radical movements, the UFO community is prone to sectarianism and schism.) "I left because the leadership was bringing in conspiracy people talking about communing with blue aliens and claiming Obama was on the moon," he says. "They'd become very unscientific, and their credibility was being dashed by their stupid decisions."

Hoffman refers to the SCU as a "think tank" populated primarily by professional scientists from both academia and industry who want to study the UFO question seriously, grind through the data, and publish legitimate papers and articles. These are the guys who do the frame-by-frame, pixel-by-pixel trigonometry and telemetry stuff. Their big projects often require months of work from dozens of contributors. Since its founding in 2018, the SCU has grown to nearly four hundred active members. Its publications have been read on Capitol Hill and in the U.S. intelligence community, and Hoffman has been invited to speak at NATO conferences and the American Institute for Aeronautics and Astronautics. Perhaps the group's biggest claim to fame is its meticulous analysis of the so-called "Aguadilla" video, shot by a CBP reconnaissance plane launched from the Aguadilla airport in Puerto Rico in 2013. The video purports to show a UAP not only flying around the airport, but then diving into the ocean and reemerging after changing shape.

The government's recent debunking of the Aguadilla incident as a pair of balloons notwithstanding, the SCU thinks the video captures a legit anomaly—in this case, a "transmedium" object that moves through both air and water. Its confidence derives from the bounty of metadata that came with the footage, as the video was shot on a military-grade camera. This wasn't just a dot in the sky like the Mexican FedEx UFO—SCU analysts could track its speed, altitude, and even its temperature. That's the gold standard for UFO footage these days, and Hoffman has little use for the silver and bronze standards: "Over the course of the past sixty years, I've heard a ton of horseshit stories. People making wild claims about having implants in their arms, people hawking video that's never been validated and can't be analyzed."

With the dawn of the UFO Renaissance, the spike in interest and legitimacy for UFO studies has made it possible for the SCU to flourish, but it's also made it easier for others to attract an audience simply by spouting outlandish and unverifiable claims. There's a weariness in Hoffman's voice as he surveys the landscape: "I'm tired of being distracted from the scientific study of UFOs by things that get us nowhere at all." In part, that's the reason he does the show: to resist, however hopelessly, the tsunami of ignorance and magical thinking that contaminates the topic. "There's an element of the show that is educating the public. As a society, we're extremely gullible, extremely fallible, and extremely ignorant about what's up in the air. My job is to help people with 'IFOs'—the *Identifiable* Flying Objects that are so often misidentified as alien craft. Of course for a lot of people, especially 'eyewitnesses,' evidence doesn't mean anything. It will always be a UFO to them, and instead of accepting a prosaic explanation, they will prefer to attack you."

Tim McMillan, Journalist, Ex-cop . . . Spy?

Tim McMillan is a former Georgia police lieutenant with deep ties to the military and intelligence communities. Tim took early retirement in 2017 and began writing about defense tech for outlets like *Vice* and *Popular Mechanics* before co-founding a website called *The Debrief*. When the current "UFO Renaissance" erupted in 2017, McMillan started peppering his sources in the Pentagon and CIA with questions. The answers, he says, led him to pursue the topic with rigor. "I kind of expected to hear, 'Aw, man, it's just a bunch of nuts.' But the people I talked to about it behind the scenes said otherwise. It's not often, but there's some unexplained stuff."

That was enough to send him down the rabbit hole. McMillan has since become one of the most respected and leading voices in the space, applying his law enforcement investigative skills and extensive contacts within the government to break dozens of exclusives about anomalous incidents past and present. To add an air of mystery to his résumé, some people within the UFO community suspect that McMillan himself is a CIA asset, more specifically a "NOC," a spy working under nonofficial cover. There are crazier allegations to concoct—McMillan lives in Germany, his wife and many other family members are in the military, and his network of contacts far exceeds that of your average journalist. McMillan ascribes those rumors to his hesitancy to support every claim advanced by the Believers. "In politics, everybody you don't like gets called a Nazi," he says wryly. "In UFOlogy, everybody who says anything you don't agree with is a CIA disinformation agent. But the truth is, if there are NOCs in the UFO community, they're not going to be who you'd think they would be."

Mick West, Debunker

Skepticism is more than an attitude. For some it's an avocation; for others it becomes a job. For Mick West it's been all three, and by dint of dedication and skill, he's ascended to the highest echelon of achievement such a man can attain—being universally despised by the UFO Believers.

How did this happen? There has been a robust Skeptic community for decades, going as far back as Harry Houdini's takedowns of psychics and spiritualists in the 1920s. More recently, the magician James Randi co-founded the Committee for Skeptical Inquiry in the 1970s. Aside from Randi's several books and countless TV appearances, he helped engineer Johnny Carson's famous debunking of psychic Uri Geller on *The Tonight Show*.

But in recent years, as the UFO Renaissance has come into full bloom, so too has West's prominence as the community's most loathed bête noir. A retired video game programmer, he's honed a formidable skill set in video analysis, but his success derives as much from the clean, incisive writing style he deploys on his popular website Metabunk.com, and his cool, dispassionate delivery on television (a British accent never hurts with the American audience either).

West started out not with UFOs, but with classic "first-generation" conspiracy theories like chemtrails—the notion that contrails observed in the wake of jets passing overhead are not mere condensation but part of a government plan to chemically seed the atmosphere for a variety of purposes that fall under the umbrella of social control. As belief in UFOs has gone mainstream and the videos have proliferated online, he's devoted an ever-larger share of his attention to the topic.

Why does he do it? "I first got into it as a hobby," he explains. "Solving these UFO mysteries is like solving puzzles, and this helps me exercise my programming muscles." But as he forged further into this world, he realized that this stuff can take over people's lives. That's when the hobby morphed into a cause. (West's critics would use the term "crusade.") "There's a broader good," he says. "I'm removing the noise from the signal. If there's something anomalous out there, you want to find the real thing. If we're living our lives based on misinformation, that's a bad thing. Especially with the conspiracy theories—I've seen people become overly concerned that the government is lying; they can start distrusting everything and separating themselves from society."

Given the fact that our show is more hospitable to anomalies than West is inclined to be, it's worth asking why he agreed to participate at all. "I do the show because it's worthwhile to be the voice of reason," he says, "though it can be frustrating. At least the show is better than most others because it does have balance." I reminded Mick that there have been occasions—albeit rare ones—where he's been stumped by videos we asked him to analyze. "Yes, that's true," he admits. "But just because you can't find a mundane explanation doesn't mean you have to go far away and find an extraordinary one. Maybe there's a normal explanation right around the corner, if we only had some data we're currently missing. We find things that are mysterious; it doesn't mean that they're magic."

I've been fortunate to work with these guys for years, and their insights have been essential to the success and longevity of the show. They comprise only a fraction of our full roster of experts, but on this topic they are the all-stars. While they are all passionate and committed to the subject, they each bring a unique constellation of skills and perspectives, which means they are rarely unanimous and never boring. Nevertheless, they were in broad agreement that the modern UFO Canon looks something like this:

THE MUSSOLINI UFOS

We begin by stipulating that *Homo sapiens* have been taking note of anomalous phenomena in the skies for millennia. The Old Testament prophet Ezekiel wrote at length about a flaming celestial circle, and ancient cultures around the globe also described similar sightings. Were UFOs visiting Earth as early as the Stone Age? I will deal with the controversial and politically charged subject of "ancient aliens" in another chapter. For the moment I want to focus on the modern UFO era, which is roughly coeval with the age of human aviation.

The earliest episode in our Canon is one that's only recently risen to prominence—the so-called Mussolini UFOs. The theory, originally advanced by Italian UFOlogist Roberto Pinotti and later exalted by Pentagon UFO whistleblower David Grusch, is built largely around a set of documents procured by Pinotti but never independently verified. They purport to document a UFO crash in northern Italy near the town of Magenta in 1933. The crash allegedly prompted dictator Benito Mussolini to form a government department called Gabinetto RS/33 dedicated to retrieving and studying the wreckage.

It doesn't end there. Believers maintain that the United States got wind of the incident, intentionally avoided bombing the aircraft facility where the wreckage was being stored, and arranged with the aid of Pope Pius XII to have it secretly transported to America after Italy was liberated and Mussolini was strung up. This marks the beginning of what is commonly referred as the Pentagon's "Legacy Program" for the retrieval and reverse engineering of alien craft. It is a central theme threaded throughout the Canon, and remains a thriving trope throughout the discourse to this day. Keep in mind, however, that the Mussolini UFO theory has only garnered widespread attention in the past few years.

THE FOO FIGHTERS

The first Canonical event that made waves at the time was another World War II incident that took place with some regularity in the skies over Europe as Allied fighters and bombers conducted their missions and engaged in dogfights with German pilots. During these sorties, American airmen repeatedly reported encountering glowing orbs that appeared to maneuver under intelligent control. (One of those pilots, Ted Stevens, would later become a U.S. senator—he rejoins this narrative later.) They nicknamed these orbs Foo Fighters, and to this day they defy explanation. Some have said they were examples of a rare and little-understood meteorological phenomenon called ball lightning, which takes the shape of a luminous orb, not the forked bolts we usually see during thunderstorms. However, the Foo Fighters' reported erratic maneuvers disqualify that hypothesis. Ball lightning doesn't move like that.

The official explanation at the time was that the Foo Fighters were some sort of advanced, experimental Nazi weapon. That made sense since the Third Reich was quite adept at developing innovative military technology ("Though not quite adept enough," Robert Oppenheimer might remark.) And yet, after the war, the Allies were stunned to discover that *the German pilots had been reporting the same thing*. They thought the Foo Fighters were *our* secret weapon.

The episode is vital for modern UFOlogy for two reasons. First, it's an early data point in support of the enduring theory that UFOs have a keen and lasting interest in humans' military weaponry and combat operations. Some of the first AARO congressional hearings in 2023 included footage of an airborne object crossing over an unspecified Middle Eastern military operation. It could not be identified.

Second, the orb-shaped UFO has proved to be one of the most consistent types reported over the decades, landing at number one in AARO's first published report on sighting statistics. No other shape—not flying saucers, not triangles, not cigars—is reported so frequently. Captain Delgado's Mexican FedEx UFO was just such an orb. So was AARO's Middle Eastern UFO. It seems they will be with us for the duration.

ROSWELL AND FLYING SAUCERS

While the Foo Fighters garnered attention within the U.S. military, the official flying saucer craze that inaugurated the modern UFO era in the popular culture didn't kick off until 1947, a seminal year in the Canon. On June 24, Idaho search and rescue pilot Kenneth Arnold was en route to an air show in Pendleton, Oregon, in his single-engine Call Air A2. He'd made a fuel stop in Yakima, Washington, and shortly after getting airborne again he made a slight detour in the area of Mount Rainier to see if he could locate a crashed military plane that had recently gone down with thirty-two Marines on board. Conditions were clear; winds were light. At around 3:00 pm, Arnold would say he saw nine objects flying in formation at what he judged to be 1200 mph, far faster than any extant aircraft of the time. Arnold would deny ever using the term "flying saucer"; his own description of the objects changed over time from "disk" and "pie-pan" to something resembling a shoe heel. Nevertheless, after he told his story to local reporters the next day, the Associated Press and other wire services picked it up, the news spread far and wide (despite the lack of any corroborative evidence besides Arnold's statements), and somewhere along the way the term "flying saucer" was coined. It's been with us ever since.

At almost that exact same time, a rancher in Roswell, New Mexico, named W. W. Brazel discovered some strange debris on his property. That July he brought it to the local sheriff, who in turn alerted the Roswell Army Air Field. The Army dispatched a small team including Major Jesse Marcel to collect the debris. It then issued one of the strangest and most influential press releases in U.S. military history, announcing that it had retrieved a "flying disk." The following day the *Roswell Daily Record* printed the story with a headline that endures to this day: "RAAF Captures Flying Saucer on Ranch in Roswell Region." The Army almost immediately retracted the statement and said that in fact the debris was from a downed weather balloon.

Interest in the story petered out shortly thereafter—an interesting indicator of public trust in the credibility of the government back then. It was not until the late seventies that the Roswell legend we know today was born. That was when Major Marcel, by then retired, told a UFOlogist author that he believed the debris was of alien origin and the weather balloon explanation was a cover story.

Since then, the government has tried repeatedly to put the flying saucer theory to bed. First in 1994, the Pentagon admitted that yes, the weather balloon story was cover, not for an alien craft crash, but for a top-secret program called Project Mogul, which employed spy balloons in an attempt to monitor Soviet nuclear tests. Then in 1997 the Air Force published a lengthy and detailed report: "The Roswell Report: Case Closed." But by then the Roswell incident had become *the* central event in the UFO Canon, sustained in part thanks to Marcel's son, Jesse Jr., who claimed for decades that his father, who died in 1986, had shown him debris from the crash site that was indisputably alien. By then several Roswell locals had come forward with accounts corroborating the UFO theory, including W. W. Brazel himself, who agreed that the debris he'd discovered was no balloon. Ever since, any attempt by the government to disprove the UFO narrative has been interpreted by the Believers as further evidence of a vast, tentacular conspiracy. "It's the epitome UFO case," says Tim McMillan. "You can have a firm opinion about it one way or the other, and any position you land on, some other new information will come and you'll be like 'Shit, that changes my opinion.' For me, Roswell continues to linger. I'd almost firmly made up my mind that it wasn't an alien spaceship, but then I saw an interview with Jesse Marcel and he was saying the material he handled was not normal. I have a tough time mitigating that because he was the guy who was there. It's a conundrum."

I considered it a professional duty to visit Roswell myself, and found it something of a paradox. On the one hand, a fully articulated UFO tourist economy has mushroomed in the downtown district, where an impressive UFO museum anchors a string of similarly themed retail stores and restaurants. Even the local McDonald's has been custom-designed into congruence with the theme-park aesthetic, and business is brisk when the annual UFO festival clogs the main roads with traffic. But those looking to get access to the key sites are in for disappointment. The ranch where the debris was found has been purchased by a family who wants it kept private. There is no public access or luxury tour that can get visitors to the original crash site. And the Roswell Army Air Field, where the debris was allegedly taken, is now a commercial facility where jets go to be repainted, the former barracks repurposed for affordable housing and the local Job Corps center. The only surviving relic from those fateful days in 1947 is the *Roswell Daily Record* newspaper itself, where an antique Goss Urbanite printing press still churns out local news for the remaining five thousand subscribers. When people ask what my visit was like, I tell them to imagine Mecca with no Kaaba stone.

Given the paucity of forensic evidence supporting the Roswell incident—there's just that one photo of Marcel and the debris—its supremacy in the UFO Canon has always struck me as peculiar. Yet its mighty cultural influence cannot be overstated. It is directly due to the Roswell case, I submit, that the proud tradition of alien corpse footage continues to this day, despite the fact that those videos are among the easiest to debunk. Their provenance is always suspect, the alleged eyewitnesses never come forward, the corpses are biomechanical impossibilities (the tiny necks are never thick enough to support the massive heads), and the bodies are impossibly intact given that they were just subjected to the impact of a fatal crash landing.

Are there credible accounts of UFOs touching down in the Roswell tradition? Absolutely. One of the stronger cases we've explored is the 1971 Delphos, Kansas, incident, in which the Johnson family claimed to have witnessed a bright mushroom-shaped craft on their farm. This UFO may have been damaged, but it was still intact. It allegedly hovered below tree level, then flew off, leaving a glowing ring on the ground. When Erma Johnson touched the ring, she claimed her fingers went numb.

The family called the police and Officer Harlan Enlow was one of the first on the scene.

"It was an eye-opening surprise," he told us. "Here's this white dry ring. It looks like a big donut sitting in the middle of a mud field. We took statements. We photographed it. And then we took actual soil samples."

Those "glowing" soil samples have been studied at length, and the most anomalous discovery was the presence of hydrophobic (water-repellent) elements. Prosaic explanations have been put forth, including bacteria interacting with a chemical that had seeped into the groundwater; and a "fairy ring" of fungus. All of them can explain a portion of the fact pattern, but not all. We concluded this case was an unexplained phenomenon, and though eyewitness testimony is notoriously unreliable, Officer Enlow became a Believer. "I'm one hundred percent convinced that an incident happened," he says. "The story the family told us was credible."

THE McMINNVILLE PHOTOS

By the time the 1950s rolled around, the public was hungry for solid photographic proof of UFOs. The next Canonical event would provide them. These are the McMinnville photos, shot by the Trent family on their Oregon farm on May 11, 1950. As the story goes, Evelyn Trent was coming back to the house that evening after feeding rabbits when she noticed a flying disk hovering over the property. She called for her husband, Paul, who grabbed the family Kodak and emerged from the house in time to snap two shots of the object before it allegedly whizzed off. It was some time before Paul used up the rest of the film on that roll and had the photos developed. The prints clearly show something in the air, just beyond the family home and some telephone wires. They eventually came to the attention of a local reporter, got picked up by a national news service, and made the Trents famous.

What happened thereafter is a convoluted saga that has fueled the arguments of Believers and Skeptics alike. For one thing, the negatives of the photos changed hands several times and were suspiciously "lost" or "misplaced" before finally being returned to the Trents decades later. Secondly, the photos were subjected to a series of scientific analyses, which provide ammunition to both sides of the debate.

Note that by the 1950s, the government was taking UFOs sightings seriously enough to officially dedicate resources to studying them. Project Blue Book, run by the Air Force out of Wright-Patterson Air Force Base in Ohio, systematically studied select cases from 1952 till it shut down in 1969, with the stated goals of investigating potential national security threats, potential technological advances, and mitigating public panic. In addition, in the 1960s an academic team known as the Condon Commission took up the topic as well. This was a government-funded project run out of the University of Colorado.

William Hartman, an astronomer working for the Condon Commission, conducted a photometric analysis of the McMinnville images, interviewed the Trents (who never profited from the photos or sought publicity), and concluded their photos were among the few genuine UFO photos ever taken, though he acknowledged a possible discrepancy in the shadows of other objects in the photo—the house, the telephone pole—which suggested the photos were taken midmorning, not in the evening as the Trents had always claimed. That conclusion was reinforced by optical physicist Bruce Maccabee, who dispelled the lighting discrepancy by ascribing the variation in shadows to weather conditions and cloud cover at the time.

The Skeptics would have none of it. Building off the shadows issue, they argued that the Trents, who'd expressed prior interest in UFOs, were not the honest aw-shucks farm folk they claimed to be, but frauds who'd taken a side mirror from a Ford vehicle, strung it up on the overhead telephone wires, and perpetrated a mighty hoax. The Trents died in the late 1990s, insisting till the very end that the incident and the photos were genuine.

Since there are images to analyze—some of the most famous UFO photos in history, no less—we knew we had to give the McMinnville photos our full attention. (While we generally focus on more recent, "breaking" sightings, we revisit the classics too. We air on the HISTORY® network, after all.) We quickly ruled out common hoaxing techniques like throwing a hubcap, Frisbee, or side door mirror into the air—since there was no motion blur, the object was certainly "hovering." But was it hovering because the Trents had deviously tied it to a string and dangled it from the overhead wires, as the Skeptics have long claimed?

Richard Hoffman of the SCU reviewed the images and prior official analyses. He came down on the side of the Believers on this one, in part because he had trouble seeing the Trents as hoaxers. Not only had they avoided the limelight; they'd expressed trepidation that what they'd captured was not an alien craft but the test flight of a secret military craft they weren't supposed to see. And Hoffman was convinced by Macabee's photo analysis, which calculated the lines of sight from the photos, proving the object was far in the distance. "The lines converged beyond the telephone wires, which indicates that [the object] was not connected at all to the telephone lines," he said on-camera. "So I completely rule out that it's a hoax or anything contrived. I go with this being a UFO."

ABDUCTIONS, PROBES, AND IMPLANTS: THE HILL CASE AND ITS DESCENDANTS

Throughout the UFO era, a central question has been that of the putative aliens' attitude and motives. Were they ruthless conquerors as imagined in *War of the Worlds*, or benevolent visitors here to bestow upon us primitive earthlings the knowledge and harmony only an advanced civilization could attain. That debate shifted with the case of Betty and Barney Hill, who introduced—perhaps "implanted" is the better word—several major tropes into the discourse that are with us to this day.

The first is the theme of alien abduction. The Hills claimed that on the night of September 19, 1961, they were driving along a rural road in New Hampshire when a mysterious light began tracking their Chevy Bel Air as they returned from a trip to Niagara Falls to their home in Portsmouth. The light eventually revealed itself to be a craft that Barney later described as a large pancake. At one point the craft descended rapidly in front of their car, forcing it to stop, and the Hills observed several humanoid creatures inside. They loosely matched the anatomical description of what are now commonly referred to as "greys"—a little taller than five feet, oblong black eyes, gray skin. The greys are the second major contribution of the Hill story to the Canon.

The aliens issued orders telepathically. The Hills initially claimed they escaped, but that they heard a beeping sound that altered their consciousness in such a manner that after they finally made it home, they had no recollection of the three hours after the initial encounter. (The concept of "missing time" is the third major contribution.) After Betty had a series of vivid dreams, the Hills both submitted to hypnosis, during which they recalled similar, though not identical, memories of being abducted and subjected to medical experiments. (The fourth.)

The Hills' account would become the definitive alien abduction story in the UFOlogy Canon, spawning books, at least one movie, and countless TV segments. After Barney died in 1969, Betty enjoyed another forty-odd years as a UFO celebrity and guest speaker. During that time her musings about other sightings, abductions, and extraterrestrial encounters grew increasingly dubious.

Skeptics have long feasted on various vulnerabilities in the Hills' story, not least of which is a fair degree of overlap between details of their account and some episodes of the *Outer Limits* TV show that aired in 1964, years after their alleged abduction, but just a few weeks before the commencement of the Hills' hypnosis sessions. Why might they fabricate such a tale? A general thesis has emerged in the academic psychology literature that "alien abduction" victims are often child abuse victims living in denial, thus the frequency of accounts of probes in the rectal and genital areas. A variation of the trauma theory applied to the Hill case posits that they were suppressing racial trauma—Barney was Black, Betty was white, and aside from being a rare mixed-race couple at the time, they were both civil rights activists. They'd experienced the racial toxicity of mid-twentieth-century America firsthand, perhaps so intensely it triggered some kind of shared neurotic delusion. I'm leery of this theory, if only because millions of Black people have, tragically, experienced traumatic racism; it would follow that Black people would be overrepresented among abduction experiencers. Yet in my observations, the UFO community is whiter than a Connecticut yacht club.

Whether or not the Hills were delusional, their case has been enshrined in the Canon, and in its wake, countless other people have come forward with stories that align with its central themes. It's become the UFOlogy equivalent of a frequently covered classic pop tune like "Love Me Tender" or "All Along the Watchtower." Everybody does their own version. Eventually abduction cases would expand to include domesticated animals, and a whole subgenre of mutilated cattle cases would be added to the literature. And aside from the specifics of the case, the Hill abduction has been interwoven into a meta-narrative about UFOs, an attempt at a "grand unified theory" that connects the tech retrieval piece of it with the abductions. In its most basic formulation, the theory is that an American president (usually Eisenhower, sometimes Truman or Kennedy) made a cosmic bargain with his alien counterpart: every so often we get to take their tech for research; every so often they get to take some of our people for the same purpose. That's the real story behind breakthroughs such as Kevlar and the integrated circuit.

Granted, then, that the Hill abduction narrative has a powerful internal magnetism, regardless of its veracity. That means something. But what physical evidence was there that their account was true? The best we have is their clothing—Barney said his shoes had been scuffed somehow; then there's Betty's dress, recently purchased, which she claimed had been torn near the hem and stained an odd pinkish-purple color.

The Hill case has been covered so exhaustively we didn't want to devote an entire episode to it; instead, we came at it through the lens of a more recent, lesser-known case that illuminates the abduction genre overall. It's the 2014 incident known as the Salt Fork abductions, in which two men (who've never revealed their names) went on an overnight fishing trip in Salt Fork State Park in Ohio. They came back reporting much more than your average fish tale. They claimed they'd endured anomalous experiences much like those described in the Hill template. They say they saw strange lights near their nocturnal fishing spot; they "lost" the next four hours; they were so disturbed by what little they could recollect of that night that they stayed home for weeks afterward; and—key for us—they said they noticed strange stains on their shorts and tops. The older man also attested that his shirt was suddenly inside-out, as if it had been taken off, then put back on incorrectly.

In both the Hill and Salt Fork cases, those clothing stains became the focus of the forensic investigation. And in both cases, chemical spectroscopic analysis revealed something curious—carboxylic acid. The compound is found in nature—in some fruits and in vinegar, for instance—so it's not as if the clothes had traces of plutonium 239. But the fact that the stains were found on a new dress, near the hem where one wouldn't expect to make contact with fruit juice or vinegar, is interesting to some investigators, especially since in the account Betty revealed under hypnosis this is the area where the "greys" grabbed her.

The stains on the dress also match the pinkish hue of the stains on the shirt in the Salt Fork case, and both glowed when put under ultraviolet light. What does it all mean? For Marc D'Antonio, the coincidences are interesting, but not probative: "There are a number of things that naturally fluoresce, and if you wipe something on your clothing that might have a UV signature like that, sure, it'll show up really brightly. Does it mean that you were abducted by an alien? Maybe. But we can't say that it's a definitive indicator."

Since the show's inception, we've been on the lookout for credible abduction experiencers who will go on-camera *and* who have compelling documentation of their experience. It would be an exaggeration to say the challenge is akin to finding the Yeti, but not a gross one. Part of the problem is personal—I consider myself a sympathetic listener, and, as a journalist, a professional one. Still, I find interviewing abductees hard. Their experience is so difficult to swallow, and their storytelling style inevitably so earnest and pure, it's difficult for me not to find myself maintaining a tight-lipped smile and partially furrowed brow on my nodding head while they share their stories, all the while thinking, *This person is not just speaking a foreign language; they're using a different alphabet.*

That's pretty much what I was doing during the first three minutes of my introductory conversation with Mindy Tautfest, a leader in the present-day experiencer community. Tony Harris and I had come to Pasadena to speak at AlienCon2023. She was on a separate panel, and after we met in the green room, Mindy was recounting details of her truly phantasmagoric abduction. It involved a brain aneurysm, being transported to a place called the Void, and what she claims is a remarkable and common overlap between encounters with nonhuman intelligence and near-death experiences. I was expecting that after explaining her communion with the aliens she would proceed to recall relaxing summers on Vega or Alpha Centauri. Instead, she pivoted quickly to the extensive work she's done building the experiencer community, codifying investigative methods for others looking to get into this kind of work, and the techniques she's developed to help tweeze out genuine experiencers from fabulists or the mentally ill. Some are borrowed from law enforcement interrogation tricks, like asking a witness to recount their initial sequence of events in reverse. (If you've made up a story, that's hard to do.)

Mindy also described candidly the troubles she'd had reconciling her background as a devout Christian with her new belief in alien intelligence, all the while speaking with the precision and measured tone of an ICU nurse, which is what she was before she decided to dedicate her life to UFOs. In other words, she was a serious person, worthy of not only my attention but my respect.

"So Mindy, let me cut right to it," I said a bit brusquely, as I needed to wrap our conversation, meet up with Tony, and head to our panel. "I hear these abduction stories all the time, but nobody I've met ever has any physical evidence. It's all just these campfire stories. I'd love to have you on the show as an expert, but we'd need to focus on some case that has pictures or video we can analyze."

"You need to meet Sev Tok," she declared. "Yeah, she's named after the star system in *Star Wars*."

Shortly after the conference, Mindy connected me with Sev Tok and our team got both her story and her photographic evidence on-camera.

On September 16, 2017, Sev and her boyfriend had just moved to Arapahoe, North Carolina. They were still unpacking when Sev felt something peculiar on her rear end. When she looked, she was shocked at what she saw—nine dots arranged on her skin in a perfect X formation. The mark didn't hurt or itch badly, and the dots were neither raised nor indented on her skin. "We were both stunned," she said, "wondering how did this red X show up on the left cheek of my tush?"

Nine nights later, vexed to nightmare by a rush of disturbing memory fragments, Sev awoke in her bed and, she claims, realized that she'd been abducted somehow in her sleep.

"I was lying on this bed that resembled a hospital bed," she told us. "I turned my head around, and standing right behind me, right there, just inches from me, was a grey. We locked eyes, and *ding*, I'm back in my bedroom." Suspicious that this was not just a bad dream, Sev checked her body in the mirror, and says she discovered a *second* X mark on her backside, directly opposite the first. The marks lasted about three weeks before fading from her skin. "I was so afraid and so confused," she recalls. "There was no logical explanation for this."

Mindy Tautfest says abductees frequently come away from their experience with all kinds of markings, including bruising and scratches, and she's catalogued cases of marks similar to those Sev discovered on her derrière. One famous Los Angeles area doctor even claimed to have removed implants from abductees, and Lue Elizondo says the Pentagon has documented alien implant cases too. Sev didn't have an extracted implant to share with us, but she did have some photos of those strange X marks.

We had the photos analyzed by our medical and biological team, who considered the obvious explanations. Could the Xs have been bugbites? Bedbugs are known to group their bites together, but our biologist Dr. Stephanie Manka says it would be highly unlikely for any insect to bite in a pattern so straight and evenly spaced. We wondered if instead the marks were man-made, perhaps during a practice called a Kambo cleanse, in which shamans burn shallow wounds into the skin to apply secretions of a monkey frog (you can look this up) for the purpose of curing a wide variety of ailments. Again, Manka eliminated that hypothesis, because there was no scarring of the kind seen after Kambo rituals, and Kambo leaves marks that are lighter than the skin color around it. These spots were darker. Even our ER trauma doctor Ed Hope was stumped. "I'm not sure *what* kind of object would create this pattern," he confessed. "I don't know what's going on here." He was highly skeptical the greys were responsible for Sev Tok's marks, but we had to conclude these were an unknown skin trauma.

Sev has since parlayed that experience into speaking engagements and has become something of a folk hero within the community. "I believe this contact was part of my spiritual journey," she told me. "I do believe those two X marks saved my life. They spiritually awakened me and changed my perspective. We're all connected through consciousness, and we meet on the playground of consciousness. That's why we come into contact with these beings."

UFOS AND NUKES: THE MALMSTROM INCIDENT

While abduction experiences are intensely personal, other encounters engage matters of national security. And a Canonical incident from the late 1960s highlights a key theme in this part of the UFO conversation: the connection between UFOs and nukes. The seminal case here took place at Malmstrom Air Force Base in Montana on the night of March 24,1967. While Lt. Robert Salas was manning a subterranean storage and launch site for ten nuclear-equipped Minutemen 1 ICBMs, he received a frenzied call from a security officer on the surface, claiming there was an oval-shaped form with a pulsing orange light hovering over the facility, making extreme maneuvers like ninety-degree turns no known aircraft could perform. Moments later, Salas reported, the guidance and control systems of the nukes went on the fritz. Salas would later learn that a similar incident had occurred just eight days earlier, and yet another had happened at Minot Air Force Base in North Dakota the year before.

Nukes going off-line unexpectedly is the kind of event that would be documented rigorously, and indeed there are declassified communications confirming Salas' story. "All ten missiles in Echo Flight at Malmstrom lost strategic alert within ten seconds of each other," reads a memorandum from the earlier Malmstrom incident. After staying silent on the matter for years, Salas and other Malmstrom officers held a media event at the National Press Club in Washington in 2010; he's since shared his information and documentation with UAP investigators from AARO.

The Malmstrom case was not widely publicized at the time and didn't ascend into the Canon until Salas went public decades later, but it is compelling not only because of the official documentation surrounding it, but because it explains so much. Note that UFO sightings accelerate as the nuclear era begins—Mount Rainier and Roswell occurring just two years after Hiroshima. (A lesser-known incident from 1948 involves "green fireballs" reported in the skies above Los Alamos.) This dovetails with what's sometimes referred to as "Galactic Zoo" theory, which posits that aliens have been observing and monitoring us for millennia but are now taking a more active interest since we've learned how to split the atom, a watershed moment for our species that warrants closer observation.

Some say incidents like Malmstrom are meant as a message that we should forswear further development and deployment of nuclear weapons. Benevolent aliens are trying to persuade us not to destroy ourselves. An opposite interpretation claims that such incidents are trial runs for a pending invasion—belligerent aliens sending advance scouts to confirm that they can disable our most advanced weaponry before launching their attack. In either framework, stealth is the key. Just as a professional wildlife photographer learns to avoid the notice of a snow leopard, the aliens usually cloak themselves, so we won't be alerted to their presence and take appropriate countermeasures. Incidents such as Malmstrom are the rare close encounters when their cloaking tech is inactive and they've ended up revealing themselves, unintentionally or on purpose.

Malmstrom is the prime example of a UFO-nuke incident, even though there's no video of it (that we know of). That's due to the extensive documentation of the case, and because Salas and others like him have been so outspoken. The incident was even mentioned in the May 2022 congressional hearing on UFOs.

Given the awesome and unforgiving power of our nuclear technology, and the gravity of the UFO-nukes narrative, it's unsurprising that videos of alleged public sightings of UFOs near nuclear facilities pop up regularly. One such case garnered some buzz in 2019, when a Marine Corps veteran in Two Creeks, Wisconsin, claimed to have noticed a bright light outside his window, hovering over the nearby Point Beach Nuclear Plant. He claims he called a neighbor to record it. The video shows a large glowing orange orb in the darkness, and if you zoom in you can see additional smaller, dimmer lights nearby it. "You gotta be kidding me!" he exclaims on the footage. "You're not going to believe me, but there's a freaking UFO out there!"

Perhaps. Or perhaps not. The hovering of the orb quickly eliminated the possibility that it was an airplane, the lack of engine or rotor noise ruled out a helicopter, and the absence of FAA-mandated red and green lights—there was just that orange glow—ruled out a drone. Plus, the airspace above nuclear power plants is highly restricted. This was not any kind of standard aircraft.

But the object didn't make any strange maneuvers or defy physics as we understand it, the way the most credible alleged UFOs do. It just hung there. Our forensic video analyst Michael Primeau didn't think the footage was faked, though the best version we could provide him didn't have much metadata. So if the recording did capture a real object, what was it?

Rich Hoffman rode to the rescue, noting that seventeen seconds into the clip the orb flickers, and as it flashes one can see what looks like a building, illuminated momentarily, just in front and below the light. That means the light was at a much lower altitude than originally described. Then there was the telling coincidence that the neighborhood's streetlights were designed with high-pressure sodium vapor lamps, which emit an orange hue. Mystery solved: in this case, aliens were not conducting reconnaissance on a nuclear power plant. However, the municipality of Point Beach might want to check for voltage fluctuations in its power grid.

Those risible misidentifications notwithstanding, the UFO-nukes thesis is still going strong, and not just on YouTube. Former Pentagon UFO investigator Lue Elizondo has written at length about a plan he and his team proposed to take advantage of UFOs' attraction to nuclear technology and capture one using electromagnetic pulses. He says it was called Operation Interloper: "So you have a nuclear-powered carrier, with other nuclear-powered vessels, potentially nuclear-powered submarines, which also may have potentially nuclear weapons. And so the idea is to create a nuclear footprint that is so irresistible to these things. We would create a trap, and then that trap would be sprung." Operation Interloper never made it past the planning phase, but Elizondo continues to believe the UFO-nukes connection is very real.

Whether or not Malmstrom will remain a Canonical event is an open question. In June 2025, the incident was featured prominently in an explosive *Wall Street Journal* investigation that revealed that the Pentagon has *intentionally* spread disinformation to fuel UFO theories for decades, to distract the attention of the public and America's enemies from the military's secret programs, and its vulnerabilities. Citing more than a dozen sources, the article claimed the Malmstrom incident was really a secret test to confirm if the nuclear missiles there could be disabled by electromagnetic interference. The "orange orb" central to Salas' account was in fact part of a testing device that would glow orange as it charged. He and the rest of the eyewitnesses to the event were kept in the dark for decades.

This Pentagon disinformation debunk has been around at least since 2013. It was the central thesis of the fascinating 2013 documentary *Mirage Men*, which featured Richard Doty, a retired special agent with the Air Force Office of Special Investigations. According to Doty and others featured in the film, they spent years cooking up and spreading disinformation about UFOs and impending alien invasions to hoodwink people who had actually seen glimpses of secret Air Force projects.

Still, for the Skeptics, the *Wall Street Journal* piece was like Christmas coming early. In their opinion a pillar of the entire UFOlogy narrative has been demolished. But for the Believers, it is merely proof that the government lies not only to the public, but to its own people.

RENDLESHAM AND THE UFO INJURIES

By 1969 we enter a period Hoffman refers to as "The Dark Ages," during which interest in UFOs subsided considerably: "The Condon Committee issued its report and basically said no one should spend their time with this. Then Project Blue Book shut down—even though it had concluded that most of the reported sightings were misidentifications, more than seven hundred of its cases remained unexplained. Nevertheless, the National Academy of Sciences blessed the Condon report and the whole field was shelved as 'fringe science.'"

Two major incidents punctuate "The Dark Ages." The first is the Rendlesham Forest incident of 1980, often referred to as "Britain's Roswell." Like most of these Canonical incidents, you can spend months reading books and watching documentaries about the case. The rabbit hole goes deep.

It happened on December 26, 1980, in the forest just outside the Royal Air Force Woodbridge base, which at the time was being used by the U.S. Air Force. On the night in question, a patrol reported seeing lights descending into the forest. Some testimony claims that as the team approached the site, they observed a glowing metallic object with colored lights moving through the trees, emitting a noise that agitated nearby farm animals. The next morning the airmen noticed impressions in the ground in a triangular pattern. Two days later the deputy base commander, Lt. Col. Charles Halt, visited the site again with a team. They took radiation readings, allegedly recording elevated levels at the "hotspot." Halt's team also reported seeing the strange lights again that night.

The incident has been dismissed as a misidentification of the light from the beacon coming from the nearby Orfordness Lighthouse, a falling meteor, or even an elaborate prank. Local police investigated at the time and found nothing anomalous. To be sure, there are inconsistencies in the eyewitness accounts and explanations for each piece of evidence. (The impressions in the ground, for instance, could have been made by rabbits digging.) And despite claims of a massive government cover-up, complete with death threats, it's hard not to notice that many of the principal characters in the event have been speaking publicly about it for decades. None have disappeared or turned up dead under fishy circumstances. If the government is willing to kill to keep this secret buried, it needs to try harder.

And yet . . . One aspect of the case has not only helped keep the glow of Rendlesham alight; it's recharged the entire discussion of encounters that injure the eyewitness. Recall those alleged elevated radiation readings at the site. One of the eyewitnesses at Rendlesham, AFC John Burroughs, claims he not only saw the craft but got close to it, experienced intense light, and then passed out. Afterward, he would spend years fighting the Veterans Affairs Administration for disability benefits for injuries he insisted were the result of the encounter. Lue Elizondo knows Burroughs personally: "Burroughs indicated to me directly that injuries he sustained from this UAP created havoc to his health. Heart complications, loss of vision, all very consistent with radiation poisoning." The VA denied his claims for many years, and—curiously—his case was stuck in quicksand forever because the Department of Defense had classified his health records. That's strange. It was only after the personal intervention of Senator John McCain that Burroughs was awarded benefits for his condition in 2015.

The fact that the United States is paying a man for injuries allegedly sustained during a UFO encounter has, understandably, lent the Rendlesham Forest incident and others like it a new patina of legitimacy. The case came up during Elizondo's congressional testimony in November 2024. It has also boosted interest in the ongoing work of Stanford immunologist Dr. Garry Nolan, who has tracked similar injuries consistent with radiation poisoning among other servicemen who claim to have encountered UFOs.

On the show the Burroughs case and the Rendlesham incident came up in the context of a case with perhaps the best-known photo evidence of these alleged UFO injuries. That came from the 1967 case of World War II veteran Stefan Michalak, who claimed he'd encountered a glowing cigar-shaped craft while on a prospecting trip near Falcon Lake in Manitoba, Canada. When he returned, he told his family he needed immediate medical attention for burns he'd suffered on his abdomen. A photo of Michalak taken in his hospital bed revealed a grid of dark circular burns on the front of his torso. His son Stan remembers the day vividly. "He was scared," Stan told us. "Here's a man who has been through the Second World War, who's been to the concentration camps and was in one himself. It was like somebody had implanted little buttons underneath his skin."

What caused Michalak's wounds? Our ER medicine expert Dr. Lisa Dabby says his other symptoms—nausea, headaches, fatigue—all aligned with the presentation of radiation poisoning, but they lasted much longer than the usual two or three days. Also, Michalak's bloodwork was normal—in radiation poisoning cases, white blood cells often drop precipitously, like a patient undergoing radiation therapy for cancer. And the peculiar pattern of the burns also made her doubtful: "Usually the zone of damage is going to be bigger. It's not just going to be a small pattern. This looks like something made contact with just that area of skin."

On the other hand, one of our physicists, Prof. Matthew Szydagis, is open to the UFO hypothesis. "If this is actually an injury from ionizing radiation, that would imply some sort of very collimated beams of radiation. You can have ionizing radiation from radio isotopes used perhaps as fuel for some sort of black ops, exotic aircraft, or spacecraft." Of course that's highly speculative, but Szydagis points to subsequent investigation of the site of Michalak's alleged encounter. It bears similarities to Rendlesham. "Radiation was found, not only in the soil, but pieces of metal found in the crushed vegetation. That does track with other UFO encounters, such as Burroughs'. In my opinion, this is an unexplained story. And I think that it is valid to suggest that this might have been an example of an actual craft from some sort of nonhuman intelligence." More than fifty years later, the case remains one of Canada's greatest UFO mysteries.

MASS SIGHTINGS: THE PHOENIX LIGHTS

After Rendlesham, seventeen years passed until the other major Canonical event that punctuates the "Dark Ages," the 1997 Phoenix Lights incident. As with all our Canonical entries, this case isn't merely enduringly popular; it is additive to overall conversation. What did the Phoenix Lights add? Easily the most important UFO event of the 1990s, the event highlights an important category of incident—the phenomenon of the mass sighting.

It is often assumed that the Phoenix Lights was a singular event. In fact, it was at least two, and depending on whom you ask, possibly many more. The central events took place on the evening of March 13, 1997, when hundreds, if not thousands, of people in the Phoenix area reported seeing a formation of lights in a boomerang or V formation in the night sky. The objects were actually observed in a much wider area than Phoenix proper. They allegedly flew from southwest Nevada through the Phoenix area, then proceeded toward Tucson. Hours later a second sighting was reported, a string of stationary glowing orbs spotted near the Sierra Estrella mountains.

The lights were witnessed by so many people that the incident instantly became a news story. Media requests deluged Governor Fife Symington's office, and the next day he held an impromptu press conference making a mockery of the event. With a staffer dressed as an alien standing next to him by the podium, Symington chided: "Let me just say that I believe it is a serious offense for anyone, be it human, space alien, or otherwise, to engage in mysterious activity in our nighttime skies."

That didn't suffice for committed UFO investigators, people like Dr. Lynne Kitei, who has since dedicated much of her life and her reputation to the incident. As Kitei and others pressed every military base in the area for an explanation, one eventually came. The original V formation was a group of A-10 Thunderbolt jets flying in formation, and the series of orbs was parachute flares dropped by a different squadron of jets. Both exercises were part of a pilot training program run by the Air National Guard called Operation Snowbird. Years later, one of the pilots confirmed he flew one of the planes.

Case closed? Nope. Although comparisons between the Phoenix Lights footage and known military flare exercises have shown similarities, Kitei and others don't believe the Phoenix Lights have ever been replicated. "Three Air National Guards came into town right before the third anniversary to show everyone," she told NewsNation. "They really publicized it. And talk about a joke. Not only did [the flares] fall apart immediately; they tried to make a triangle, and one of the lights just fizzled out. To date, the Phoenix Lights have never been reenacted or explained."

Lue Elizondo has also analyzed the footage. His conclusion: "They weren't flares, we know that . . . white phosphorus flares usually drop out the end of an aircraft . . . they flare up, they come down on a parachute, and then they dissipate, they burn out. That did not happen."

And for what it's worth, a decade after his dismissive press conference, Governor Symington himself admitted he'd witnessed the lights and initially believed he'd seen an alien craft.

By this point the UFO community was even less inclined to trust official government efforts to explain away UFO sightings, in part because of a man named Bob Lazar, a self-proclaimed physicist who had come forward in 1989 to say he'd been working on a government program to reverse engineer captured alien craft. This program was located at Area 51 in Nevada, now ground zero of American UFO mania. Almost everything about Bob Lazar's credentials and employment history has been thoroughly debunked. Even in the UFO community, which grants wide berths to "whistleblower" types, he's considered a nut. Nevertheless, it's fair to say that if a single man is to be credited for inserting the story of Area 51 into the popular culture, it would be he.

With the popularity of TV shows like *The X-Files* and conspiracy-minded political phenomena like the militia movement, it was clear by the 1990s that UFOlogy would always have a place in the culture beyond fans of science fiction. Yet it remained largely the stuff of entertainment or paranoid delusion—fun at best, often silly, sometimes sinister, depending on how thoroughly people were willing to order their lives around its Canon. Believers were often compared to the religiously devout, using UFOs to fill Pascal's "God-shaped hole" in their hearts. And the comparison didn't seem like much of a stretch when formal, organized UFO religions made news.

On March 26, 1997, less than two weeks after the Phoenix Lights sighting, members of the Heaven's Gate cult, a UFO religion based in San Diego, committed mass suicide. (It was the passing of the Hale-Bopp comet, not the Phoenix Lights incident, that triggered their decision to "graduate" from human evolution.) It was this kind of thing that underscored, in macabre detail, the element of kookiness within the UFO community, disincentivizing serious scientists and journalists from embracing the topic. UFOlogy's "Dark Age" would extend into the new millennium.

THE *NIMITZ* TIC TAC

The most impactful UFO event of our young millennium occurred in 2004, but the public didn't learn of it until 2017. It is the watershed moment that launched the current UFO Renaissance. I'm referring, of course, to the famed USS *Nimitz* Tic Tac incident I touched upon in the introduction to this book. It is commonly grouped with two similar incidents in 2015–16 involving the USS *Roosevelt*. Each of these was, crucially, recorded on military-grade cameras, and leaked to the public in conjunction with a groundbreaking *New York Times* article. Together, the three pieces of footage are known simply as "The Pentagon Videos," or by their individual nicknames—"GIMBAL," "GOFAST," and "FLIR." Among UFOlogists, this footage is the equivalent of the Zapruder film.

The incidents themselves are truly remarkable, for both the reported details of the events and the quality and credibility of the eyewitnesses and the footage. On November 14, 2004, U.S. Navy Cdr. David Fravor and other aviators were flying F/A-18 Hornets from the USS *Nimitz* aircraft carrier off the Southern California coast. Fravor would later report that he encountered a UFO that resembled a "Tic Tac," which moved with previously undocumented speed, acceleration, and maneuverability. In short, it neither looked nor behaved like any known asset of the U.S. or other rival militaries. A second group of fighters was launched off the *Nimitz* to investigate, one of which was equipped with an advanced infrared camera that recorded the object, logging crucial telemetry data that would help corroborate Fravor's account. Then, in late 2014 and early 2015, similar incidents were recorded by fighter pilots from the USS *Roosevelt* strike group off the east coast of Florida. These videos include cockpit audio, and you can clearly hear the pilots exclaiming in amazement as they track something they've never seen before. "Ohhhh got it! . . . Oh my gosh, dude."

When the videos were leaked to the public it wasn't simply the footage that set off the frenzy. It was the *New York Times* article from December 16, 2017, which revealed that the Pentagon had been taking these incidents and others like them seriously for years. Headlined "Glowing Auras and 'Black Money': The Pentagon's Mysterious UFO Program," the article detailed a $22 million program called the Advanced Aerospace Threat Identification Program, or AATIP, which had been officially, if secretly, authorized by Congress at the behest of Senators Harry Reid of Nevada, Daniel Inouye of Hawaii, and Ted Stevens of Alaska—the same Ted Stevens who'd encountered a Foo Fighter as a pilot back in World War II. In other words, despite decades of denials going back at least as far as Roswell, it turned out that the Pentagon was spending millions of taxpayer dollars investigating UFO incidents.

The story broke because Lue Elizondo, who ran AATIP, and Chris Mellon, former deputy assistant secretary of defense for intelligence, had grown concerned that the Pentagon had curtailed funding for AATIP and wasn't taking the national security threat these UFOs represented seriously enough. Frustrated that his work was being stymied, Elizondo would leave the Pentagon, go public, and become the face of the UFO Renaissance. Mellon, Fravor, and other characters from the Pentagon Video incidents have now become household names in the UFO community.

The impact of those revelations has been profound and enduring. In Washington, there is now an outspoken cadre of congressmen—sometimes referred to as the UAP Caucus—who believe these incidents are credible enough to justify more transparency from the Pentagon. That's why we now have AARO, the dedicated Defense Department team tasked with investigating these incidents and reporting on them publicly to Congress. AARO has confirmed that some of its cases still cannot be explained; but has consistently maintained that it has yet to find any conclusive proof of extraterrestrial technology or intelligence. Consequently, many in the UFO community think AARO is part of the broader ongoing cover-up.

But that's just part of it. With the Pentagon videos, the whole game has changed. Richard Hoffman has seen it firsthand: "Suddenly there's a new awareness in the scientific community saying, 'Hey, the USG is taking it seriously; why can't we?' We started seeing a whole plethora of scientists coming forward wanting to talk to other scientists" and devote real time to the topic. Marc D'Antonio agrees: "There is a tremendous amount of people coming forward because they feel like they can. Pilots are not shunned, it's not frowned upon anymore, because the military says they exist." According to D'Antonio, a central element to this sea change has been the adoption of a new term for the phenomenon. "Unidentified Flying Object, UFO," is out. "Unidentified Aerial Phenomenon, UAP," is in. "They've rebranded UFO as UAP," says D'Antonio. "When we talk about UAP it's not inflatable alien dolls and tinfoil hat guys in their basements." The incidents also established v hat are now known as "the five observables," the criteria by which all UAPs are judged: sudden acceleration, hypersonic velocity with no signature like a vapor trail, cloaking, anti-gravity lift, and trans-medium travel.

The funny thing is, people have debunked the Pentagon Videos, or at least tried to. In 2024 AARO announced that it had done a detailed trigonometric analysis of the "GOFAST" video from the 2016 *Roosevelt* video and discovered that the object that seemed to be moving very fast and close to the water was actually at an altitude of thirteen thousand feet and moving slowly, like a piece of floating debris might. The video looks anomalous only because of a trick of the eye known as the parallax effect, which deceives a moving observer into thinking close objects are moving much faster than distant ones. Similarly, our resident debunker Mick West is convinced the *Nimitz* Tic Tac merely captures other planes flying away from the fighter jets. "You can say there are Canonical events in the history of UFOlogy," he scolds, "but it's all Canonical crap."

That hasn't dampened an intense new public appetite for military-grade UFO footage, and indeed there's been a steady supply, for which we are gushingly grateful. Documentarian Jeremy Corbell, an impressively sourced journalist, has broken several scoops in recent years with leaked video of more recent incidents. Some, like the so-called Mosul Orb recorded over Iraq, have been deemed worthy of the attention of AARO's investigators. Others have made a splash in the global press, like a second Tic Tac video recorded by the USS *Jackson* in the same area off the coast of San Diego as the 2004 *Nimitz* video. Our experts believe that is truly anomalous.

To be sure, other Corbell scoops have been quickly determined to be misidentifications. A video known as the "Green Pyramid," which purports to show a triangular UAP above another U.S. warship, was revealed to be a regular plane, its FAA lights flashing at the required one cycle per second. It's true that the craft's airframe appears as a green triangle on the video, but that's because of a blurring effect known as bokeh that happens with cameras using wide aperture lenses. When the aperture isn't fully open, the bokeh typically forms around the object in the shape of the aperture blades within the lens, which in this case was a triangle. There you have it.

It doesn't take much to get Hoffman audibly agitated on this topic. "I'm getting sick of watching Corbell come out with stuff that just looks like bird shit on a camera lens. Where'd you get this video? Can you tell me if anybody serious has analyzed it? Just because your source is in the military doesn't mean they're correct. I'm not going to buy something without evidence that shows it's been properly treated, because over sixty years I've heard too many horseshit stories."

So . . . are there any more cases that withstand scrutiny? Certainly. They may one day be debunked conclusively, but at the time of broadcast, these are some examples of military-grade footage we've deemed unexplained:

- The aforementioned "Aguadilla" video out of Puerto Rico, which the SCU studied exhaustively and concluded has no known explanation, even in the face of a recent government report concluding it was two balloons.
- The "Rubber Duck" video, leaked by a Customs and Border Patrol agent as part of a trove of videos of UAPs along the Arizona border. Some of those have been identified as birds, but the "Rubber Duck"—so named because of

its duck-like appearance on the thermal video—is trickier. The SCU also examined this, and concluded that because of its temperature and flight path it cannot be a balloon (it was going in circles, against the wind) nor a drone (it was too cold).

- The "Mideastern Orb" mentioned earlier—a metallic sphere shot by a Reaper drone over an undisclosed location in the Middle East in 2022, which AARO released and declared unidentified. Our experts agreed—not that it was an extraterrestrial craft, but that there wasn't enough data to make a confident determination about what it was. A subsequent geolocation analysis by the open-source intelligence outfit Bellingcat made a sound case that the object was a balloon, but until we get confirmation from AARO that the case is closed we're being cautious.
- There's also the case of the "*Omaha* USO"—another Corbell-leaked video, this one showing an orb-like object shot from the USS *Omaha* during another war games exercise. The footage is interesting, but it's shot off a monitor and doesn't include telemetry readings, so our analysis is impaired by a paucity of hard data. Yet the case merits deeper investigation because it raises the bigger issue of USOs—Unidentified Submerged Objects that can operate in both air and water. The idea plays into an intriguing thesis of nonhuman intelligence—that they're not coming from outer space but from the bottom of the ocean. In addition, the case engages a competing hypothesis about the hot-button trend of encounters between U.S. Naval warships and UAPs—

could we instead be seeing high-tech attempts by rival militaries to gather data on our naval capabilities? More on that in the next chapter.

- One case has even stumped our debunker-in-chief, Mick West. This was a video shot by Ukrainian troops in February 2024. Soldiers from the 406th Battalion, operating a camera-equipped quadcopter drone, spotted an oblong UFO on the horizon. Their equipment indicated the object was thirty miles away, which would mean it was truly massive. We ruled out any conventional aircraft, including drones or blimps. Tim McMillan thought it was likely a mirage, but Mick geolocated the location and determined that the geological and atmospheric conditions also eliminated that possibility. His conclusion: "It's maybe not as far away as they think it is. Perhaps not quite as big as they think it is. But I don't actually know what this is."

These are some of the meatiest cases that keep the burgeoning UFO community fed, yet still hungry for more. But personally, the video I find most important and to some extent most chilling was one quickly revealed as fake. In fact, its creators never claimed otherwise.

This video was posted in September of 2018. We see an F-18 Hornet approaching the deck of the USS *Ford*. The camera is clearly positioned on another aircraft above and to the left to record the landing. As the F-18 touches down and decelerates, the camera follows it along the deck as we see it pass other aircraft parked on the side of the jetway. They are all known military aircraft, except one—a triangular craft that looks like something straight out of a science fiction movie. In fact, it's something straight out of the UFOlogy Canon: the TR-3B, a legendary aircraft said to have been reverse-engineered from a crashed alien ship. Nuclear-powered, equipped with a vaunted anti-gravity drive, and shielded from enemy radar by a plasma field, the TR-3B is the ultimate stealth weapon. It's so renowned, model TR-3Bs are for sale online.

There were several reasons not to take the video seriously, the first being that an official version of the same video was released by the Department of Defense showing the exact same plane landing on the exact same ship under the exact same conditions, but with no TR-3B on the deck. Still, a conspiracy-minded viewer might think the "official" video had simply been edited to remove the TR-3B to protect the secret of the government's alien tech.

To eliminate any doubt, we showed the footage to Mick West and Tim McMillan. They noticed that the shadow cast by the TR-3B onto the deck was at a more obtuse angle than those cast by the adjacent planes. How could that be if they are being lit by the same source—the sun—at the same time of day in a nearly identical location? Also, once the footage is stabilized so that the ship's deck stays fixed in the frame, the TR-3B (and only the TR-3B) is seen jiggling around as the video plays, a telltale sign that it's been edited into the footage without properly registering the motion tracking with the ship's deck at the sub-pixel level. "That is a hoax," McMillan declared. "Not the worst I've seen. Not the best." Indeed, we traced the footage back to a video effects house in France. They told us they made the video and posted it for fun, and had no idea it would go so viral.

Why is it worth mentioning? Because someone *did* take the video seriously: Iranian state media presented it on national television as proof the United States is plotting with aliens to take over the world. In our post-*Nimitz* era, these videos can have a lasting impact as weapons of information warfare, even when they are clearly fake. The USS *Ford* video is not proof of aliens, but it is proof that this business is not all fun and games. When UFOlogy gets exploited by hostile governments, it can sow distrust and anger toward the U.S. military. We concluded that sure, this was a hoax, but not such a harmless hoax.

THE PARADE OF WHISTLEBLOWERS

The most recent entrant into our UFOlogy Canon centers around a different type of event altogether. Since 2023 some of the biggest buzz has centered around a string of highly credentialed, highly serious men with impressive military careers coming forward to tell slightly different versions of the same story: nonhuman intelligence is real; the government's Legacy Program has been retrieving and reverse engineering alien craft for decades, and a massive cover-up has been perpetuated to keep the truth submerged.

The Parade of Whistleblowers began with Lue Elzondo, though when he first went public in 2017, it was merely to disclose the existence of AATIP and his role in it. It wasn't until 2024, when he published a best-selling book, that he really told all. By that time, the floodgates had already opened after David Grusch, a former Pentagon military intelligence officer, was granted official whistleblower status by the Inspector General of the Intelligence Community (IGIC). In 2023 he went on to tell his version of the story on television and later, under oath to Congress. Others have followed, including retired rear admiral Tim Gallaudet, retired Army colonel Karl Nell, and former Air Force airman Jake Barber, who says he knows the retrieval program exists because he worked on it himself for years. Others will most certainly have emerged before this book is published.

I have personal experience with Elizondo, Grusch, and Barber, having produced specials for NewsNation built around their exclusive interviews with correspondent Ross Coulthart, one of the world's preeminent UFO journalists and an unabashed Believer. Just as when I first spoke with Captain Delgado about the "FedEx UFO," I was taken aback by the experience of hearing these men of honor—their faces unflinching, their gazes unwavering, their voices projecting supreme confidence—utter some of the most outlandish statements I'd ever heard from anyone who wasn't tripping on acid.

With such credible and aligned accounts, there are only a few plausible explanations:

- The Parade of Whistleblowers is, either knowingly or unwittingly, part of a massive disinformation campaign, à la *The Mirage Men*. Some believe the UFO Canon has been promoted to prevent us from probing into what's really flying around in the sky that we shouldn't be seeing: experimental, next-gen weaponry of ours, or unchecked incursions into U.S. airspace by equally high-tech craft belonging to our enemies. In this scenario whistleblowers are given "secret knowledge" and then goaded or manipulated into perpetuating the Canon in public.
- The whistleblowers are hucksters, selling books, getting booked for paid appearances, or seeking investors in UAP-related business enterprises. It is a fact that UFOlogy drives an economy where things are bought

and sold, and where demand will be filled by supply. I'm a for-profit participant in this economy too and don't begrudge anyone making a buck, though I'd prefer they do it honestly.

There are well-known charlatans out there. Dr. Steven Greer sells handsets and training techniques for people eager to join the "CE5" movement (meaning close encounters of the fifth kind)—the kind initiated by a human observer who has developed the capability to summon UFOs. Greer charges stiff prices to take people on summoning tours and was once credibly accused of hiring a Cessna pilot to drop flares to make Greer's customers believe extraterrestrials had indeed been summoned.

- The Parade of Whistleblowers are victims of a mass psychosis or hysteria. It wouldn't be the first time this happened: see the Dancing Plague of 1518 in Strasburg (it's exactly what it sounds like); the Salem Witch Trials of the 1690s, or the Seattle windshield pitting epidemic of 1954—all cases in which delusions and paranoia "infected" a community of like-minded or physically proximate people. There is truth to the fact that a substantial proportion, large though uncountable by me, of those who submit UAP evidence and testimonies have been through traumatic experiences during their military service. Could UFOlogy be an informal mechanism for coping with PTSD? This isn't me spitballing, it's derived directly from the accounts of troubled veterans who've sent in videos for us to analyze, certain that they've had an encounter—sometimes more than one—that has imbued them with a transcendent, uplifting, curative experience that salvaged their mental health out of an abyss of despair.

- What they are telling is at least some version of the truth. It is not a stretch to say that with their security clearances the Parade of Whistleblowers has likely seen and heard things kept from the public, and at least partly kept from the whistleblowers themselves. It is equally possible that they observed things that nobody in the military could explain and still cannot.

With so much gray area on the board, one might hope that a minimalist position would hold sway, some version of "Can't we all get along?" which accepts that some UAPs remain inexplicable, while acknowledging that the possibility of extraterrestrials visiting earth remains an unlikely explanation and has yet to be confirmed. But for the Parade of Whistleblowers this is not good enough, and that's where they open themselves to the criticism that they've gotten far ahead of their skis. Grusch not only believes in the retrieval and reverse engineering program; he supports the Mussolini UFO story, which is among the most outlandish and thinly documented entries in the Canon. He's gone as far as suggesting some anomalies may have entered into an alliance with the Kremlin. Elizondo claims that after he began working on UAPs, aliens began appearing at his home in Maryland—both he and his wife claim they would observe green orbs passing through the walls in their hallway. Jake Barber says that the Legacy Program screens recruits for psychic abilities and trains them to operate as "psionics"—assets who can not only summon but usurp control of alien craft.

But let's not judge too harshly. We're along for this journey till the end, and now that we've taken in the lay of the land and scanned the Canon of modern UFOlogy, we must confront the next question—or perhaps we should have done that first. If UFOs are indeed the technology of nonhuman intelligence, where might they be coming from and how could they get here?

Chapter 4

QUESTIONING THE COSMOS

A VERY LARGE ASPIRATION

Drive south from Albuquerque. In about seventy-five miles you'll turn west at Socorro, making your way through a downtown strip dotted with Old West clothing stores, Mexican restaurants, and cannabis dispensaries. Keep going, past Magdalena. The demographics of the road traffic shift—the cars are older, many crying out for a new paint job or muffler; the commercial vehicles grow more exotic, as the ubiquitous eighteen-wheelers that dominate the interstate are replaced by massive trucks with wider wheelbases, bigger tires, and esoteric industrial configurations and appendages used for—what exactly? Resource extraction, construction, salvaging even larger machines?

I first saw the VLA antennae from nine miles away. They struck me at first like a cluster of white desert flowers in bloom, which I smugly regarded as an original thought until I saw Carl Sagan make the same observation in the film they show at the visitor center. But more than that, from a distance, they reminded me of eager uniformed students or choir singers, faces turned up, awaiting instruction and enlightenment from an unseen educator or conductor positioned somewhere above.

The twenty-seven telescopes of the Very Large Array are, for my money, the most impressive monument to human curiosity ever built. For only the most inquisitive of species would have such a compelling desire to understand its place in the universe and events that took place in remote galaxies trillions of miles away, millions of years ago—a desire that spawned the impulse not only to design this place, but to make it a reality. A curious species, no doubt. Also a prosperous one. Perhaps a lonely one as well, longing not only for knowledge, but for company.

The VLA is the world's largest radio telescope. The individual 230-ton antennae are themselves gargantuan, each parabolic dish eighty-two feet in diameter. But the telescope is not one antenna. It is all of them, working in unison. Things are big here and they have to be—the VLA observes radio waves, the lowest end of the light spectrum, where the wavelengths are so long and the signals so weak you need a radio telescope of this size to detect them so far away. Building a Very Small Array is not an option.

I came in March, when the VLA was at its most accessible—what they call Configuration D. In the course of every year, to provide a variety of images and resolutions, the antennae are repositioned along custom rail tracks that extend in three arms from the command center like a gigantic Mercedes-Benz symbol—what the folks there call "the WYE." In Configuration D, they are all bunched together near the center. In Configuration A, the widest, they spread out along 13 miles of track, together forming a simulated dish 22 miles wide.

The VLA is always on. Unlike terrestrial light telescopes that can only be used at night when the stars are visible, radio waves can be "seen" twenty-four hours a day. But even though it's cranking out mountains of data every minute, the place has the feel of an abandoned ruin. It's so remote you'll rarely have crowds of tourists, except the occasional school group. The Statue of Liberty, it ain't. And the staff largely remain out of view in secure areas like the central building, a generic cement block that could pass as an airport's lost luggage storage facility, but within which, entombed in its own Faraday cage–equipped room, one of the world's most powerful supercomputers digests a flood of incoming data, performing 16 quadrillion calculations per second. I guess that's where the scientists were. The only people I saw working on the entire site were an elderly janitor changing a light bulb in the visitor center hallway and a young woman behind the counter in the gift shop—friendly, bespectacled, mildly emaciated, and attired like a refugee from a Phish concert.

It's quiet. As you walk among the antennae, the only sounds are the chirping of the native sparrows and mockingbirds, and the constant hum of the antennae themselves, especially the cryogenic systems needed to keep their receivers cool (like −270 Celsius cool). It needs to be that way, because while the VLA is a mighty human achievement, the presence of humans themselves is a hindrance. A single cell phone, which emits radio signals thousands of times more powerful than a distant galaxy, can disturb an antenna like a mouse scaring an elephant. This is strictly an "Airplane Mode" facility.

The aggregate experience emits an anticipatory vibe—the feeling that something's about to happen. It spikes whenever the dishes suddenly move in unison, adjusting azimuth. What did they just notice? Are we on the brink of the world's biggest eureka moment since Archimedes took a bath? That wouldn't be surprising. The

VLA cranks out new discoveries faster than Apple releases iPhone upgrades—ice on Mercury, Gamma-Ray Burst afterglows, supermassive black holes. It is a fire hose of cosmic information. And, quietly piggybacking on astronomers' data stream, a group known as the SETI Institute—the Search for Extraterrestrial Intelligence—is searching for proof of alien life. If and when contact is made, it will likely happen here in the New Mexican desert, while someone like me is buying an overpriced baseball cap in the gift shop.

DRAKE, FERMI, AND HART

At the end of the movie *Contact*, Jodie Foster's Dr. Ellie Arroway tells a kid on a school tour of the VLA: "*The universe is a pretty big place. It's bigger than anything anyone has ever dreamed of before. So if it's just us, it seems like an awful waste of space.*"

That sums up the most foundational tenet of the Believers. Sure, they have their personal experiences and Canonical UFO incidents to sustain them, but beyond that, they are *certain* they have overwhelming odds in their favor. There are a minimum of 200 billion galaxies in the universe (some estimates go up to 2 trillion), each of which contains 100 billion stars on average. How many planets does that net out to? Estimates vary from a mere 70 quintillion to 100 sextillion.

Fine, but how many of those planets could sustain life, and not just microbes and fungi but life that has advanced to a level of sophistication that we could communicate with them? That gets more complicated. Thankfully, a visionary astrophysicist named Frank Drake took up that challenge. In 1961, he formulated the now-famous Drake Equation to introduce formal probability into the conversation:

$$N = R^{*} \times f_p \times n_e \times f_l \times f_i \times f_c \times L$$

Many of the variables that need to get plugged into this polynomial are difficult to pin down—such as the fraction of life-sustaining planets where life actually evolves—so estimates vary wildly. But in 2016, using new data about recent discoveries of exoplanets, a pair of scientists published an article in the journal *Astrobiology* concluding that the odds that we are the only civilization to have ever developed on a habitable planet are about one in 10 billion trillion. So how could anyone swallow the proposition that Earth is the *only* place where intelligent life has emerged? It sounds absurd.

The problem is, to date that absurd assumption has proved to be correct. Can it really be that absurd if every datum from centuries of scientific observation of the universe confirms it? Aside from devising his famous equation, Drake and a bunch of other heavy hitters including Carl Sagan founded SETI more than sixty years ago. It's been on the case ever since. Today, with dozens of PhDs in its ranks and millions of dollars in its coffers, SETI's slick website lays out its mission statement with enviable eloquence: "Whether looking for signs of life on the surface of Mars, under the ice of Jupiter's moon Europa, or sweeping the sky for alien transmissions, SETI Institute scientists investigate the prospects for biology in our solar system and beyond." And SETI is not the only outfit on the hunt. Other groups include The Breakthrough Listen Project and NASA. They each have different names and approaches, but they're all on the same epic quest for a signal that only another intelligent species could transmit. This signal is called a technosignature—an anomalous radio wave determined to be, by process of elimination, generated exclusively by alien technology. Once a genuine technosignature is found, one that can't be disputed as a natural phenomenon or a glitch in the equipment, then alien life—nay, an advanced alien civilization—will be confirmed.

So what solid evidence have they found so far?

Bupkis. Nada. The null set.

That perplexing fact is at the crux of the single most important problem with which the UFO community must contend—the Fermi Paradox. If the laws of probability insist that life exists on other planets, why does the evidentiary record insist that it doesn't? Phrased another way: If we are not alone, then where the heck is everybody?

There are a handful of thoughtful answers worth ticking off here. The first is—they're *really* far away, so even if they've been transmitting personal love notes to us constantly for a million years, none of those transmissions would have gotten here yet if they're separated from us by more than a million light-years. This explanation is buoyed by the Copernican Principle, which states that humans don't occupy some privileged or central place in the universe. (Sounds obvious today, but it was radical back in the sixteenth century when Nicolaus Copernicus first floated it.) That means that life in the universe should be evenly or at least randomly distributed. Since the universe is so vast, it stands to reason that our alien neighbors are nowhere near shouting distance.

Even so, they should be here by now. That's the classic argument put forth by Harvard astronomer Michael Hart in response to Drake's equation. Hart's "Fact A"—that there is no definitive proof aliens have colonized Earth—flies in the face of Hart's calculations that, judging by rates of human evolution, it should only take 650,000 years for an alien race to colonize the galaxy with self-replicating robotic craft known as Von Neumann probes. Since Earth has been around for 4.4 billion years, that obstinate Fact A means the aliens simply aren't out there.

It's important to note that there's a big difference between saying we're not the only intelligent species that's *ever* existed and saying we're not the only intelligent species that exists *right now*. If there's one thing human history has taught us, it's that great civilizations have a striking tendency to rise and fall in dramatic Ozymandian arcs. One doesn't have to listen to today's prophets of doom for long to grow pessimistic about our entire species' projected life expectancy in the face of anticipated environmental calamity, nuclear apocalypse, pandemic eradication, or an irreversible Malthusian crisis. Extinction is always an option. We've managed to keep this hustle we call civilization going for about ten thousand years. Should that be considered an eternity, or just a little while? Who's to say an alien race could do the same, much less sustain itself long enough to master interstellar telecommunication or even travel? Maybe they rose and collapsed like the Mayans. Maybe they scoped out Earth sometime during the 700 million years before any life had emerged here and just moved on without planting a flag. Or, as many astrobiologists suggest, there may well be *some* form of life on other planets—recent research shows that some microbes, called extremophiles, can even survive in space—but that life may be in a much simpler and earlier stage of evolution than anything approaching our level of intelligence and technological achievement. In other words, as we earnestly aim our radio telescopes into the sky, interrogating the heavens for signs of nonhuman intelligence, a potential tragedy of bad timing hangs over the entire enterprise. We may have launched our search too early or too late.

UFOS ON THE SUN

Imagine, then, the Keatsian wild surmise with which retired Army aviation officer David Toon reacted when, while analyzing NASA satellite images of our own modest sun, he spotted the first of several hard-edged objects in various colors, shapes, and sizes, all hovering in proximity to the star's blazing surface. They look nothing like common solar flares, and David claims he's sifted through more than 5 million images over the course of the past twenty years, identifying thousands on which these objects were captured. He's convinced they're technosignatures. As he explained to us, "The images indicate there is a more organized pattern to these objects. They have multiple lights associated with them that may be linear or have basic shapes like triangles or squares. The lines, the shapes, are all basic evidence that there's intelligence behind it. It's not just a natural phenomenon."

His guess about what they are aligns with a theory that's been around for years—that alien civilizations use our sun as a way station. "I think there are advanced civilizations that use the sun as a navigating point and refuel point," he says. "As a navigator, I used to do the same thing. Every pilot flies from point to point. If you're in space, it's no different. It's not really far-fetched for me to think they're visiting or passing through."

Our experts were less enthusiastic about David's discoveries. Most thought the objects were most likely natural gases or plasma coming out of the sun, interacting with camera artifacts that make the gas bursts look more geometric than they really are. So we showed the images to our astrophotographer Andrew McCarthy, who agreed that camera artifacts are the most likely culprits: "The CCD technology used by NASA [on its solar satellites] has a side effect—as the camera pixels fill up, they tend to bleed into the surrounding areas. Sometimes that creates unusual shapes in the photos. It's not a sign of any kind of object floating out there near the sun. It's just a sign of how the technology actually works."

STELLIVORES AND DYSON SPHERES

David Toon's solar imagery analysis may have been misguided, but the notion of alien civilizations harnessing the energy of stars in a manner that would generate technosignatures is being taken seriously in the scientific community. A cosmological philosopher named Clément Vidal published a paper arguing that some binary star systems might not be two separate stars at all but a single star paired with a massive, advanced construction or artificial structure designed to harness and convert the star's energy to feed and fuel an alien civilization that need not be dependent on oxygen or carbon. Such civilizations, which thrive on thermodynamics, are termed "stellivores" ("star-eaters") by Vidal, who've constructed their life-fueling technology around the star much like humans harness the power of waterfalls with hydroelectric generators.

Vidal suggests SETI and other groups searching for technosignatures should focus on what he considers the most promising binary star systems, looking for evidence of high energy rate density as the telltale sign. Some researchers are taking the thesis seriously as they decide where to concentrate their cosmic searches.

Others are pursuing a progenitor of the stellivore theory, one proposed by the great physicist Freeman Dyson. In 1960, Dyson proposed that advanced aliens might build a large structure that wouldn't adjoin a fuel-cell star as the stellivore thesis posits, but surround it entirely. These "Dyson spheres" could be entire shells engulfing the star, or perhaps a connected network of smaller objects—say, solar panels the size of Jupiter.

Dyson spheres were in the news in May 2024 when an international team of scientists who called their endeavor Project Hephaistos released a groundbreaking study in the *Royal Astronomical Journal.* The team had sifted through decades of research on millions of stars, and found some infrared readings from deep-space telescopes that, they claimed, could be Dyson spheres. The images show dense black dots, remarkable for the massive amounts of infrared heat they are emitting. Those anomalous infrared emissions align with what would be expected of a Dyson sphere, which would soak up solar energy and run hot like a car engine.

Was there a natural explanation for those intriguing black dots? Disks of dust and debris, which usually surround young stars as they form planetary systems, can generate excess infrared radiation, but these black dots were identified as red dwarf stars, which rarely have those kinds of debris disks. We took the images to famed theoretical physicist Michio Kaku, who came to another conclusion: "Maybe we're looking at a galaxy that is hiding behind this star. And the infrared radiation that we're picking up is from a galaxy. It gets confusing because the picture is flat. A picture is two-dimensional. Reality is three-dimensional. And therefore, what could be masquerading as a Dyson sphere is really a galaxy hiding behind your star." Kaku's analysis was in line with the American Astronomical Society's—a false positive for Dyson spheres due to infrared-emitting galaxies coincidentally positioned behind the stars in question.

(A similar, if more amusing, confusion occurred with the wildly viral "cosmic question mark" of 2023, a distant celestial body in the distinct shape of a question mark, spotted in the bottom right quadrant of a photo from the Webb telescope. Was it an alien species asking us to clarify a transmission it couldn't decipher, or maybe the universe itself posing an existential question? After further detailed analysis, our esteemed physicists again concluded that the punctuation mark was formed by two separate galaxies—one which formed the hook, the other, perhaps millions of light-years behind it, forming the dot beneath it.)

MIXED SIGNALS

Every once in a while, a suspected technosignature pops up without anyone deliberately looking for it. On August 31, 2024, two astronauts had arrived at the International Space Station via the Starliner spacecraft (which, owing to a rocket malfunction, was unable return them home, stranding them in space for nine months until a Space X rocket pulled off the return trip). While the craft was docked at the ISS, mission commander Butch Wilmore heard an odd sound coming out of a speaker. It was pulsing, rhythmic, and disturbing enough that Commander Wilmore alerted mission control:

> ***Mission Control:*** *"Houston is with you Butch. Go ahead . . ."*
>
> ***Wilmore:*** *"There's a strange noise coming through the speaker, . . . I don't know what's making it. . . . I'm gonna put the mic up next to the speaker. . . . Here we go. . . ."*

This wasn't the first time astronauts had heard surprising sounds that could be perceived as interstellar communications. In 1969, the crew of the Apollo 10 mission heard a sound they described as otherworldly "music." In that case it was soon discovered that the "music" was interference between the mission's lunar module and command service module, both of which used VHF radios. In the recent Starliner case, our forensic audio analyst Dr. Robert Maher recognized the sound as similar to acoustic feedback sometimes picked up by cell phones—the pulses are the giveaway. Commander Wilmore was simply hearing feedback created by the complicated interconnection between the microphones on the Starliner and the ISS.

And yet, for all these duds and disappointments, new technosignature candidates are announced all the time. Only a few days before I began writing this chapter, the Very Large Array yielded another promising signal—a "coherent" radio signal from a rocky exoplanet named "YZ Ceti b," located about 70 trillion miles from Earth. The signal is a strong indicator that the planet may have a magnetic field, one of the likely preconditions for a stable atmosphere, and thus life. "We saw the initial burst, and it looked beautiful," Dr. Sebastian Pineda was quoted as saying. "And when we saw it again, it was very indicative that, OK, maybe we really have something here." To be clear, this isn't proof of advanced technology like a Dyson sphere, merely an indicator that the YZ Ceti b *could* be hospitable for life. But until someone comes up with a prosaic explanation for that signal, it may be the closest thing to a true technosignature we've found yet. It's certainly motivation to keep looking, hoping, and, should one so choose, believing, Fermi paradox be damned.

OUMUAMUA

Remember, though, hardcore UFO Believers aren't content with the claim that nonhuman intelligence (NHI) may exist in the present, too far away for contact. They assert that the NHI has arrived on Earth (in the flesh or by proxy with robotic emissaries)—right here, right now, close enough to be detected by military radar, and in some cases even our consumer cameras. Lined up against the daunting data from SETI's fruitless interstellar searches, it would seem the Believers have some explaining to do.

They do not shy from the challenge. Nor do they lack champions. Among contemporary astronomers, none may be more widely known than Harvard's Avi Loeb, who rose to prominence in 2018 with his buzzy take on a truly anomalous astronomical discovery—the first interstellar object (ISO) confirmed to be passing through our solar system. Named Oumuamua (meaning "messenger from afar" in Hawaiian), the ISO was also distinguished by its odd shape—it was elongated, almost cigar shaped.

The vast majority of scientists were certain it was either a comet or an asteroid—a debate that resulted in multiple classifications. But Loeb had his own hypothesis—that the object was an artificial solar sail, launched by an extraterrestrial intelligence. To repeat, that's a minority opinion. Still, there are enough deep-pocketed individuals and institutions compelled by his work that Loeb has since attracted both funding and attention for further research into both Oumuamua and other objects of interest, such as a meteor named IM1 that landed in the Pacific Ocean in 2014. Owing to its known speed and unusual composition, Loeb thinks it might have been an interstellar visitor as well. And in 2025, Loeb was frequently on TV making the case that another interstellar object known was 3I/Atlas might also be alien tech.

HOW WOULD THEY GET HERE?

Yet even if we go along with Loeb, he doesn't get us all the way to the Roswell flying saucer or the *Nimitz* Tic Tac—piloted, maneuverable craft that have been witnessed at low altitudes on Earth. Fortunately for the Believers, other scientists and theorists have enlisted to get us there. Among them is physicist Matthew Szydagis, professor at SUNY Albany and a member of the SCU. Szydagis has spoken and published in favor of the proposition that, contrary to Einstein, it is physically possible to travel faster than the speed of light; and feasible to design anti-gravity technology—both capabilities are probably prerequisites for UFOs to get here from other solar systems and maneuver the way they've been alleged to do. Szydagis is one of the regulars on *The Proof Is Out There*® series, and has been a great asset for the show.

How long might it take to develop such technology? Whatever your guess, it might not matter. For one thing, we don't know how long the aliens have been around and hard at work. For another, we shouldn't impose an anthropomorphic estimate of an alien species' potential rate of progress. They're alien, remember? Who's to say their brains aren't ten times bigger than ours, or that they can't link their minds like ants to tackle big projects as a superorganism? And—perhaps most importantly—why should we assume that progress is linear? The great futurist Ray Kurzweil's magnum opus *The Singularity Is Near* argued that technological progress should be understood instead as an exponential function. Once a species hits the bend in the curve, it's not only progress that begins to accelerate rapidly; the rate of acceleration itself starts accelerating. If an alien species had their singularity even ten thousand years ago, they could well have God-like powers by now. (We'll delve deeper into the Singularity later.)

That opens up another possibility that could surmount the challenges of long-haul space travel. As Pentagon whistleblower David Grusch has opined, it's likely that the NHI are interdimensional creatures who jump between points in space-time. Marc D'Antonio likes this hypothesis too: "UFOs often appear as orbs or saucers or lenticular-shaped objects because they are large particle accelerators. They're generating particles and popping in and out of dimensions. They don't travel from point A to point B, crossing all the space in between. They just toggle from one point to the other."

Or perhaps the aliens aren't traveling far at all. Maybe they've been here the entire time. This is the so-called crypto-terrestrial theory Lue Elizondo has promoted. Recall that many of the most impressive unresolved UAP incidents happen in and around the water—the *Nimitz* and *Roosevelt* UAPs, the Aguadilla transmedium USO, the various incidents reported during the 2019 naval exercises involving the USS *Omaha* off the coast of Southern California. Could it be that the aliens aren't coming from outer space, but from the bottom of the ocean? Remember that cool James Cameron movie *The Abyss*? Something like that. Here's Lue's take from his NewsNation interview:

> *You know, people will say, "Well, you know, these things are clearly from outer space." And I say, "Well, you know, let's, let's hold off on that . . ." We're always discovering new capabilities of life, right. When I was growing up, we were always taught that photosynthesis was the source of all life; we now realize that's not true. There's life in the bottom of the ocean, and they survive off chemosynthesis, not the sun. . . . And so is it possible the things come from outer space? Sure. Is it possible they're from underwater? Sure. Is it possible that they've been here all along? Sure. We don't know yet. I mean, maybe we do, but I don't. What I do know is: it's not us.*

Another theory that's gained some traction in recent years comes from biological anthropologist Michael Masters, who has come on our show several times. His claim to fame is the time travel hypothesis, which posits that UFOs aren't alien craft at all; *they're humans from the future* who have mastered time travel. Our distant descendants have come back to our time to study us the way today's anthropologists poke around caves in Russian mountains and archaeologists comb over Machu Picchu. This theory pops up when people send us videos of UFO sightings near cultural events like Independence Day fireworks shows. Those almost always turn out to be drones, but the time travel theory is fascinating.

Pick whichever of the above theories you like to explain how the aliens (or future humans) got here. We still have to account for their stealthy, even shy behavior. OK, they may be exposing themselves on rare occasions to our warships or nuke bases, but why aren't they simply landing in Times Square and announcing their intentions?

There are two mainstream theories currently in wide circulation that address this question. The first, which I touched upon in the previous chapter, is "Galactic Zoo" theory. The aliens are observing us for their entertainment, research, or security. They don't want to disturb us by making themselves known because that would pollute their data, or trigger some response that would tangle up their master plan. (Masters' time-traveling humans dovetail nicely into this line of thought.)

The second is known as "Dark Forest Theory," popularized in the 2007 science fiction novel *The Three-Body Problem*. It's interesting because it engages with some of the logic of game theory. It's also extremely potent, as it addresses the "shy UFO" problem, Hart's Fact A, and the Fermi Paradox in one fell swoop. Dark Forest Theory goes right at the common assumption that aliens are peaceful and benevolent. To the contrary, it argues, they are hostile and paranoid—not necessarily because they are naturally malevolent, but because, following the logic of game theory, any creature concerned primarily for its own survival must assume that any unknown creature it encounters for the first time could well be predisposed to destroy it. This logic obligates any civilization to avoid interstellar outreach; to camouflage and hide, and to strike with annihilating force if it feels it's been spotted. All civilizations are like hunters in a dark forest, creeping silently through the trees, and taking out anything they come across to avoid suffering a similar fate. Maybe they peek out every once in a while, maybe they even form secret alliances with the leaders of other civilizations, but for the most part they stay out of sight. That's why we don't see much with our telescopes—everybody is hiding or dead. Stealth is the supreme law of the universe. By this logic, of course, dispatching uncamouflaged probes into deep space as we've done with the Voyager missions is tantamount to a death wish.

So we've established the reasoning—not proof, but reasoning—that helps us get closer to where the UFO community wants us to be, accepting that: 1) civilizations of advanced nonhuman intelligence exist in the present day; 2) they've had the capability and motivation to visit Earth repeatedly in the past one hundred years, quite possibly for far longer; 3) for whatever reason, they've committed to a measure of stealth that has kept them more or less hidden from the vast majority of the world's population.

But that's still not enough. For modern UFOlogy, from Roswell through the present, holds as a central tenet that the U.S. government has been aware of the UFO presence for decades; has been retrieving and reverse engineering crashed craft through a long-running top-secret operation often called the Legacy Program; has quite possibly formed some sort of agreement or alliance with non-human intelligence; and has successfully kept all the hard evidence that would conclusively prove any of this from the public, the press, Congress, and possibly the president. As Sean Kirkpatrick, the first head of the Pentagon's All-domain Anomaly Resolution Office (AARO), once told me, "If you're talking about alien life in other galaxies, that's science. If you're talking about it near our solar system, that's science fiction. If you're talking about it within Earth's atmosphere, that's conspiracy theory."

It's time to address that issue directly.

Chapter 5

CONSPIRACY

A VISIT TO WHITE SANDS

"Sir, are you carrying any weapons or drugs in the vehicle?" The military policeman at the entrance to the White Sands Missile Range must have asked that question ten thousand times. Yet his voice lacked the robotic, disengaged tone of your standard "Welcome to McDonald's; may I take your order, please?" Somehow he managed to convey a sense of genuine personal interest in my threat potential. That's a skill.

I'd come here, to this 256,000-acre rectangle in southern New Mexico where the Buffalo Soldiers once helped subjugate the Apache, because despite its remote location, White Sands sits at the center of two of the twentieth century's greatest developments: the dawn of the nuclear age and the dawn of the space age. It was here, at the Trinity site, where Robert Oppenheimer officially became the destroyer of worlds, and where the Apollo rocket team took many small steps before Neil Armstrong took his.

The vast range tests America's most cutting-edge missile technology, but the general public never sees more than the WSMR museum and its impressive "missile park," displaying the myriad weapons systems WSMR claims as its own. It's like a sculpture garden, except instead of Henry Moores and Rodins it exhibits Pershing IIs and Patriots. It even has the original casing of the Fat Man bomb that helped make Nagasaki what it is today.

Owing to its track record of impressive projects and imposing security, White Sands also occupies a place of prominence in various conspiracy theories that pop up regularly on our show. If you harbor sinister thoughts about America's military industrial complex, your mind has likely passed through the gates of the WSMR with considerably more ease and frequency than my body.

WSMR Museum Director Darren Court has heard more wild theories than he'd care to remember. He's a former Army mechanic who spent years stationed here working on the Chaparral missile system. Like many who've passed through, he decided to come back at the first opportunity. Why? "It's because White Sands is a different world. Not just from civilian life, but from life on other Army bases. We don't have a major training and deployment schedule which has troops constantly rotating in and out. We have a testing mission, so people come and stay. A strong community has developed here over time."

Court prides himself on his work as a serious historian. He's written the definitive history of White Sands and appeared on C-SPAN, so you can imagine his general attitude toward conspiracy theories: "I don't deal with it. As much as possible, I push it away."

If only it were that easy. Capital H Historians like Court put their faith in primary sources. Fine—but some primary sources *lend credence to outlandish theories*. Take, for example, a 1950 Air Force memo that reads:

December 1948 through May 1950: "Phenomena have continuously occurred in the New Mexico skies during the past 18 months and are continuing to occur. . . . These phenomena are occurring in the vicinity of sensitive military and government installations."

That's why, at least once a week, Court will get either an email or an in-person visit from someone in thrall to one theory or another. Despite his efforts to forget them, some stick in his head, like the guy who claimed one of the abandoned Redstone rocket test stands was actually an entrance to a vast twelve-level subterranean base, each level of which, like Dante's inferno, houses stratified diabolical secrets. A variation of this same theory claims the WSMR is merely one of a chain of such underground bases, connected by magnetic rail of course, that includes the mythical "Dulce" base near the New Mexico–Colorado border, jointly run by humans and aliens. In some iterations of this theory, Area 51 is merely a red herring designed to distract the public from the true locations of the activities alleged to take place there. White Sands is where it's at.

Court does get a kick out of some of the more esoteric theories that interweave elements of documented history. He recalled one email from a guy working on a book making the case that White Sands was the true launching point for the craft that crashed at Roswell. It was neither a UFO nor a military balloon; it was a next-gen V-2 rocket developed at White Sands after Operation Paperclip, in which Americans seized Nazi rocket tech and scientists after World War II. There were bodies recovered there, but they were not aliens—at least not entirely. They were mutants created by the Japanese during the war at their notorious human experimentation

Unit 731 in occupied Manchuria—a cross-breeding of enslaved Chinese test subjects and extraterrestrials.

I told Court about one video in particular that had attracted our attention. Allegedly leaked by a WSMR scientist in the mid-nineties, and first presented at a 1997 UFO conference, it is "FLIR" footage that purports to show a glowing, cigar-shaped object hurtling toward one of the White Sands impact areas. It strikes the ground, then bounces back up into the air, then crashes again, fragmenting into dozens of pieces that appear as glowing sparks on the footage. At first glance, there's nothing unusual about the object's trajectory—it makes no anomalous accelerations or puzzling maneuvers like right-angle turns. You could think it's just a standard missile test, illuminated strangely on the video by the glow of its propulsion system. But a frame-by-frame analysis of the footage shows the object appearing to nose up near the moment of impact, as if it's trying to avoid crashing. That's prompted UFO investigators like Lue Elizondo to speculate: "Is this video the deliberate shooting down or neutralizing of a UFO for the sole purposes of capturing it and reverse engineering it?"

Court's response? "It's certainly egotistical to assume we're alone in the universe, and there are many things we don't understand, but it's a huge jump to say it's aliens." As for the 1997 video? "I haven't seen any tangible proof that would make me take it seriously," though he forgives people for being fascinated with video of failed missile tests. He's a sucker for them too: "It's always fun to watch things blow up when they're not supposed to." So, if this is just another failed missile test and not a downed UFO, what missile could have behaved in that way?

"I can't talk about current testing," he answered, stone-faced. "That's a question for public affairs."

The term "conspiracy theory" might be derogatory, but there's no avoiding it. Today's mainstream UFOlogy does not exist without this core belief in the government cover-up, the more flowery versions of which involve exhaustive disinformation campaigns and even extralegal killings to either discredit or liquidate any insiders who dare to go public. And like any conspiracy theory—and I've gone deep on more than my fair share—a central paradox hangs at its center.

On the one hand, the design and execution of any of the big conspiracy theories you've heard about—not just those related to UFOs—require the simultaneous occurrence of three extreme right-tail rarities on the bell curve. They are:

- Extreme malevolence—the motivation to perpetrate a massive cover-up and commit the attendant crimes necessary to keep the top-secret activity secret.
- Extreme competence—the brains and skill to execute such diabolical plans.
- Extreme discipline—the ability to keep explosive secrets quiet for years on end, even through a proverbial deathbed confession moment, despite the immense temptations of the co-conspirators to be the ones who blew the whistle on a matter of historical significance.

What's the likelihood of those three very low probability conditions being met? As the lawyers say, *de minimis*.

On the other hand, just when you're ready to dismiss some lunatic fringe theory as pure paranoid fantasy, documented evidence of something almost as outrageous comes to light. Yes, the QAnon conspiracy is a fiction, but the Jeffey Epstein case is true. Yes, it's a stretch to think a cabal of unelected government officials devised and executed an elaborate plot to gain control of the White House by removing a young and energetic John F. Kennedy from the Oval Office, as was argued in the film *JFK*. But the CIA's MKUltra program, the FBI's COINTELPRO—these things *happened*. And if one makes the reasonable deduction that what's been disclosed is only a fraction of what's taken place, the mind can be forgiven for filling in the blanks with fevered speculation. In other words, the documented facts are sufficiently bizarre to fertilize the soil of undocumented theory.

The pull and popularity of conspiracy theory brings us back to Pascal's "God-shaped hole." It is no surprise that many people feeling lonely, powerless, and alienated (basically everybody at one time or another) would seek to explain their world as a creation designed by large, impersonal forces that far outweigh the will of the individual. For most of human history, that large force was God. The twentieth century saw the emergence of the idea, actualized in all its brutality by totalitarian regimes, that a godless but almighty state could fulfill that role too, with the proper doses of propaganda and violence. Modern conspiracy theories can be understood as a byproduct of this development.

EMPCOE

We've investigated several government conspiracy theories on the show, prompted by the proliferation of viral videos that purport to prove they're real. Some relate to UFOs; many do not. Counterintuitively, it feels like the more outlandish its claims, the more popularity and longevity a given theory enjoys. Their power shouldn't be underestimated. As ridiculous as you may find them, their reach extends far beyond the comments sections of YouTube. In some cases they've impacted people's lives deeply, negatively, and permanently.

Take, for example, a conspiracy known as EMPCOE, short for the Electro-Magnetic Plasma Changeover Event. The name alone already sounds too over-the-top for anything but a plot point in a bad Marvel movie. Nobody would take such a thing seriously. Or would they? The video record suggests otherwise.

On an overcast evening in 2018, in the skies over Brooklyn, a startled pedestrian noticed something in the sky. It was not a UFO. It was a pulsating blue light in the airspace above the city. The massive, amorphous glow turned the sky around it an eerie shade of blue. You can hear the witness struggling to contain himself as he gives his girlfriend a play-by-play over the phone. After the footage was posted, the internet quickly connected this Brooklyn glow to similar sightings around the world—one in Latvia, another in France. Put them all together and you get "proof" of the bizarre apocalyptic theory called EMPCOE.

In a nutshell, EMPCOE adherents believe that the Earth is on the verge of a cataclysmic event in which the poles of the planet will be rocked by a "plasma apocalypse," a celestial event that will flip the planet's magnetic field and throw civilization into an extinction-level tailspin. One of the stages of this apocalypse is the opening of mysterious portals in the sky that unleash plasma onto the world. It's said to have a blueish hue, so there you go. Only the "elites" know when and where this is going to happen and they are poised to launch a new world order once the rubble is cleared. The rest of us have to prepare to defend our endangered liberties . . . and wait.

Like any viable conspiracy theory, EMPCOE pulls from something very real. It is true that the threat of an electromagnetic attack on our grid from a foreign adversary, or a strong enough electromagnetic pulse from the sun, could be devastating. Congress took the issue seriously enough to create a special commission to study the threat. It's also a fact that Earth's magnetic poles switch naturally every two hundred thousand years or so (and we're overdue!).

Still, the EMPCOE threat has been so filigreed with exaggerations about its imminence and attendant diabolical schemes that it has upended people's lives. We interviewed a woman named Sarah whose boyfriend became obsessed. "I had started to notice packages coming to the house," she said. "And this was very extreme survival gear. Weapons, life jackets, night vision goggles, and he told me that this was essential in order to survive this event, which he explained was going to be this rainfall of plasma." The situation deteriorated to the point where he became violent with Sarah and she called the cops: "I told them about the stockpiling of fuel, weapons, and ammunition. And that led to them charging him with a number of offenses."

Sarah has since moved on with her life, but committed EMPCOE Believers have not. So we felt not just a curiosity but a sense of obligation to explain what that blue light over Brooklyn really was.

Enter Mick West. Our lead debunker geolocated the eyewitness' position and the direction of the camera. Checking local news reports from that night, he noticed that there was a fire at a transformer station just over the horizon in Queens. When a transformer blows up, the large arcs of electricity that result make very bright blue light. As for why the light appeared to be coming from the sky, our meteorologist Deanna Hence explained it ties back to the cloud conditions that night—a layer of stratus clouds was hanging low over the city: "It's exceedingly common that these kinds of low clouds will reflect either ambient or point light sources that are underneath them." I'd like to think our reporting spared the next Sarah from a similar ordeal.

WILDFIRES AND DIRECTED ENERGY WEAPONS

Like swamps for mosquitos, natural disasters are breeding grounds for conspiracy theories, for at least two reasons. First, they provoke government responses that trigger the minds of the paranoid. Floods, earthquakes, and other disasters clearly cripple the communities hit hardest, making them more dependent than ever on the state for survival and recovery. If your a priori principle is that the government has an insatiable appetite for social control and fantasizes about a populace of spineless slaves, it follows that "natural" disasters are the quickest way to create the prerequisite helplessness among the citizenry, motivating them to run to the embrace of the state as it asserts vast emergency powers.

The second is that natural disasters upend our expectations that the world is orderly and generally safe. Believing it wasn't a random "Act of God" but the result of a meticulous master plan, however sinister, at least plucks the world out of the grip of random chaos and restores a modicum of order in our minds. History and psychology have taught us that many social pathologies stem from this need for order.

Thus and so, it was unsurprising that in the aftermath of the 2018 California wildfires some drone footage sparked a frenzied rumor that the government had caused the destruction. You see, as the drones surveyed the damage, they noticed some anomalies among the incinerated wastelands that had recently been leafy rural communities. In one popular video, the drone camera passed over blocks where some houses had burned to the ground—sometimes even the brick chimneys were destroyed—but strangely, the charred ruins were surrounded by trees left untouched by the flames.

Soon word was spreading that the fires were not caused by lightning, improperly extinguished campfires, or cigarettes—the U.S. government was using space-based directed energy weapons to start the fires, clear out the rural towns, and force the population into urban centers where they can be controlled more thoroughly and efficiently.

Directed energy weapons are real. They have been developed by the U.S. military and in some cases put into the field. In the 2000s, the Air Force commissioned Boeing to build the YAL-1, a custom 747 with a laser weapon in its nose to shoot down enemy missiles. It successfully destroyed two test missiles, but that was at a range much closer than could ever be achieved in the real world, unless the YAL-1 were to be in North Korean airspace at the moment Kim Jong Un pushes the button. The program was soon scrapped, but development of DEW weapons continues to this day. In 2024, the Army officially deployed the P-HEL laser weapons system as an anti-drone platform. It's been put into the field in an undisclosed conflict zone.

That's enough to fuel the DEW conspiracy theory, which sustains entire conferences, sells books, and rakes in speaker fees for those who espouse it with conviction. (One of those speaker/authors, whom I will not name, refused to appear on the show because, after seven rounds of an interrogatory email exchange, I could not convince her that I was not a federal agent working undercover to entrap her.)

Nevertheless, the California wildfire footage is explained with relative ease. First, we know a space laser couldn't successfully take out a single California home, graciously sparing the surrounding landscaping, for the same reason the YAL-1 was scrapped—the target would be too far from the weapon for it to work. As our military and aviation expert Tim McMillan explained, "Whenever the laser is being projected down, it's going to travel from the atmosphere to clouds. Any type of inclement weather is going to cause what is called 'atmospheric blowing.' And by the time it reaches Earth, it's not going to have the amount of energy to start a fire and burn something. And it's certainly not going to be pinpoint accurate to where you're going to make these precise laser shots from space. It's just not possible with the technology we have today."

So what accounts for that bizarre video? Start with the fact that, despite how we imagine them, fires don't sweep across a given area continuously like a tidal wave. As they burn, they cast off embers, which can be carried by the wind. What happens next depends on where the embers land. If it's on something combustible like a dry dead tree on the ground or the dry dead wood in a house, it's likely to catch fire; if it's on something moist or damp, like a living tree, it won't. (That's why you see homeowners watering down their roofs as a wildfire approaches.)

"Live trees actually have a lot of water in them," Mick West says. "They're constantly sucking up water from the ground. They're not dead. And so it's actually quite hard to burn greenwood." Mick was kind enough to demonstrate the difference by attempting to light fires with two separate stacks of logs—fresh and moist versus old and desiccated. The first refused to do anything other than emit a few feeble wisps of smoke; the second ignited faster than Match Light charcoal.

TRUTHERS EVERYWHERE

Some conspiracy theories have become as embedded into the culture as classic rock hits like "Don't Stop Believing" or holiday chestnuts like "Jingle Bell Rock." Whether you go looking for them or not, they'll pop up in conversation as you navigate your way through either polite or impolite society.

The conspiracists can be found in every zip code and tax bracket. Not long ago my wife and I were grabbing a quick bite with a wealthy widow we'd met at an invite-only social function. Between nibbles of her tuna tartare, she launched into a soliloquy on chemtrails, the theory that first inspired Mick West to get into the debunking game. It's been around since the Bee Gees were big. The claim: vapor trails seen in the wake of passing overhead jets are laced with chemicals by the government for the usual nefarious purposes—poisoning, social control, or, in this woman's version, manipulating crop growth in her native Ontario so "the elites" could reap windfalls on the commodities markets.

At the other end of the spectrum, I vividly recall listening in on a couple of reformed gangsters on the South Side of Chicago having a chat about the universe and the meaning of life. We were in a storefront nutraceuticals shop one of them had opened with his wife (also a notorious former "driller") on the corner of 75th Street and South Jeffery. They were affirming to each other, with an impressive degree of erudition, all the reasons Flat Earth theory was true. Who knew that one was even still around?

Other theories have local followings, like sports teams. During the thirty years I lived in New York, I lost track of how many acquaintances and even colleagues in the network news business bought into the 9/11 Truther movement or—a personal favorite—

the belief that TWA 800 was downed by the U.S. Navy conducting a test of a surface-to-air missile that went lethally awry.

What's both interesting and fun is tracking how some theories evolve and adapt over time as history advances and new technology emerges. Example—the "Moon Truther" theory that asserts the Apollo moon landings were all propaganda stunts staged in a Hollywood studio. (See that American flag rippling in the wind as Neil Armstrong plants it on the Sea of Tranquility? How could that have happened when *there's no wind on the moon*!)

Moon Trutherism has recently been updated for the twenty-first century and reemerged as the "Mars Truther" theory. This new, improved version claims that the Mars rovers never went to Mars, they've just been rolling around Devon Island in Nunavut, Canada, which boasts Earth's most Martian landscape. The evidence in this case consists of blown-up images "allegedly" transmitted back from Mars by the rovers, which inadvertently documented the proof that gives everything away: bones of dead sea mammals indigenous to Canada, but of course nonexistent on Mars.

We investigated those images with NASA Mars mission geologist Dr. Robert Anderson. He confirmed that NASA does in fact use Devon Island for rover training. But he pointed out that the "bones" in the pictures are pareidolian misreadings of rocks that have been weathered into bone-looking shapes by the Martian winds. The rovers' current location on Mars can be confirmed by satellite imagery, and even consumer-grade radio telescopes. The Mars Truther theory suffers even further from the fact that the Chinese and Soviets have put rovers on Mars too, snapping images of some of the same places. Why would they be cooperating with us to that extent?

BIRDS AREN'T REAL . . . ISN'T REAL

Less amusing are the cases when tongue-in-cheek theories go viral initially for their entertainment value, and then wind up being taken seriously. Such is the case with the recent "Birds Aren't Real" movement, an internet stunt engineered by performance artist Peter McIndoe back in 2010, intended as a satire of people's susceptibility to misinformation. The "theory" is that birds aren't living creatures; they're robots engineered by the government to keep us under surveillance. Not content with mere internet chicanery, McIndoe fleshed out the idea "IRL" by staging rallies complete with signs and bullhorns. Perhaps the movement's most daring stunt was storming Twitter's headquarters demanding the company change its logo. (Perhaps Mr. Musk was listening. Shortly after the BAR siege he acquired the company and renamed it X.)

We brushed up against the theory when we saw it mentioned in comments for a YouTube video that recorded a bird suspended mid-flight above a street in Surrey, British Columbia. The footage included the obligatory open-jawed "That's freakin' weird, man" provided by the witness documenting the sight. Commenters claimed the footage "proved" that birds aren't real, since here we had video of a bird-drone malfunctioning and stuck in hover mode. Yes, the video shows a power line a few feet above the hovering bird, so sure, it could have been a prank, but who would risk electrocution solely for the sick satisfaction of hanging a dead bird over a public street?

We did the story half in jest, making it clear that the BAR movement was not meant to be taken seriously. We proceeded to solve the mystery by consulting ornithologist Bryce Robinson. He identified the bird as a gull that had suffered a common fate. He believed it had tried to eat a piece of fisherman's bait that had been cut when the fishing line got tangled. The gull likely got the hook caught in its mouth and was flying around with a long string of fishing line trailing from its beak, which in turn got tangled in the overhead power line and ended up trapping the gull till it strangled or starved to death. A sad conclusion to the story, but—in case you needed it—proof that birds are real animals, and like every other member of the animal kingdom, they die with breathtaking frequency as a result of human irresponsibility.

After our piece aired, I gave little thought to the Birds Aren't Real conspiracy theory until I saw a news story out of St. Louis. Six people, including two children, had gone missing after joining a cult whose leader, an incarcerated child molester, preached, among other things, that Birds Aren't Real . . . was real. It was a haunting thought—something created purely in jest had come to be taken literally, to the point where it had contributed to the potential ruination of people's lives.

ADDICTED TO SECRECY

How is it possible that such wacky theories gain such tenacious holds on people's minds? There is plenty of rigorous academic work on the topic, incorporating compendious expertise on psychology and sociology I do not pretend to have. But from my own experience, I will say simply this: conspiracy theories proliferate and survive mostly because the U.S. government gives them reason to.

For one thing, the federal government has been obsessed with secrecy for decades. Every year, authorized officials make classification decisions on 50 million documents, and out of "an abundance of caution" or the basic, self-protective "cover your ass" instinct, secrecy becomes the default option. At a 2016 congressional hearing on the problem of overclassification, it was argued that at least 30 percent of a random sampling of classified documents actually contained no information that met the current standard for classification. Other estimates say that between 50 and 90 percent of all classified documents could be released to the public without any threat to national security.

The costs of overclassification have been decried by everyone from Republican legislators to the left-leaning Brennan Center for Justice. It costs billions of dollars each year, it prevents Congress from holding agencies accountable, and it makes a mockery of the public's right to know in a country that claims to value transparency. I will add that the rampant silence and secrecy invites the imagination to run in the direction of conspiracy. Look at a page of a heavily redacted document—what do you automatically think when you see all those blacked-out lines? The same thing you think when you see a fig leaf on the marble crotch of a Renaissance sculpture—that there must be something salacious and titillating underneath. We immediately fill in those blanks with the most outrageous theories we can imagine.

Secondly, the government has a proven record of engaging in some seriously outrageous stuff. The CIA's aforementioned notorious MKUltra program conducted illegal human experiments to test hallucinogens and other drugs for their efficacy in interrogation. The National Security Agency, working with its international partners, has deployed the Echelon program, a global surveillance project that intercepts civilian telecommunications. I could go on.

Given those two conjoined forces: the volume of information we're told we can't know, and the shocking government secrets we've pried loose, it's not irrational to believe that we've only scratched the surface. Under those conditions, the proposition that the government has been engaging in a UFO crash retrieval and reverse-engineering program fits in snugly with the known fact pattern. Even what is arguably the UFOlogists' kookiest claim—that the government has been recruiting and training children with psychic abilities to work as "psionic agents" in the Legacy Program to communicate with and even steer alien craft—can draw from the documented history of the CIA's Project Stargate, which spent years pursuing the potential for psychics to engage in "remote viewing" for purposes of espionage and interrogation. You can easily look up the documents stating that the program was discontinued when it found remote viewing to be of no provable use, but that means little to the Believers. It only means the program went underground.

Returning to the triad of unlikely probabilities required for the success of any large conspiracy—extreme malevolence, competence, and discipline—we can take solace in the fact that, in the long run, those conditions will rarely sustain. But ultimately, any conspiracy theory that attains critical mass is usually an extrapolation from something one government or another has really done. Even my Canadian widow, the aforementioned advocate of the long-discredited chemtrails conspiracy theory, can point to the historical record and say she's not far off base. As it happens, the Canadian government *is* using planes to put chemicals into the atmosphere to manipulate the weather and crop harvests. The Alberta Hail Suppression Project uses sodium iodine and a process called cloud seeding to prevent the massive thunderstorms that produce large hailstones that have traditionally inflicted hundreds of millions of dollars of damage on crops (and homes). Cloud-seeding technology was also exploited by the U.S. Air Force during the Vietnam War: "Operation Popeye" laced sodium iodine into clouds to extend the monsoon season in Cambodia, Laos, and Vietnam, making it more difficult for the enemy to transport troops and matériel.

Can any government be trusted not to direct its massive resources, technological wizardry, and its monopoly on the legitimate use of force for some self-serving or illegal purpose at the expense of its own citizens? It is up to our leaders to earn that trust. Judging from our interactions with a suspicious public, they have some work to do.

Fortunately, many of the world's mysteries don't carry the same scent of the sinister. Some of the most captivating anomalies we investigate won't be solved in the third subbasement of a government office building, but out in the wilderness, where nature's enduring riddles attract Believers and Skeptics alike. Put on some hiking boots and pack bug spray. Let's go.

Chapter 6

THE BIGFOOT FILES

A NIGHT IN THE WOODS

Stacy Brown was worried about his dad. Stacy Brown Sr., a retired Army Ranger, had been diagnosed with cancer. Among other things, Stacy Jr. was taking measure of the reality that he might not have much time left to engage in the father-son activity that had formed the foundation of their relationship since his childhood: hunting for Bigfoot. It was their thing.

So when his dad called on a Tuesday afternoon in May 2012 and asked if he was up for one of their overnight camping trips in search of Sasquatch, Stacy was elated. This outing would be even more fun than usual, since his dad had recently sold his boat to buy a thermal camera specifically for the purpose of documenting any encounters. This was a bit out of character, since his dad had always been the more skeptical of the pair. It often felt that Stacy Sr. had initiated this tradition primarily to indulge his son's fantasies of finding the legendary creature in the woods outside their hometown of Quincy, Florida, population 7,913.

It had been more than fifteen years since their first expedition, but Stacy Jr.'s passion had not waned. He was now twenty-seven and in recent years he'd been finding what he called "weird structures in the woods that definitely looked like they were made by something with thumbs." And, on one trip, he'd heard what he characterized as "deep breathing" in the dark coming from just fifteen feet beyond the glow of a campfire. As both Browns headed into Torreya State Park, Brown the Younger was ruminating on the thought: Would tonight be the night they proved the legend of Bigfoot—or, more specifically, the smelly southern variant known as the Florida Skunk Ape—was true?

Around midnight they had their answer. Startled by the sound of animal footfalls and a strange knocking noise that seemed to be moving around their camp, Stacy Sr. grabbed the thermal camera and started rolling. "At first, he was convinced it was two raccoons, and they were fighting or squabbling," Stacy Jr. said. But then his dad saw something through the viewfinder that made him freak. "He goes into a full-blown panic mode. He's like, 'We got to go, we got to go. Do you have your gun?' "

Stacy says he'd never seen his dad so scared. After they hurriedly tore down their campsite and made it back to the safety of their truck, he was able to review the footage and see why. The thermal imagery clearly shows a humanoid figure moving between a gap between two trees. Its arms seem disproportionately long, its stride strikingly simian. "I knew exactly what we had on-camera. Even if nobody else believed it, it was proof to me and my dad, because who on a Tuesday night is a mile and a half into the woods, running around with no flashlight?"

Stacy's dad never went back to those woods. He found all the proof he needed, and he didn't need to be terrified any further. Stacy Jr., on the other hand, continues to devote much of his spare time to the Bigfoot quest, returning to the site regularly to look for a carcass or some DNA sample that will convince the rest of the world of what they saw. That hasn't turned up yet, but the Bigfoot community at large (and it is *large*) doesn't need more convincing. The video achieved iconic status and is known the world over as the Brown Footage.

Stacy is proud to have contributed to the case for Bigfoot, but sharing that moment with his father is what he treasures most. Stacy Sr. died in 2018 shortly after his cancer returned. The memory of that night will never fade.

"It was like winning the Super Bowl with your best friend. That's the best way I can explain it. . . . My dad, the only thing he was doing it for was so he could hang out with his son. He didn't believe these things were real at all . . . and he didn't think in a million years that we would come across something that ended up being so important."

YOU CAN'T BE SERIOUS

Maybe we should stop right here. Bigfoot? Are you kidding me? Of all the anomalous phenomena to ponder, the Bigfoot legend seems the least likely to have persevered into the digital age. With the billions of smartphones and trail cameras in the world today, how could a large hominid be roaming the forests of North America with no incontrovertible evidence of its existence? And even if we grant the creature is sufficiently elusive to avoid being caught on-camera in anything but the blurry, shaky, exasperatingly inscrutable footage we've seen to date, where are the Bigfoot skeletons and fossils? Where are the Bigfoot droppings? The abandoned dwellings?

And yet, Bigfoot's popularity is not just enduring; it's growing, even among the scientific community. I recall in 4k resolution the morning of September 21, 2022, when, between spoonfuls of Honey Nut Cheerios, I flipped over that morning's *Wall Street Journal* to find the following spit take–worthy headline: "More Scientists Dip Their Toes into the Bigfoot World." The article described how respected zoologists, anthropologists, and primatologists are devoting serious time to the hunt for Bigfoot, though usually anonymously due to the ongoing reputational risk. Whether attending conferences or trudging along on Bigfoot hunting expeditions, these academics are inching Sasquatch studies, however incrementally, toward mainstream acceptance. We have no trouble finding viral videos of alleged Sasquatch sightings, so it appears the general public seems to find the topic worthwhile too.

Why?

Academics have numerous explanations for the prevalence of the Bigfoot tradition throughout diverse cultures worldwide, and its persistence in the face of regular debunkings. Anthropologists have argued the creature is a common symbol of the balance between humanity and nature, a protector of both tribe and forest. Jungians invoke the "Wild Man" archetype, a representation of the untamed instincts still lurking beneath our socialized personas. And if you've read the earlier chapters, you know what Blaise Pascal and his intellectual heirs would say about this kind of thing and the God-shaped hole.

The Bigfoot community contests those diagnoses. They say they have hard evidence the creature is no mere myth, and they have affirmative answers to all of Skeptics' lines of attack. Many of those answers have been verbalized on our show in the measured, avuncular tenor of Dr. Jeff Meldrum, professor of anatomy and biological anthropology at Idaho State University, and one of the few, possibly the sole, tenured academics who openly advocated for the existence of Bigfoot. Meldrum's magnum opus on the topic, *Sasquatch: Legend Meets Science*, is a must-read for a deep dive on the topic. When Dr. Meldrum passed away in 2025, the community lost one of its most committed champions.

Meldrum's passion for this fringe subject, which burned in his breast since childhood, cost him dearly in terms of job offers, citations of his published work, and speaking invitations at academic symposia. And because he became known as "The Bigfoot Guy," many dismissed his non-Bigfoot research categorically. But in recent years, he became less of a pariah. "I've felt a bit chagrined at times about the path I've chosen," he told me shortly before his passing, "but it's been interesting to watch the science catch up with my position, and recognize that Bigfoot might exist, or at least *might have existed* at one point. Now I can talk to my colleagues about it."

Author and longtime Bigfoot researcher Kathy Strain, who also has a background in anthropology, is another of our go-to contributors. Strain is known for advancing the argument that the folklore of Native Americans and other indigenous peoples around the world should not simply be dismissed as myth and superstition, but rather early reportage—what one might call proto-data. Strain has studied and published well-regarded work on the so-called Hairy Man pictographs drawn by the Tule River Indians, who occupied California's San Joaquin Valley. The pictographs show a family of "Hairy Man" that matches most descriptions of Bigfoot, and the creature was revered by the tribe as a protector and spirit guide. Hairy Man of lore can also be mischievous and steal food, and is clever enough to outsmart the coyote. But perhaps the most intriguing detail of the pictographs is that other animals are represented—a fish, an eagle, a coyote, all of which are real. Why would a single fantastic beast be represented when all the others are known creatures that survive through the present day?

Rounding out our Bigfoot all-stars is Cliff Barackman, a leading voice among layman Bigfoot hunters and the director of the North American Bigfoot Museum in Oregon. Cliff has been doing television forever, and he's known for his extensive field research. He spends between one and three days every week walking in the woods in search of evidence, and he's traveled to far corners of the country and even overseas to investigate current reported Bigfoot sightings, often leading expeditions with other like-minded explorers.

Collectively, these three honed ready-made rapid responses for the usual battery of questions. Had they desired, they could have collaborated on a Bigfooter's analog to the *Baltimore Catechism*. It would go a little like this:

Why has no Bigfoot skeleton ever been found?
Well, have you ever stumbled across a bear skeleton? No, but we know the woods are teeming with them.

Why have no Bigfoot fossils ever been found?
Well, the environment and soil of the American Northwest is notoriously inhospitable to the process of fossilization. Furthermore, we regularly discover fossils of species we never knew existed, so there could well be Bigfoot fossils we simply haven't come across yet. Paleontology is notoriously serendipitous.

How can a large primate hominid be living in North America when there are no other known primates on this continent?

Well, the majority of animal species in North America emigrated from somewhere else. And we know there are primates in Asia. Like many other mammals, Bigfoot could have migrated from Asia to North America over the now-submerged Bering Land Bridge.

Why isn't there better footage of Bigfoot if it exists?

Because most people aren't expecting to be surprised by Bigfoot in the woods; when it happens they freak out. Lacking the composure to hold their cameras steady, and often more focused on fleeing than documenting, they end up with blurry, fragmented video that characterizes almost all Bigfootage.

Yet surely if the Sasquatch were real it should not have taken this long to find the proof that it's out there?

Perhaps, but think of all the species that were once considered myths. The African gorilla might be the best example—the same creature we now see in every zoo on earth. It was believed to be a fictitious monster until European explorers officially observed it in the mid-nineteenth century. Then there's Australia's duckbilled platypus—it was considered such an absurdity that even when one was captured and shipped back to England, British naturalists initially suspected it was a hoax perpetrated by an unscrupulous taxidermist. The point here is that some legends . . . are true.

Indeed, fantastic creatures have always existed throughout human history—not just in epic poems or carved on totem poles, but out there in the wild, eating, mating, and pooping. "Cryptozoology," as it's called, is not simply a fancy word for deluded people taking campfire stories literally. At least not always. It's simply that once a legendary creature or "cryptid" is confirmed to be real, it stops being legendary. That specimen of cryptozoology becomes a species of regular zoology. Once a creature is assimilated into mainstream science, it becomes domesticated in our minds, and we have difficulty recalling the awe and mystery that once trailed in the creature's wake back when it emitted the scent of lore.

FLORES MAN AND THE ORANG PENDEK

A recent development in anthropology is exceptionally useful as we delve into the Bigfoot question. For centuries, the Nage people of Indonesia's Flores Island have spoken of hobbit-like creatures they called Ebu Gogo, short, hairy, broad-featured hominids who spoke their own language. Ebu Gogo could mimic and interact intelligently with villagers, though some spooky tales alleged that they have kidnapped children. More recently, anthropologist Gregory Forth has documented local accounts of an "ape-man" with similar characteristics, known by the Lio people as *lai hoʼa.*

The tales sound like a local instantiation of the "little people" archetype that appears in cultures the world over, from Kentucky goblins to Canadian Mannegishi to Germanic dwarfs. Purely the stuff of legend. But that perception—or prejudice—was punctured when, in 2003, anthropologists working on Flores Island dug up the remains of a hominid that came to be known as *Homo floresiensis.* It matched the description of the "legendary" Ebu Gogo and *lai ho'a* almost perfectly. Most scientists believe *Homo floresiensis* or "Flores Man" went extinct fifty thousand years ago, but the discovery establishes that the "ascent of man" was not a straight evolutionary progression but a variegated multi-pronged process during which numerous hominids were roaming the planet. "It's not an evolutionary tree trunk; it's a bush," says Barackman. "All these other species of hominids lasted longer than previously thought, and some were in the same place and overlapping time periods." This raises the fascinating question of whether the local legends could indeed have derived from physical encounters between people and these creatures or their current descendants. Could there still be some version of Flores Man deep in the island's jungles?

Of course that's unlikely, but given the alignment of the fossil record and ethnographic accounts, it would be obtuse to dismiss the possibility outright. And while we consider just how drastically to reset the epsilon for this particular probability function, we need to account for a truly remarkable piece of video that emerged in 2017. A YouTuber in Aceh, Indonesia, named Fredo Pastrana, whose content usually features him and his friends dirt biking around the country, uploaded a clip that shows Fredo coming around a slight bend and nearly hitting a diminutive, nearly naked humanoid figure that appears to be carrying a spear. The figure darts across the road and disappears into the tall grass as it tries to avoid the dirt bikers.

The footage blew up online, with some claiming it was a legendary Indonesian creature known as the Orang Pendek—a smaller local version of Bigfoot—or a member of a semi-mythical uncontacted tribe known as the Mante. Our experts agreed this was unlikely to be a hoax, and if that's so, it makes the case that there are human or humanoid creatures of some kind that have yet to be "discovered."

This helps explain that *Wall Street Journal* article, and the emergence of a new generation of academic paleoanthropologists who might not be comfortable using the word "Bigfoot" in the faculty lounge but would be eager to discuss "relict hominids"—surviving populations of these once-abundant primates that, like Flores Man, branched off the evolutionary trunk and could possibly be extant today. (Note how, just as the new term "UAP" has adequately laundered the topic of UFOs for the mainstream, "relict hominids" has legitimized Bigfoot, at least partially.)

Professor Meldrum was overjoyed by this development. "The old-timers in the anthropology world always asserted that Bigfoot *didn't* exist because it *couldn't* exist," he said. "There was no place in the paradigm for it to fit. But in the late eighties and nineties, there was this paleoanthropology revolution. Now we're seeing all this evidence, and folkloric stories persisting where the fossils are found. A lot of the young up-and-coming anthropologists are interested because they see there's a place in the paradigm for the creature to still be existing."

So let us grant that the Bigfoot quest is a valid endeavor. The possibility of a large bipedal primate—a relict hominid—residing in North America is more than a hallucinatory notion. Still, cogent as the pro-Sasquatch arguments might be, after a while the collective weight of the Believers' apologetics begins to become a burden. Where is the physical proof? That's where we come in.

FACE MASKS AND FOOTPRINTS

IMHO one of the most convincing artifacts supporting the case for Bigfoot is one of the earliest. It is not a video, film, or photo. It is a ceremonial mask from the mid-nineteenth century, made by the Tsimshian people of British Columbia, Canada, to represent the "Bukwus"—the wild man of the woods. The mask has several facial and cranial features that align to near perfection with known primate anatomy. "This mask was such an accurate and naturalistic depiction of what could only be a great ape," Meldrum pointed out. "The very prominent eyebrows with very sunken eye sockets, the nose with nostrils that are laterally directed, a broad nose."

The problem is this: as noted earlier, *there are no known primates native to North America*. So where did the Tsimshian get the inspiration for such a detailed primate likeness, if not from a genuine "Bukwus"?

If we are to believe the mask depicts a real creature, we still have to explain how it got to North America. Meldrum long advocated the theory that Bigfoot originated from a common Asian ancestor, possibly Gigantopithecus, which branched into other legendary hominids like the Yeti of Asia or the Yowie of Australia, while the subspecies we call Bigfoot migrated across the Bering Land Bridge: "The most likely scenario is that a population of giant terrestrial bipedal apes that had dispersed through southern and eastern Asia expanded its range into North America."

Of course, no fossils have been found of Bigfoot, Bukwus, or any other bipedal primate in North America. The Bigfoot community, as previously noted, says there are good reasons for that, and regardless, they argue there's ample evidence from other sources, specifically footprints. Over his last thirty years, Professor Meldrum amassed a collection of more than three hundred footprint casts in his Boise lab.

The most impactful for him personally was a set he examined back in the mid-nineties, in the Blue Mountains of Washington State. It was here that a former U.S. Forest Service Patrolman named Paul Freeman claimed he'd found multiple sets of Bigfoot tracks, in 1991, '92, and '96. Freeman was an avid outdoorsman who claimed to have seen his first Bigfoot in 1992, and became obsessed with tracking them, ultimately becoming one of the core researchers in the area.

Freeman made casts of the prints he found, and the feet were certainly big—fourteen inches long. They'd penetrated the soft forest ground, leaving an indentation commensurate with a creature weighing at least five hundred pounds. And, most intriguingly, there was a line across the bottom of the foot, indicating what's known as the "midtarsal ridge." Meldrum argued this detail is key to distinguishing any human foot from Sasquatch's: "Behind the metatarsals is a big jumble of bone right beneath the ankle. In human beings that jumble of bones doesn't bend at all because we have an arch that holds our foot stiff. But Sasquatches can actually *bend* their foot to some degree at that location." That is the location of the midtarsal joint. This might sound like a throwaway detail, but to the Bigfoot community, it's essential.

Could the Freeman footprints have been faked? Certainly. The ongoing public fascination with Bigfoot means there will always be hoaxers (more on them in a bit). That makes it that much harder for the serious researchers to get their work taken seriously, but in a way it's a blessing, at least in this case. That's because hoaxed footprints, almost always made by someone stomping around the woods wearing a pair of carved wooden feet, can be easily identified, documented, and compared against new discoveries.

For one thing, faked prints made with a prosthesis are too clean and even, the toes perfectly arranged like gumdrops because the weight is coming down on the soil evenly like a stamp. Real foot-prints have a far "dirtier" imprint, since the weight is rolling on and off as the creature strides. Real prints also have dermal ridges (the foot's equivalent of fingerprints), whereas carved feet typically lack those minute details.

Meldrum heard about Freeman's 1996 find, and to put any doubts about a possible hoax to rest in his own mind, he drove unannounced to Freeman's property for a surprise inspection. He was soon convinced the prints were authentic, and that they weren't made by any of the common local fauna. The most likely candidate was the bear, but the prints didn't match. "The bear isn't completely flat-footed," Meldrum stated. "Its heel does not entirely rest on the ground. The heel of a bear has a very pointed appearance, as opposed to the very rounded, full heel pad of the Sasquatch foot." The prints also showed a "Morton's toe"—the second longer than the first—which again deviated from the standard fake. And then there was that midtarsal ridge. Bingo.

The Proof Is Out There® series producer Marley Jaeger found all that interesting, but what propelled her most forcefully toward the notion that Paul Freeman may have found authentic Bigfoot tracks was the story of Freeman himself. "Paul Freeman lived in the woods, he knew every plant and animal, and he never had any intention of being a Bigfoot guy," she says. "It drove him crazy that he couldn't explain what he saw and that nobody believed him. He was so obsessed with the Bigfoot hunt, everyone in town thought he was nuts, and it strained his relationship with his wife and kids. This almost cost him his family, so he finally backed off and repaired his relationships."

A NEW LOOK AT AN OLD CLASSIC: THE PATTERSON-GIMLIN FILM

Masks and footprints are cool, but what about the Bigfootage? No discussion of the topic can begin anywhere else—the classic Patterson-Gimlin film. This is the forty-second 16mm movie footage shot of a figure now affectionately known as "Patty" on October 20, 1967, in the Six Rivers Forest in Northern California. Two Bigfoot researchers, Roger Patterson and Bob Gimlin, had heard reports of Bigfoot activity in the area and had been searching for the creature for weeks. On that afternoon, they were riding on horseback when they came around a bend and approached a downed tree by a creek. That's when they say they saw the hair-covered manlike creature, which proceeded to stand up and stride off.

Patterson dismounted his horse, scrambled to get out the camera, and started shooting. By the time the shot stabilizes, you can see the figure already loping off along the creek bed. That's when the famous "lookback" occurs, as the figure turns to the camera for a moment, then proceeds to amble off into the woods. The creature seemed to match folkloric descriptions of Sasquatch—a bipedal primate, ranging from six to ten feet tall and weighing up to seven hundred pounds.

The "PGF," as it is commonly known, is the most compelling photographic evidence for the existence of Sasquatch. That's a problem, because it's not very good. It's grainy, shaky, and of such mediocre quality overall that for more than fifty years most people dismissed "Patty" as just a man in a suit. There's even a costume maker in North Carolina who came forward years later claiming he was the co-hoaxer who manufactured the outfit for Patterson.

If the incident was a hoax, it ranks among the most successful and remunerative of all time. The film was shown in theaters, generating a tidy profit from Bigfoot fans like a young Jeff Meldrum, who claimed the experience changed his life. Since then, as Bigfoot content continues to generate ratings, the Patterson estate has been charging stratospheric licensing fees for anyone who wants to broadcast it—north of $30,000 and rising. That hasn't inhibited documentary projects from forking over the ransom, and the PGF now ranks with the Zapruder film as some of the most microscopically and exhaustively analyzed pieces of footage ever shot.

For all these reasons, I was disinclined to do anything with the PGF for the show. There's a steady pipeline of fresh, user-generated Bigfoot video that makes its way into the public sphere every year. None of it is as jaw dropping as the PGF, but we can still make strong segments with it. No need to pay that kind of money for a clip more than fifty years old. Was there anything really fresh to say about it anyway? The prospect of revisiting the PGF for the thousandth time was as appetizing as the thought of eating a prechewed steak.

That all changed when Meldrum introduced me to Isaac Tian, a computer scientist and engineer who'd found a way to present the PGF as it had never been seen before. Assembling twenty-two different copies of the film (the original has been lost), Isaac used an AI program to integrate them and eliminate camera artifacts and imperfections in the film itself; then he stabilized the images using computer vision algorithms, and the result was as clear, clean, and steady as if Patterson had been shooting on a tripod with a digital camera. "It's a game changer," said Meldrum. "Really illuminating."

So we went for it—bringing Meldrum, Isaac, and a noted monster movie costume designer named Bill Munns to a Los Angeles studio to break down this new improved version frame by frame.

According to the team, the footage strongly suggests the following:

- The bottom of Patty's foot, now visible with unprecedented resolution, evinces the same midtarsal flexing motion suggested by Meldrum's "midtarsal break" theory. According to Munns, since monster costumes are built around athletic shoes, that flex in the foot mitigates strongly against the "guy in a suit" debunk.
- Clear subdermal flexing of the calf muscle as Patty strides is further evidence against the costume theory. The most sophisticated costumes of the time were those made for the *Planet of the Apes* and *2001: A Space Odyssey*, and those required big movie studio budgets. The average Bigfoot costume goes over the legs like a pair of pants—"stovepipe legs" that are never customized to be that tight on the skin.
- The creature is too tall and its limb proportions too abnormal to be that of a normal human. Sure, a major movie studio's casting department could find someone like Peter Mayhew, the seven-foot actor who played Chewbacca in *Star Wars*, to pull off the prank. But again, that requires pockets much deeper than Patterson's and Gimlin's.
- A line observed on the hair of the right thigh, previously thought to be the seam of the costume, is instead more likely to be the fur being brushed forward and back as Patty's right arm swings by her leg.
- The figure seems to have an observable "natal cleft"—the anatomists' term for butt crack—and pendulous mam-

maries. (That's why "Patty" is referred to as a female.) Hollywood creature costumes never show genitalia or butt cracks; and prosthetic breasts don't sway with the fluid motion observed on Patty's. The case against the "guy in a costume" theory has an evidentiary basis.

- The upgraded image of the head and neck area at the moment of the "lookback" shows no signs of the gap or seam typically included in costume designs so the costume's head can be removed from its torso to keep actors from overheating. And from an anatomical perspective, the head shows signs of a "sagittal crest"—the ridge of bone along the top of the cranium—and the musculature and morphology of the neck region bears little resemblance to human anatomy.

Our anthropologist Kathy Strain was persuaded. To be fair, she was always sympathetic to Meldrum's position, as her own research on the "Hairy Man" pictographs would suggest. But after reviewing the enhancement, she was adamant. "There is just no way that can be a costume," she declared. "After this analysis, if you don't believe what you're seeing on that film is a true Bigfoot, then nothing will convince you."

Interesting stuff, but what did the Bigfoot *Skeptics* have to say about this new version of the PGF? We've had a handful of mainstream wildlife biologists on the show to provide precisely this perspective. One of them, Dr. Stephanie Manka, was not swayed by the upgraded footage or the Meldrum/Munns analysis of it. "To me, the fur looks fake," she declared. "It just doesn't look like real animal fur . . . too uniform and too shiny." She found the creature's behavior even less authentic. "Assuming this creature has never seen humans or doesn't interact with them frequently, it shouldn't have just walked calmly. I would think if it were truly a Bigfoot-like animal, it would back away. It wouldn't turn its back to these people going after it."

We figured we'd get a similar response from biologist Floyd Hayes, an avowed Bigfoot Skeptic who needed persuading to participate in this PGF project at all. He just thought it was all too absurd. But, to our amazement, he found the upgraded version and Meldrum's analysis compelling. "Having watched the analysis," he concluded, "it makes it more difficult for Skeptics like me to remain skeptical. I was rather surprised by the detail that they could come up with on the shape of the foot. [And] the rather thick neck and the shape of the head is very similar to Australopithecus. I still think it's possible that it's a fake, but it would be kind of difficult to come up with all those different coincidences. And if it is a genuine film, then it's going to shatter our preconceived notions of primate evolution."

That's pretty much where the show landed on the PGF too. The new version and analysis weren't conclusive, but they increased the likelihood that it *might* be legit.

What *decreases* that likelihood is the PGF's singularity. Jeff Meldrum recalled the dissipation of the optimism that first surrounded the footage back in 1967. "At the time of the Patterson-Gimlin sighting, everybody thought it was just a matter of months till it was all locked up," he told me. "New, higher-quality footage would emerge; a carcass would be found; one of Patty's band might be captured alive, perhaps even the star of the PGF herself." Meldrum waxed wistful when he thought back on the evidentiary vacuum of the intervening decades. "That was not the way it went."

Instead, what do we have? More footprints, yes. Meldrum had his voluminous collection and Barackman's museum boasts its own. "I find footprints in remote places where no one knows I'm going," Barackman says proudly. "Abandoned logging roads, places so untraversed I could get lost. So if I'm finding evidence there, it's hard to explain away." There's even a celebrated butt print. I'll let you google that at your leisure.

As for video? A compendium of fragmentary, often indecipherable caught-on-camera moments, the footage usually of lamentable quality and dubious provenance. In an age where professional nature photographers and random trail cameras are able to capture beasts as rare as Sumatran rhinos and Himalayan snow leopards, how could nearly sixty years have passed without another PGF?

Perhaps they haven't. While we've explained away at least 80 percent of the alleged Bigfoot sightings we've analyzed, there are a handful which have withstood our scrutiny. They're worth mentioning.

A BABY BIGFOOT? THE PRIDGEN FOOTAGE

One of my favorites—and definitely one to know if you want to impress the crowd at your next Bigfoot conference—is referred to as the Pridgen Footage. It was shot on May 23, 1997, by the eponymous Doug Pridgen, who was camping in the Catskill Mountains in upstate New York with a group of friends who'd gathered to attend a nearby music festival. While Doug records the merriment around the campfire, a shape emerges in the trees in the background—a small, bipedal creature that proceeds to climb and swing from the branches. When you slow down and push in, you can also make out a second figure in the trees.

Barackman is convinced this proves that Bigfoot is not a singular legendary creature but a normal species that mates and breeds. What we're seeing here is a mamma and baby Sasquatch. They're rarely seen like this for the same reason you never see baby squirrels: they're usually kept secluded in lairs until they're big enough to venture out into the world.

Meldrum was equally sure the figures aren't people. "Humans, for all their agility, don't have the capacity to cavort around amongst the branches of trees like that." He was also certain it's not any of the local wildlife like a bear—the limb proportions don't match. He could accept the possibility of it being a chimpanzee, except of course chimps aren't indigenous to upstate New York; the campground didn't allow pets for insurance liability; and there were no reports of escaped chimps or monkeys from zoos, labs, or private owners in the area. (Private investigator Steve Kulls, who takes on Bigfoot cases, checked all this. Fun job, right?)

Is there an explanation besides baby Bigfoot? Yes, if you agree with Stephanie Manka that primates generally wouldn't let their young go anywhere near human activity like an active campground; whereas bears are notorious scavengers, uninhibited about rummaging through trash even when people are in the immediate vicinity. They're also skillfully arboreal. It comes down to which anatomical analysis you want to go with—can the limbs be those of a bear or are they too long, as Meldrum asserts? Due to the low light and shakiness of the footage, it can be argued either way. But when we consider the provenance of the footage—it was shot by a guy out with friends at a music festival, not some Bigfoot hunter prowling around the woods with a camera—we didn't think this was a hoax. Pridgen did not try to get his film theatrical distribution; he didn't even want to appear on-camera with us. It's safe to say some kind of creature was up in those trees. It remains unidentified.

A SOUTHERN SIGHTING: THE FLORIDA SKUNK APE

Then there's the Stacy Brown footage that kicked off this chapter. Unlike Doug Pridgen and his friends, the Browns were avid Bigfooters, and arguably prone to an acute case of confirmation bias. That's why Cliff Barackman wasn't satisfied just watching the footage; he traveled to Florida to conduct his own investigation.

Barackman examined the exact spot where the figure was captured on video. He concluded that, measured against the foliage in the frame site, it was much larger than any normal person. Also of note—the thermal signature on the image was a uniform shade. People wearing clothing give off different heat signatures depending on what parts of the body are covered, which would mean the creature is either an animal with a uniform coat of fur or a person running through the woods at night naked or in a full body suit. Furthermore, the anatomy of the creature was odd. It resembled a primate, with no visible neck and beefy arms, but its legs were too long to be a chimpanzee or a gorilla, too short to be a human. And its loping gait, sometimes called a Groucho walk, was nearly identical to what's observed in the PGF at the moment of Patty's "lookback."

Wait a minute, though; the footage was shot in Florida, not the Pacific Northwest. What reason is there to believe that Bigfoot has spread throughout North America and adapted to its diverse climates? Again, Native American folklore provides helpful context. The Seminoles and Muscogee tribes spoke of a creature they called the Esti Capcaki or Tall Man, characterized as a protector of the forest. The lore has evolved into a modern version, the Florida Skunk Ape, which is said by some to be slightly smaller, a little more belligerent, and a lot more foul smelling than its northwestern cousin. In accordance with the new paradigm of paleoanthropology—the evolutionary bush, not the tree—it jibes that there could be more than one subspecies of Bigfoot alive at the same time.

Even our staunchest Bigfoot Skeptic, Stephanie Manka, agrees that the Brown Footage captured something that looks like a large primate, but one that doesn't match the body structure of living apes. That being said, she's reflexively suspicious of any footage proffered by dedicated Bigfoot hunters: "In order to consider this video credible, I would need to see more of this creature in the forest. And I would expect to see a lot more thermal imagery through the trees. I wouldn't expect it to just completely disappear."

So we're left with the two likeliest possibilities—the Brown Footage either captured a large unknown animal or it caught a large person in the woods either running around naked or wearing a suit to perpetrate a hoax. Maybe that person was an unnamed co-conspirator, or even Stacy himself if you think he's lying about the whole story. (Neither Meldrum, Barackman, nor our producers do, and they're more eager to denounce hoaxers than anyone.)

The "naked guy running around the woods" hypothesis seems the least likely. But now here's a twist that threw me for a loop—*there's a documented history of just such an occurrence in this immediate vicinity.* Newspaper reports from August of 1884 describe residents of nearby Ocheesee Pond encountering a "Wild Man" much like the Esti Capcaki wading in the water, eating berries, and occasionally disturbing the peace with primitive cries and howls. The story doesn't end there—a party of men with guns in boats went searching for the creature . . . and soon found him. He was described as a man, "entirely destitute of clothing, emaciated, and covered with a phenomenal growth of hair." The sparse news reports say he could not identify himself and was assumed to be an escaped inmate from an asylum. What ultimately became of this "Wild Man" remains unknown.

Yet cases of hermits, fugitives, and other "Wild Men" living off the grid still pop up today, and as we've delved into the world of Bigfoot sightings I've become more open to the possibility that some might be explained this way. The most famous case is that of Christopher Thomas Knight, the "North Pond Hermit," who lived for twenty-seven years without human contact in the area around Maine's Belgrade Lakes, surviving the harsh winters by burglarizing homes and stockpiling supplies. Did the Brown Footage capture another such hermit? I've been living in the Sunshine State myself for three years now. If it turns out this Wild Man was merely a subspecies of Florida Man, I wouldn't bat an eyelid.

BIGFOOT LINGUISTICS: THE SIERRA SOUNDS

Some of the most impressive evidence for Bigfoot is not video, but audio. We're frequently sent recordings of what are alleged to be calls, roars, howls, and grunts of the Sasquatch. Of course we analyze them against known animal noises. The experience has provided a valuable education in the vast variety of unexpected sounds animals produce—the mating call of an elk in estrus, to cite but one, is as otherworldly as anything George Lucas ever put on film.

A set of recordings known as the Sierra Sounds has proved to be the gold standard of alleged Sasquatch audio. They originate from an expedition in Northern California undertaken back in 1971 by two friends, Al Berry and Ron Morehead, who'd ventured into an area near Lake Tahoe and Yosemite to investigate mysterious noises reported by bewildered hunters. They dangled a microphone from a tree branch, began recording on a portable reel to reel (kids, that's what people used back then), and picked up a series of guttural grunts and howls that changed Ron's life. "The very first sounds were very aggressive and could be considered very scary," he recalls. "But we don't know the intent. We don't know their agenda."

Ron would return to the site frequently over the course of the next five years, recording several times. Eventually he became convinced the Sasquatch had its own language, which he tried to mimic. At one point, he claims he was even communicating with them: "I was responding back to them. That was the most unique Bigfoot encounter I've ever had."

Barackman, along with many in the Bigfoot community, gives credence to the Sierra Sounds, and he has his reasons. First, many other eyewitnesses over the years have reported hearing Bigfoot "protolanguage" similar to what's heard on a portion of the Sierra Sounds known as the "Samurai chatter"—a passage during which the utterances evoke images of a curt Japanese warrior barking orders. Second, the recordings have been analyzed by independent experts, including a retired crypto-linguist from the U.S. Navy, who concluded that the sounds included phonetic patterns that repeated. This indicates that the Sierra Sounds may have captured multiple creatures communicating with each other.

As for our own analysis, sound ecologist Dr. Ben Gottesman compared the Sierra Sounds with the most obvious candidates known to inhabit the area—elk and black bear. He also noticed a truly remarkable acoustic diversity and enormous vocal range on the recordings. It would be highly unlikely for a human voice to be able to go from a very low growl to a very high pitch.

Might the sounds have come from . . . a monkey? We've already established there are no primates native to California, though there was a famous case of a pet chimp, Moe, who escaped from the animal sanctuary to which he'd been remanded by the state after biting off someone's finger. Moe got free and eloped into the San Bernardino National Forest. Despite a desperate search—with a helicopter and everything—launched by the couple who'd raised him, Moe was never seen again.

That incident happened much farther south, and it happened in 2018, much later than the Sierra Sounds recordings of the mid-seventies. I mention it only to point out that people do keep primates as pets, and in California exotic animals are frequently trained for use in the entertainment industry. So it's possible, albeit unlikely, that a similar mishap occurred back in the era of bell-bottoms, went unreported, and those escaped monkeys were responsible for what Morehead and Berry caught on tape. (Actually—full disclosure—I'm throwing in the Moe mention only because the story is too nuts not to include in this book. The detail that gets me: at a teary press conference, Moe's owners bemoaned their loss while reminiscing over their innumerable fond memories with the beloved chimp. "He meant the world to us," said the husband. "He was the best man at my wedding.")

So what was it? While experts like Barackman and Strain are sure Morehead did indeed record a Bigfoot, the furthest we'd stretch was to call this the sound of an unidentified animal. The problem, as Meldrum himself noted, is that while other Bigfoot experiencers have *claimed* to have heard sounds much like the "Samurai chatter," nobody else has independently captured anything that matches Morehead and Berry's originals. You'd think if there's a species out there making that much memorable noise, someone else would have caught it on tape.

THE YETI, THE YOWIE, AND OTHER DISTANT RELATIVES

As I mentioned earlier, variations on the Bigfoot legend pop up around the world. This might be interpreted as support for the Jungian or structural anthropology argument that the "Wild Man" is not a real creature but an archetype to which human cultures are drawn the world over. Bigfoot, these arguments claim, is part of our shared human consciousness but not part of our natural history.

Conversely, this recurrence could be read as ratification of Meldrum's take on hominid evolution, which we mentioned briefly earlier. In layman's terms it lays out like this: the early human ancestor Australopithecus (of which the famed "Lucy" was a celebrated specimen) lived in Africa about 3 million years ago. Mainstream paleoanthropology has it going extinct roughly 2.1 million years ago, but Meldrum proposes another narrative: "One can speculate that perhaps this lineage did not go extinct, but expanded into Asia and attained gigantism during the Pleistocene, as did so many other northern latitude mammal species like the wooly mammoth." (Exactly why mammals became huge in the Ice Age is an ongoing debate. Some argue the colder temperatures made larger creatures more fit for survival because they retain heat well; others argue the extinction of the dinosaurs meant less competition for food.) From there, the evolutionary "bush" branches in several directions, spawning numerous Bigfoot-like species that differentiate from each other over the millennia as the continents drift and animals migrate. In the Pacific Northwest we get Bigfoot; in parts of Russia and the Himalayas, they get the Yeti; and in Australia, they have the Yowie, to name but three.

If that's the case, and those other distant relatives are as real as Bigfoot, surely there must be some proof they exist too? Well, let's start with the Yowie. We know the creature appears on aboriginal cave paintings and in storytelling traditions; and for those who only trust Europeans, there are accounts from eighteenth-century colonizers as well.

As for present-day video? The best we've come across came from a team of Yowie researchers who zeroed in on an area of Springbrook National Park just south of Brisbane, where they believed they'd found traces of Yowie activity. In May 2021, they set up thermal imaging cameras at this "hot spot," where they claim they hit pay dirt. Their footage shows not one but two figures, hiding behind a large tree trunk, then revealing themselves as one bends down to pick something up off the forest floor. The creatures appear to have vaguely cone-shaped heads, large shoulders, and apelike limb proportions. When we put the image through a filter, the head comes into better view. Like Patty in the PGF, and the alleged common ancestor Australopithecus, this potential Yowie appears to have a pronounced sagittal crest.

Our zoologist Roxy Furman was certain the creatures were bipedal, which presents a puzzle because the only bipedal wild animals in Australia are the cassowary, the emu, the kangaroo, and the wallaby. It's obvious that's not what the video captured. This led Furman to conclude that the creatures were *non-wild* bipeds: people, whose heads appeared conical because they were wearing head lamps. In short, she was positive this was either a case of misidentification or a massive hoax.

Fair enough—but that wasn't the last word. The research team went back to the spot the next morning and measured the tree to get a sense of scale of the figures on the video. Kathy Strain found their results dispositive: "Whatever it is, it is more than eight feet tall. The possibility of them being human is highly unlikely. What this video shows are two real Yowie. I think it is one of the most significant films taken in at least fifty years." Strain advocates for more scientists to dedicate resources to Yowie research "so that these animals can be studied and protected." But to date, this Yowie footage has not been the game changer many hoped it would be.

As for the Yeti? The closest we've ever come to validating a sighting was one that came out of the Russian republic of Bashkortostan in 2016. A camera is rolling inside a car as a family of three records a drive down a desolate stretch of road; suddenly one of them spots something strange in the distance. As the driver backs up for a better look, the video captures a mysterious hunched figure peeking out from the tall greenery. Then it suddenly lurches forward, arms flailing. The driver tears out, but the dark figure pursues, frenzied, chasing the vehicle until it speeds off. The lighting is so dark and the camera so shaky it's difficult to tell whether or not this is a person, a primate, or something in between. In some frames the arms look inhuman, though that could just be a camera effect in the low light.

Analyzing Russian Yeti footage comes with extra challenges. The waters are clouded by a noxious stream of hoaxed footage created to keep the lucrative Yeti tourism industry humming. The problem is so widespread that even government officials are in on it. In 2021 a story broke that Aman Tuleyev, a Putin-picked governor of the Kemerovo Oblast in Siberia from 1997 to 2018, ordered one of the tall bureaucrats on his staff to don an outfit and help produce videotaped Yeti sightings to lure visitors to their impoverished region. The Tuleyev stunt is actually quite primitive compared to others we've debunked—including a viral clip of a Yeti running across a snow-covered road at night, startling the passengers in a dashcam-equipped car. In that case, the producers did an admirable job staging the event and making the encounter seem spontaneous, but the awkward angle of the creature's leg as it kicks up the snow in its path is a dead giveaway for a man in a suit.

Nor do the Russians have a monopoly on Yeti disinformation. In 2019, the Indian Army released photos on its official Twitter account purporting to show that its mountaineering team had encountered Yeti footprints measuring thirty-two inches by fifteen inches near a base camp in the Makalu Barun National Park. The post was widely ridiculed, the prints identified as those of a bear, and there was no further comment from the Indian Army.

When we spoke to Igor Burtsev of Russia's International Center of Hominology, he told us their investigation of the Bashkortostan car-chase case put them squarely on team Yeti. "We checked the trees, bushes, and we found many signs of Yeti activity there. Broken branches . . ." Still, with the maximum possible respect to Mr. Burtsev, we wouldn't go beyond saying it was an unidentifiable bipedal animal, if for no other reason than the footage made more specific identification impossible.

HOAXES AND HOKUM

The hoaxing problem bedevils domestic Bigfoot research too, as it gives Skeptics an excuse to dismiss any sighting and inhibits cautious scientists from even dipping their toes into the subject for fear of being suckered. (It's happened—Cliff Barackman has been specifically targeted by people who've made fake footprints and tried to get him to confirm their legitimacy.)

We see them all the time. One of the more famous Florida Skunk Ape videos is clearly a guy running, awkwardly, through the Everglades in a cheap gorilla suit so ill fitting he nearly stumbles—not the gait of an indigenous species elegantly adapted to its environment.

Then there are truly shameless, Barnumesque figures like a man named Rick Dyer, who claimed to have shot Bigfoot outside San Antonio, Texas, in 2012. He was happy to let the public inspect its corpse, preserved like Lenin in a glass case, for a mere ten-dollar ticket. It was clear the "creature's" fur was a cheap fake, that it had severely chapped lips one would expect from an arctic environment, not southern Texas, and that its body showed no signs of gunshot wounds though Dyer claimed to have slayed it with a shotgun. None of that inhibited Dyer from recounting his tale to us on-camera without an iota of equivocation or shame. "I wanted to attract him so I went out and got deer urine and pork ribs," his tale goes. "And I hung the pork ribs on a tree. I scattered the deer urine all under the tree. In the middle of the night, Bigfoot came back and I jumped out of the tent with my firearm and I shot at him a couple of times." Despite the absurdity of Dyer's story, one has to salute his chutzpah. He reportedly raked in a cool $500,000 in ticket sales.

Bigfoot tourism is popular in America just as Yeti tourism is in Russia, so it's to be expected that a fraction of the hoaxes will be premeditated marketing stunts. That was most likely the case in 2023, when passengers on Colorado's Durango and Silverton Narrow Gauge Railroad captured footage of a Bigfoot lounging in the brush along the scenic tracks. Silverton-based RV company Sasquatch Expedition Campers issued a wink-wink denial both to us on-camera and on Facebook, but we all know better, don't we?

Perhaps it's to be applauded that some people are still industrious enough to don a Bigfoot suit and run around outdoors for the sake of cheap laughs or money. Our great country was built with that spirit. And in any event our experts tell us intentional hoaxes are a drop in the bucket compared to innocent misidentifications. Plus, the hoaxes can sometimes be put to practical use, as mentioned earlier with fake footprints.

What our experts find truly annoying are the "paranormal folks" and "New Agers." This is the segment of the Bigfoot community that pushes zany theories that Bigfoot is a shape-shifting interdimensional being. Or that it's a race of aliens who traveled to Earth in UFOs; or that they can communicate telepathically with the people they encounter. These are often the folks who get so caught up in the Bigfoot question that it can impact their relationships and careers. "I think there's a fair amount of mental illness in this field," Barackman laments. "When you have people promoting these New Age theories, why would anybody take [the subject] seriously?"

What does all this mean for the future of "Bigfoot studies"? Both Meldrum and Barackman told me they were optimistic about the potential for new technologies and research projects. Meldrum extolled the potential for LIDAR—Light Detection and Ranging technology that enables researchers to see what's on the ground beneath tree canopies. It is already being used to great benefit in archaeology. Meldrum believed it will someday be applied successfully to wildlife biology too. "With LIDAR, we might soon be able to differentiate large-bodied mammals like bear, moose, and then possibly identify a Sasquatch." He also liked the burgeoning field of environmental DNA (eDNA), a tool that identifies species in a given area by analyzing genetic material that has been shed into the environment and left behind in the soil. His only concern was that there may be so much overlap in the human and Bigfoot genomes that a deteriorated or fragmentary sample poses a big risk of false negatives. In other words, a degraded sample could lead us to mistake authentic Sasquatch DNA for that of a lost hiker.

For his part, Barackman sees immense potential in a project underway at NC State, under the direction of Darby Orcutt, the director of Interdisciplinary Partnerships. Orcutt's project, approved by the Institutional Review Board, is officially called the "Study of Allegedly Morphologically Anomalous Physical Samples." You have to use a convoluted string of multisyllabic words to get official approval for what's really happening: Orcutt is testing candidate samples of peculiar hair, teeth, and other body parts to see if their DNA could be that of Bigfoot or some other undiscovered species. So far Orcutt has received more than a hundred samples.

In the meantime, the search continues. As a new generation of academics looks upon the subject with unprecedented hospitality (and as the old guard literally dies off), the Bigfoot question, like the UFO question, is emerging from the shadows, even if the creature itself has yet to do so. And if solid proof never emerges? It's unlikely public interest will ever dissipate. "People love Bigfoot because we recognize in him a little bit of something we've lost," says Barackman. "He's an undomesticated version of ourselves that we miss." Taking an interest in Bigfoot, either online or in the field, brings our attention back to nature, at least for a moment.

That's good enough for him. "I don't feel like I'm on some Arthurian quest. If I go into the woods, and don't find stuff, I don't mind. I still had a great walk in the woods. I'm not trying to show people I'm right; I'm not trying to prove this species exists. I'm just enjoying the ride."

While the Bigfoot quest continues in the forest, it's time for us to turn our attention to the water, where the seas and lakes are teeming with legends equally as seductive and tenacious as the prodigious Sasquatch. If you too have been enjoying the ride, might you fancy a cruise?

Chapter 7

GOING DEEP WITH SEA MONSTERS

THE OGOPOGO EFFECT

Skaha Lake was like glass.

Jim La Rocque had been taking his family to his mother-in-law's cabin there in British Columbia for fifteen years, and on the afternoon of June 1, 2019, he was sitting on the dock with his daughter, looking out while his son was paddleboarding about fifty meters from shore. Then he remembers hearing a strange "swoosh" sound, and seeing something emerge from the water just behind the paddleboard. Familiar with the frequent tales of a local lake monster known as Ogopogo, he reached down to grab his smartphone and started recording. His daughter's amazement is evident on the video, as she repeats, "What is it? What is it?" out of frame. "I was like, 'Oh my God,'" he recalled. "'I hope I get this on video because no one's ever going to believe me about this.'"

There's a discrepancy between what Jim remembers seeing and what can be discerned on his footage. He says it was a massive creature with a white underbelly and flippers or fins. "In my head, I was like, 'That thing is massive. It must be the Ogopogo they talked about for years around here.'" In his account, the creature was only visible for about twenty seconds before it submerged again, thankfully leaving Jim's son unharmed.

The video is more ambiguous. Something unquestionably peculiar is happening in the water, and if you freeze and zoom in you can identify something that could, possibly, be a flipper, maybe two. Jim said he showed his video to several locals and experts, including some Japanese scientists who determined that there were indeed two flippers, separated by about ten feet, making the creature as long as sixty feet.

Our experts, conversely, said the hydrological evidence points in another direction. The "creature" is simply not producing the kind of wake one would expect from a swimming animal. The "bumps" in the trailing waves should be going up and down in sequence; but in the footage all the waves peak at the same time. They concluded that Jim had recorded something called a *propagating wave*. These occur seasonally when lake layers of different temperatures pass over each other. The phenomenon even has a name: the Ogopogo Effect.

But Jim is certain about what he saw. "We've been going down to our family cabin for fifteen years, at least forty to sixty times every year. I've shown the video to everyone in my family and they've never seen a wave look like that before. That's not a paddleboarder wake. That's not a kayak wake. When I first moved to the Okanagan, I heard rumblings about this Ogopogo thing and I kind of laughed it off. But after getting that on video, I'm a true Believer now that something's out there that's big."

WATERWORLDS

Humans have been telling stories of gigantic sea creatures since antiquity, and it's easy to see why. Outer space is so vast it's hard to even comprehend—the mind just categorizes it as something too big to measure, like the number gazillion. But the ocean is built to our scale. It's just small enough for us to appreciate how huge it is. Just this morning I took a bike ride that brought me to a little strip of South Florida beach I visit frequently to swim or meditate. Even though I'd been to the same spot dozens of times before, the awe and wonder inspired by the Atlantic's vastness and power were as intense as when I'd first gazed upon it as a child visiting from my little hometown of Ottawa, Kansas. What lies over that horizon, and what lurks beneath the waves? Even the most impoverished imaginations shoot up into the higher tiers of fantasy pondering the great subaqueous mysteries. (And by the way, what kind of courage and curiosity must it have taken for the great explorers—be they Portuguese, Viking, or Maori, to venture past that horizon without GPS?)

The oft-quoted stats validate the intuition that there must be entire ecosystems of marine life about which we still know precisely nothing. As every sixth grader is taught, 71 percent of the Earth is covered in water; the average depth of the oceans is twelve thousand feet, and only 5 percent of the ocean floor has been explored. Clearly a plethora of fresh discoveries awaits us, and we can say so with even greater confidence because new discoveries are made all the time.

I was born in 1970, and at the time it was commonly believed there were about 300 species of sharks on earth. Today the number is around 380. That's more than 1 new species of shark discovered every year. In my lifetime the discovery of the "megamouth" has been the most remarkable. In 1976 a Navy research vessel operating about twenty-five miles off Kahuku Point in Hawaii pulled up its parachute-shaped anchors and noticed a peculiar animal entangled in one. It was cartoonishly monstrous—about fourteen feet long, with a bulbous head and a distinctive, three-foot-wide mouth that, when open, makes it look like the shark is smiling. We've since learned that the megamouth is a deep-sea plankton feeder, seen so rarely that the scientific community has a list of each encounter that's occurred outside a single area in Taiwan where the species is seen frequently. It's living proof that there are large creatures swimming in the depths of the sea we have yet to encounter. And should we ever run out of strange unknown creatures to discover, fret not. Human pollution, especially chemical and radioactive waste, is causing increasingly frequent and monstrous mutations, like a "human-headed" shark we investigated a few seasons ago.

Bottom line: you are not wasting your time hunting for aquatic monsters. This kind of anomaly is not that anomalous. Recalibrate your epsilons accordingly.

That's what keeps Ken Gerhard going. Ken, our resident sea and lake monster expert, is a well-known cryptozoologist, lecturer, and author. As the son of a forest ranger, he grew up outdoors with a menagerie of pets that would shame Dr. Doolittle. He conducted his first research at age fifteen when his father took him to Loch Ness to spend a week camped out by the legendary Scottish lake with an 8mm movie camera gathering as much info as possible. As he got older, Ken traveled to areas where he knew there'd been reports of other local lake monster activity—Canada, Wisconsin, Texas. He even went to Zandvoort, Holland, to chase down fresh leads about sea serpents first allegedly encountered in 1906. He's spoken to eyewitnesses, examined video and photos. Has he ever seen anything truly inexplicable himself? No. Still, his curiosity persists to this day. He may be in his fifties, but he hasn't lost that boyhood sense of wonder.

"There's obviously room for skepticism," Gerhard admits. "You'd think we'd have better footage than we do. I welcome that; people should be critical thinkers." But Gerhard and others in his quirky field keep going, in part because they share the same respect—even deference—for the lore of indigenous peoples, just as the Bigfoot hunters do. "We should always look at some of those legends and take them seriously," he says. "These people have lived in their areas for thousands of years. When we say something is 'discovered' it's a bit disingenuous. It just means Western scientists have finally noticed something and taken interest. Many creatures that were 'discovered' were long said to exist by natives. For them, it's not a discovery; it's an 'I told you so.'"

Gerhard has also noticed that the stigma around cryptozoology seems to be subsiding for sea monsters as well as Bigfoot, as evidenced by the fact that the San Antonio Zoo employs him as a docent, allowing him to speak freely about his "pseudoscientific" work and writing, though the zoo is a serious research center with an accreditation to maintain.

When we come across a tantalizing water monster video, we always turn to Gerhard to help us understand the relevant lore and supporting evidence. He's been with us from day one, and he says he sticks with the show because "each subject is approached objectively. No one goes in with preconceived notions." He also appreciates our efforts to solicit a diversity of opinions, such as those from "legit" marine biologists like Dr. Shea Steingass of Oregon State University's Marine Mammal Institute.

Steingass, like me, was born and raised in a landlocked state, in her case Wyoming. She saw the ocean for the first time at age seven when her family went on a vacation in Mexico, and says she fell so deeply in love with it she cried on the flight home as it disappeared out her window. The feeling has never left, through her decision to join the Save the Manatee Club as a tween to her commitment to a career in marine biology, forsaking a prior interest in veterinary medicine. When I asked her to explain why, she said, "The ocean is the ultimate mystery. We know so little about it. From the shore, looking at the waves, you can see there's a whole world under the water, filled with animals you rarely see. And though we can touch it, we can't be a part of it."

Dr. Steingass jumped at our invitation to contribute to the show. "I've spent a lot of time studying Native American folklore and traveling in India," she says. "I've learned that there are elements to human nature outside of mainstream science that are incredibly important. We don't do a good job of acknowledging all of human nature when we do science; we just tell people they're wrong. It's important to talk about out-of-the-box ideas and theories."

NESSIE, INC.

So let's get right to the most famous aquatic cryptid of all, the Loch Ness Monster. As with many legends, "Nessie's" is sustained by the thriving industry that's developed around it. Every year as many as six hundred thousand tourists flock to the lake, and while the area's castles and scenery are part of the draw, the monster is the big magnet. The Loch Ness Centre offers reasonably priced cruises on boats equipped with deepscan sonar and organizes an annual four-day "Quest Event." Separately, serious Nessie hunters including Ken Gerhard periodically conduct their own expeditions, using the latest underwater research tech. They've even requested assistance from NASA, which they hope can deploy its advanced imaging technology to locate the beast. So far that request has not been granted.

Marketing efforts aside, there are several reasons why enthusiasm for "Nessie" persists. The first is the creature's impressive history. Sightings date back to the sixth century, back before tourism was even a word, much less an industry.

The lake itself also gives the legend an assist—it's as deep as 745 feet, and believed to be big enough to fit the entire human population of planet Earth three times over. Its water is especially inky, thanks to high levels of peat washed into the water by rainfall on the surrounding hills; dark enough to hide the iconic creature.

But to justify the disposal of the tourists' disposable income, and to (hopefully) recruit NASA to its cause, the Nessie cryptid community needs a viable theory for how the monster fits into the area's natural history. The most popular hypothesis is that Nessie is some type of relict plesiosaur, which was a large marine reptile from the Mesozoic era that matches the general description—broad body, flippers, long neck, short head. They varied greatly in size, the largest growing to eighty-two feet. And they lived all over the world, so Scotland would be as likely a place to find one as any.

Hang on, though. The plesiosaurs went extinct 66 million years ago. Surely it's absurd to think one—or a breeding pod—could have survived the notorious Cretaceous-Paleogene extinction event, the same one that wiped out the T. rex and Triceratops. It is here that the Believers pipe up, pointing to a quirk of zoology known as "Lazarus species," animals thought to be long gone, but which reemerge unexpectedly, upsetting the applecart of mainstream thought.

I touched on this concept in the Bigfoot chapter amid the discussion of a potential "relict hominid" still walking the earth. In the sea, there's more than potential for Lazarus species; there are concrete examples. The coelacanth, an elusive deep-sea fish, is the rock star of this *Jeopardy!* category. The youngest fossil of the species is 66 million years old too, which had led paleontologists to the reasonable conclusion that the fish went extinct at the same time as the plesiosaurs. That was, until 1938, when one turned up in the nets of local fishermen off the east coast of South Africa.

Other Lazarus species include a variety of birds and mammals that were around in recent centuries, so their reemergence might not be that shocking, but there are a handful that date back to the heyday of the plesiosaur. The Alavesia fly, originally discovered encased in amber 100 million years old, was found buzzing around Namibia in 2010. Monoplacophora mollusks, believed to have disappeared about 380 million years ago, were found off the coast of Costa Rica in 1952. Given all that, would it really be that absurd for a relict plesiosaur to be swimming in Loch Ness?

There is no shortage of sightings. Gerhard estimates about ten good ones are reported annually. As I've been drafting this chapter, the most recent—a photo purporting to show a "dark mass" moving just under the surface—made headlines worldwide and even earned a spot on *The Today Show*. As long as that keeps up, the mystery will endure.

Our engagement with the Loch Ness legend began in our first season, with a couple of photos intriguing enough to make the *New York Post*. They'd been taken by Loch Ness tourist Steven Challice, and were being hailed as "one of the top three sightings" ever. The images showed the back of a large sea creature breaching the water's surface. No head or flippers were visible, but Challice told us it was huge. "I'm guessing that what I saw was eight foot long," he said on-camera with a straight face, "but there might have been a bit more either end of that underneath the water. So you could be talking about a fish that was ten, twelve feet long, which is massive. It really is."

"It was amazing," remembers Ken Gerhard. "I mean, here you had the classic Nessy hump. It's been described by the majority of eyewitnesses. And the quality of the photograph is incredible. Great clarity. Great detail, which is actually very rare."

Sadly, the Challice photos did not survive scrutiny. Again, Dr. Steingass saw red flags flying when she took a closer look at the physics of the water around the object: "If an object or animal is submerged in water, we would see a series of eddies and ripples around the entirety of this animal extending out pretty far. Instead, what we see are a series of regular waves surrounding this animal with a small trailing wake behind it." Her suspicions were confirmed when forensic video analyst Michael Primeau assessed the photos' authenticity. There were enough inconsistencies with the digital information for him to conclude the image had been manipulated, using an uploaded image of a catfish.

I fully expected every Nessie sighting to be equally fraudulent. But that same season we investigated a fresh sighting captured on video by a Loch Ness local, firefighter Ross MacAulay. The video was confirmed as authentic, and according to MacAulay, it captured a grayish creature twelve feet long, four feet wide, moving against the waves and into the wind. MacAulay was shooting from a distance and whatever is moving through the water isn't easy to identify, but it seems to be splashing on the surface and lollygagging in the water rather than motoring with purpose in a specific direction. That's why Gerhard was positive it wasn't a seal, which is how Loch Ness sightings are sometimes explained away: "A seal would not be staying in one spot; it would be moving swiftly through the water from point A to point B. So whatever it is, it's massive and it's not any known native species we would find in Loch Ness."

Dr. Steingass agreed it was an animal, and not a seal. She based her analysis on a recent eDNA study of the water in Loch Ness, which had turned up surprising evidence of a creature not previously believed to be native to the lake: an eel. Her conclusion: "It's possible that some of these species could be large. However, they are as of yet undefined." Perhaps the mystery of Loch Ness will be solved when a large eel species is documented conclusively, and the pattern will repeat—a legend of cryptozoology will attain legitimacy as it loses its power of enchantment and takes its place alongside the other assimilated species of the animal kingdom.

Such is the way with Nessie videos. Recently, however, Gerhard and one of his Scottish counterparts, Alan McKenna, documented an interesting *audio* event using a hydrophone. The underwater listening device was once the heart of the SOSUS system used by the U.S. Navy to detect enemy submarines (and was featured prominently in the last *Mission: Impossible* movie). McKenna positioned his hydrophone about one hundred feet underwater and was taken aback by what it recorded: a bizarre thumping that some have interpreted as Nessie's heartbeat. "This is literally the first time we've ever captured some really unusual sounds in the depths of Loch Ness," Gerhard said. "It's easy to compare it to that of any animal with a four-chambered heart very similar to ours." Gerhard pointed out some recent evidence suggesting plesiosaurs were warm-blooded and may have had a four-chambered heart that would emit a sound in line with the recording.

Dr. Steingass observed that if the sound was a heartbeat, it would not be a healthy one. Its rhythm is erratic, suggesting atrial fibrillation. Indeed, when we compared the sound to that of a manatee heartbeat, it was much more irregular and fast compared to what we'd expect. In other words, if it was Nessie, her carcass would probably have floated to the surface by now. Another theory is that the "heartbeat" was generated by a flaw in the hydrophone itself. Still, the sound was compelling enough that McKenna has vowed to return to the same spot and pursue his quarry with hydrophone at the ready. And if that device can capture Nessie's heartbeat, what other monsters might it discover elsewhere?

MEGALODON

The trusty hydrophone plays an important role in the ongoing oceanic hunt for another fan favorite: the ancient megalodon. This is the celebrated gigantic shark, as big as sixty feet long, that isn't legendary at all in one sense, since it was real. The fossil record confirms that this immense creature prowled the oceans in every corner of the globe except Antarctica, feasting on whales and other sharks. The megalodon was one of the large fraction of marine animals—as much as a third—believed to have gone extinct by the end of the Pliocene era as a result of global cooling, which chilled the tropical waters and wiped out several organisms at the base of the marine food chain. The last megalodon died and went to monster shark heaven about 2.6 million years ago.

Or did it? Saying anything with certainty about the megalodon comes with an additional set of challenges because we have such sparse data. Sharks are made of cartilage after all, so when they die they don't leave behind a large fossil record. In fact, the only hard evidence we have of the megalodon's existence are massive teeth that have been recovered whole—some more than seven inches long—and portions of which have been found embedded in whale fossils. Given the paucity of data, the vastness of the ocean depths, and the reappearance of Lazarus species, it's no surprise that many people are actively rooting for the hypothesis that a relict megalodon is still swimming.

Occasionally a photo or video will surface that purports to make the case. One internet classic shows what looks like a gigantic shark nosing up to one of those diving cages we know from *Jaws* and Discovery's Shark Week. The shark dwarfs the cage, which is typically about ten feet wide. In addition to its anomalous size, the beast has haunting white eyes that make it look ghostly and unfamiliar.

We quickly debunked this one by determining the cage was actually a crab trap, about a third the size of a diving cage; the creature's anatomy matched that of a Pacific sleeper shark, and those otherworldly eyes were the result of a parasite called *Ommatokoita elongata*, known to latch on to sharks' eyes. This was an impressive creature about which much is still unknown—Pacific sleeper sharks can grow to fourteen feet—and a rare caught-on-camera sighting, but nothing approaching the megalodon.

We also took a look at a remarkable photo of a mako shark pulled from the sea by a fisherman off the coast of Australia. It was at least twelve feet long and appeared to have been bitten in half. What gargantuan creature could have a bite radius big enough to do that, if not the megalodon? But when Dr. Steingass examined the photo, she noticed a series of scratches and lacerations on the shark's side. Those, plus a closer examination of the "cutting edge" of the bite itself, led her to conclude that this shark had been killed not by one tremendous bite, but by several smaller ones, likely inflicted by other tiger sharks in a feeding frenzy.

The strongest evidence we've had for anything resembling the megalodon came to us via our friend the hydrophone. Over the years, research teams from NOAA and other organizations have deployed these devices to monitor everything from whale migrations to underwater seismic activity, as well as submarines. On rare occasions, they will pick up noises that defy explanation. These recordings quickly become viral sensations and acquire memorable monikers like "The Bloop," "The Whistle," and "Julia."

We've had a couple of outstanding forensic audio analysts during the show's run. We started with sound ecologist Dr. Ben Gottesman, currently at Cornell's Yang Center for Conservation Bioacoustics. In recent seasons we've had Dr. Robert Maher, a Fellow of the Audio Engineering Society, and a professor of electrical and computer engineering at Montana State University. Using the same method they apply to alleged Bigfoot howls, they compare the spectrographs of the mystery deep-sea sounds to sample recordings of the most likely prosaic explanations, looking for a match. These include sources as diverse as humpback whale calls, deep-sea drilling machinery, submarines, and underwater volcanoes. In the case of "The Whistle," Maher confirmed that indeed, a significant seismic event was the most likely culprit.

With the case of "The Upsweep," however, it was another story. In 1991, a hydrophone off the western coast of Mexico picked up a bizarre sound from the middle of the Pacific Ocean more than *five thousand* miles away. It's a strange warbling, bubbling noise, rising in pitch at the end—hence the moniker "Upsweep." During our investigation, both Dr. Gottesman and Dr. Steingass agreed that given the distance the sound traveled, whatever entity produced it was Capital L *Large*. Our experts considered all the aforementioned usual suspects (including the megalodon) but found nothing that matched. Dr. Gottesman first thought the sound would match recordings of deep-sea seismic activity but found that they lacked the distinctive increase in pitch heard with "The Upsweep." Steingass concluded that "The Upsweep" was a bioacoustic sound, but no known animal's call comes close to its unique audio signature. We called this a "mystery marine mammal." At the time of this writing, "The Upsweep" is still unidentified.

So with both Nessie and the megalodon we have some acoustic evidence that's tantalizing but not rock solid, and the best Nessie video we've seen, while intriguing, is still of no more superior quality than your average Bigfoot clip. Isn't there some legendary creature with a more compelling evidentiary record? Something solid we can really sink our teeth into? The answer . . . is yes.

THE KRAKEN

The Kraken endures as one of the most captivating sea stories from the Age of Exploration—an enormous, tentacled creature that could drag entire sailing vessels beneath the waves, dooming the crew to watery graves. It's easy to imagine a gray-bearded, peg-legged sailor in an eighteenth-century harbor pub retelling his Kraken story for the thousandth time after a few quaffs of rum, but "respectable" sources also presented such accounts. In the late 1700s, the French naturalist Pierre Denys de Montfort described a Kraken attack off the coast of Angola, in which sailors succeeded in hacking off the Kraken's arms and tentacles using swords and hatchets. An artist's depiction of the attack was placed in a chapel.

It should be noted that Montfort's career went into a death spiral when he later claimed ten British ships that had vanished had been victimized by a group of giant octopi. When he was proved wrong, Montfort and his Kraken theories were roundly discredited. He died disgraced and destitute. Today a sympathetic take on his Kraken accounts chalks them up as early sightings of the giant squid, a creature that was itself considered legendary until its existence was confirmed in the 1870s.

Nevertheless, the Kraken has a loyal constituency in the cryptozoology community. And it's often the case that a video goes viral precisely because commenters upvote it as evidence of the beast's existence.

One of my favorites hit TikTok in October 2022. A young woman named Afri Gregory was walking her dogs on the beach in Queensland, Australia. As she took in some of the lovely scenery, she recorded a clip that would quickly attract more than a million views. Her narration is what takes it to the next level.

"Warm crystal-clear water? Fucking mint!" she exclaims, using the Aussie term for "cool" while holding her hand in front of the lens in a thumbs-up sign. "Incredible views surrounded by mountains and nature? Fucking mint!"

Then the camera pans down to something grotesque at Afri's feet that's drawn the attention of her dogs. She doesn't miss a beat. "Giant random animal part washed up on the beach? Fucking mint!"

The object is clearly a biological specimen. It's fleshy, smooth, and quite large—nearly the size of Afri's leg. "I had absolutely no idea what it was," she'd tell us later. "I thought if there's something that's like that washing up on the beach, there's something that's out there that could be many times the size of what I'm seeing here."

So what was it? We are intimately familiar with the otherworldly appearances dead animals can take on after prolonged exposure to the sun and sea. (Google the words "globster" or "Montauk monster" to see what I mean.) But this didn't look like anything we'd investigated before.

We quickly ruled out a giant squid or octopus. Cephalopod mollusks, the family in which they both reside, use their long tentacles to grasp objects, and those tentacles typically have a series of suckers for that purpose. This thing had none. In addition, the severed edge of the specimen showed traces of blood, a strong indicator that it came from a mammal or other vertebrate. Cephalopods don't have blood—their circulatory system relies on water.

But if it was from a vertebrate, why do we not see any bones? Dr. Steingass, who has spent plenty of time around carcasses, had a strong guess: "What we're seeing here is just a portion of the male reproductive tract of a whale—or just part of the penis. Unbelievably, blue whales, which are the largest animals on the planet, can have penises that extend ten to twelve feet."

We were startled by that conclusion, and even more taken aback by her claim that whale penises may have contributed to early Kraken lore. Steingass explained: "Often when whales are breeding, it's pretty violent. You will see these organs protruding above the surface of the water in a way that maybe looked like an enormous sea creature that is raising its head out of the water." That's right. Many scientists speculate that sightings of sea monsters like the Kraken trace back to the penises of mating whales—officially known as dorks—sticking out of the water. As for how this particular dork section got severed and washed up at Afri's feet? We think that the whale may have collided with a boat propeller, or it could have simply died at sea and disintegrated as it decomposed.

So should we toss the Kraken back onto the heap of discredited cryptids legends? I was prepared to, until we delved into the strange case of the USS *Stein*, which provides the most convincing evidence I've seen to date. In 1978, the *Stein*, a Navy destroyer, was conducting routine tests in the Pacific Ocean when its radar system suddenly went down. The *Stein* headed for port, and when she reached dry dock, an inspection of her radar dome revealed something astounding, which was recorded on film. The rubber coating of the dome was shredded, with large tears as big as four feet long. What's more, embedded at the bottom of those scratches are curved claws or teeth. Even stranger, the dome was covered in a special "no foul" coating specifically designed to create a smooth, nonstick surface so barnacles and other sea creatures wouldn't stick to it.

The Navy called in its top scientist, F. G. Wood, to investigate. He concluded that the most likely cause of the damage was a giant squid. But there was one hitch: the largest documented giant squid is sixty-six feet long. Based on the size of the teeth and the scratches, however, Wood estimated that the squid that attacked the *Stein* would have had to have been around 150 feet in length—2.5 times larger!

The squid theory is intriguing because there are documented cases of squid attacking vessels. In 2014, two Greenpeace submariners survived such an experience when a "red devil" squid got aggressive. But before we embraced that theory, we wanted to eliminate some other possibilities. Gerhard suggested we consider the frilled shark, another Lazarus species that just reemerged in 2015. Certainly F. G. Wood would not have considered it, since in 1978 it was still considered extinct. It's a deep-water shark with twenty-five rows of teeth. So could it have made those marks? Dr. Steingass eliminated that possibility when she noticed that there was no evidence of the serrated teeth the frilled shark uses to grab and tear its prey. Those teeth leave triangular tears. The tears on the *Stein*'s sonar dome were linear; they had to have been made by narrow and sharp teeth or claws.

The giant squid remained the strongest candidate—but a 150-footer that dwarfs the largest known specimen? Short answer: *yes*. According to Dr. Steingass, "The idea that there's a giant squid in our ocean that is much larger than any other documented specimen is totally possible. We've only found a few of these animals because they live in the deep-ocean environment. When a large animal dies in the deep sea they almost immediately sink because there's so much water pressure. And we probably would never see them. So imagine how many unique animals are living and dying in our oceans today that we've just never encountered. This could be one of them."

Why would such a creature attack a naval vessel? Since we know giant squid attack sperm whales, her theory is that the supersquid mistook the radar dome for one of its enemies trying to echolocate. In any event, consider the aggregate evidence: teeth and bite marks consistent with a 150-foot creature of a species known to attack ships. As far as I'm concerned, there's your Kraken. And while we might not have video of it alive, moving and breathing, that's not the case with another legendary beast, though its legend is scarcely known in the English-speaking world.

THE LAKE VAN MONSTER

It's important to note that while Nessie is easily Earth's most famous lake monster, tales of similar creatures have been starring in local folklore around the world for centuries. And truth be told, the percentage of those sightings we've ruled inexplicable is higher than what we've seen in the Nessie files.

Take the Lake Van Monster of eastern Turkey, the subject of a local legend that likely dates back to the tenth century (an ancient castle on the lake's shore displays an engraving of what appears to be some kind of sea dragon). More recently, an Ottoman newspaper published a story in 1889 about three men who were attacked by such a creature while camping by the shore. But it is a video recorded in 1997 that really gave the story (if not the creature itself) legs. A teaching assistant from Van University, hoping to capture evidence of the fabled monster, set up a camera by the waterline and, after a frustrating day observing a whole lotta nada, his fortune turned. The footage shows a creature of apparently massive proportions emerging from the surface of the lake. It has textured, copper-colored skin; a small cluster of bubbles percolates from beneath, potentially indicating a mouth or blowhole. There may even be a head or eye visible, though opinions differ.

We were not the first to examine the footage. It's been around for almost thirty years. Several universities have tried to explain it without success. The strongest reasons for skepticism derive from the composition of the lake itself. It is not connected to any ocean, and its water is highly salty—so rich in sodium carbonate that only two species of fish have been found living there. Still, Dr. Steingass concluded that "this definitely looks like something that's moving up and down in the water." It was those bubbles she found so probative: "If this were just an inanimate object in the water, we wouldn't be seeing that. It looks like a living, breathing animal to me." But how could that be, given Lake Van's inhospitable living conditions?

Steingass did not consider it likely for a large aquatic creature to be living in a landlocked lake for so long without more frequent, definitive sightings. The lake is huge—at 1,450 square miles and a maximum depth of 1,480 feet it dwarfs Loch Ness—so there's certainly room for a large creature to live there undetected. Perhaps this video is the first solid evidence, but we still have to account for the salinity of the water. "There's a lot of incredible animals that have adapted to extremely high-saltwater situations," says Steingass, "including animals that can live at saltwater concentrations of up to fifty percent. But if this were a type of animal that we're seeing, it would have to have an entirely different biology than anything that we really understand. I do think this is biological, but I can't tell you exactly what we're looking at." We concluded that the video documented an unknown biological specimen. While there was not enough evidence to confirm or disprove those centuries of lore, the creature seen on the footage is a genuine mystery. And if it's hard to figure out how any earthly creature of that size could live in water with that stifling chemical composition, maybe the answer is: it's not entirely of this earth.

THE "ALIEN GOLDEN EGG" AND THE PANSPERMIA HYPOTHESIS

This brings us to the so-called Panspermia hypothesis. In earlier chapters I touched on a theory that aliens and their craft aren't traveling from outer space, but from the ocean floor. Sightings of USOs, or Unidentified Submersible Objects, also called transmedium objects, buttress the case that extraterrestrials arrived here long ago, or have always been here, living in the deep sea via "chemosynthesis." This is the crypto-terrestrial theory referenced earlier, which famed Pentagon UFO whistleblower Lue Elizondo says we should take seriously.

A separate but perhaps complimentary theory has gained a bit of traction in recent years, and not just among the UFO and cryptozoology crowd. Known as the Panspermia hypothesis, it posits that the original seeds of life have been planted throughout the universe by a single extraterrestrial source. We know that some microorganisms, known as "extremophiles," can survive in space and can, in theory, function as space seeds dispersed throughout the universe on asteroids like cosmic dandelion seeds. (The tardigrade is the prime example here.)

Mainstream Panspermia argues that all life on earth evolved from such seeds; other versions say the seeds may have been involved in the evolution of *some* strange forms of life, but aren't the common ancestor of every living thing. One variation of the theory argues that Panspermia is the explanation for one of evolution's greatest mysteries: the Cambrian explosion that witnessed a rapid, exponential diversification of species 540 million years ago. And the crypto-terrestrial faction suggests that those seeds may have spawned life-forms wholly separate and unique from any life-form currently known to modern science—including, perhaps, the Lake Van Monster!

We're really pushing it here, I envision you thinking. And that's what I thought. Then I was alerted to a recent video that not only realigned my thinking; it convinced me after months of dithering that this book was indeed worth writing.

On August 23, 2023, NOAA researchers were live streaming a mission to find and document new life in the unexplored waters off Alaska. Their ship had dispatched a tricked-out remote-operated vehicle (ROV), and two miles below the surface the ROV's high-def camera came across a truly confounding sight. It was a strange, solitary, smooth orb, golden or copper colored. It strongly resembled an egg out of which something had recently hatched.

The trained scientists react with the exact same degree of amazement as Jim La Rocque's daughter when she thought she'd spotted Ogopogo.

Scientist 1: "I don't know what to make of that. . . ."
Scientist 2: " . . . it's definitely got a big old hole in it, so something either tried to get in or tried to get out!"
Scientist 1: "It's like the beginning of a horror movie."

Again, the event was being live streamed to scientists around the world. All of them were equally perplexed, as the audio confirms.

Scientist 2: "I don't know what I'm looking at. What's the science chat saying?"
Scientist 1: "We're all over the place at the moment."
Scientist 2: "When our collective knowledge can't identify it, that means it's something *weird*."

One of those scientists told us later that the closer they got to the orb, the more questions they had. The "alien golden egg" defied classification—it was hard to say it was a coral, due to its smooth surface and lack of corallite holes; and it couldn't really be a sponge, since it seemed too fragile. The team collected a sample and delivered it to the Smithsonian, where it remains unidentified as of this writing.

As our experts analyzed the footage, we of course considered every possibility—including the thought that this could be the hatched egg of a relict dinosaur. The notion drew from the fact that paleontologists working in Southeast Alaska recently discovered the remains of a new species of prehistoric aquatic reptile called the thalattosaur. But that seemed highly unlikely, not only because the thalattosaur went extinct 200 million years ago, but because aquatic reptiles typically lay their eggs on land, not underwater, so oxygen can diffuse through the membranes. Plus, Alaska was a lot hotter when the thalattosaur was around, and it was an ectothermic (cold-blooded) organism. It would be impossible for such a creature to maintain body heat in today's Alaskan waters.

As for the Panspermia hypothesis, Dr. Steingass thinks it's impossible for *all* life on earth to have evolved from a space seed. It's known that every living creature descends from an organism called LUCA, the "Last Universal Common Ancestor," which, she says, didn't have a fully packaged genome. Its DNA was little more than a tangle of connected proteins. This was a particularly fragile lifeform. Therefore, she believes it couldn't have been an extremophile hardy enough to hitchhike a ride to Earth on an asteroid and survive the trip intact.

But she is open to the notion that *some* life on earth may in fact have evolved with input from alien DNA. A sensational scholarly paper recently suggested the octopus might be such a creature, and Dr. Steingass can see why: "Their genetic code is so odd. They have millions more base pairs than any other species and octoradial symmetry; we can say that they aren't like any other species on the planet. Maybe there are certain types of genetic code that end up on earth from an alien species."

Where does that leave us with the alien golden egg? We concluded it was some type of egg sac that had hatched—the membrane attached to the rocky surface of the floor would give an embryonic animal time to develop in a safe and static environment. But what animal? We leaned toward it being from some undiscovered species. The golden color was such an odd feature—what kind of adaptation could it be? Dr. Steingass said we won't know for sure until molecular or genetic testing is completed and released. "And that's part of the excitement of the ocean. There's always something new."

N'HA-A-ITK

It's in that spirit that we circle back to Canada's Nessie, the fabled Ogopogo. First, we need to note that while Jim La Rocque's footage probably documented nothing more unusual than a propagating wave, other, more convincing sightings abound. Within twelve months of the La Rocque incident, an hour north in Okanagan Lake—where the Ogopogo legend originated—a teenager captured another compelling sighting on video. What's now known as the Neudorf Footage clearly shows something more than waves. The object looks like it could be the creature's dorsal side, and it matches traditional eyewitness accounts—a beast anywhere from forty to sixty feet long, moving through the water with vertical undulations. Dr. Steingass was willing to admit the possibility this could be a large animal, because in this case, the hydrology of the object's wake supports that hypothesis. "At times you can see what appear to be different 'humps' that appear throughout the images as it moves," she notes.

What makes the video a double instead of a home run is the fact that the object is moving *with* the current, not *against* it, leaving open the possibility that it's an inanimate object being tossed around by the water. "This is either an object like a log that's rotating as it's moving through the water," says Steingass, "or an animal moving through the water column." While Ogopogo Skeptics will certainly opt for the former explanation, the footage supports one of Ken Gerhard's metatheses: that many lake monsters—specifically those in deep, cold-water lakes connected to the ocean—are what's known as "anadromous" sea life, animals that migrate up rivers from the ocean to spawn. Sturgeon, salmon, and eels are well-known examples. Gerhard does not subscribe to the plesiosaur theory because he believes the recurring accounts of vertical undulation and smooth skin align with the swimming motion of sea mammals, not reptiles. Instead, he believes lake monsters like Nessie and Ogopogo (but not the landlocked Lake Van Monster) are a relict population of prehistoric whales known as basilosaurus. These colossal whales, originally thought to be reptiles, measured between fifty-six and sixty-six feet long, and resembled Nessie more than a modern-day orca. Of course, current science has the basilosaurus going extinct about 35 million years ago, leaving no descendants. But oh, those Lazarus species. Remember the coelacanth!

There's a bigger point to be made here. As exciting Ogopogo videos have gone viral, the uptick of interest in the creature has recently renewed focus on the people from which the legend originated: the First Nationers called the Sylix.

Pushing back against the rank cultural appropriation they see in the Ogopogo stuffed animals and lakeside statues, the Sylix recently sued successfully for the copyright over the name Ogopogo, though they consider it a gibberish word only loosely derived from the creature's original name, N'ha-a-itk. Why'd they bother? They want to remind people that while the creature of legend can take a fearsome form of a dark serpent with antlers, its true, original form was simply the water itself. The N'ha-a-itk was a sacred water spirit, not a mascot, a representation of everything that water is in both practical terms (a sustainer of life, a purifier, a cleanser) and metaphysical (a symbol of the subconscious, the emotions, rebirth).

Water gods appear in every polytheistic religion, from the ancient Greek Poseidon to the Yoruba deity Olokun. Water plays a major role in the Bible too. The great flood, the parting of the Red Sea, Jesus' various ministerial activities on the Sea of Galilee, and the wedding at Cana, where he memorably turned it into wine, are just a few key moments that come to mind.

And you needn't consult a sacred text to find something transcendent beneath the waves. Spend enough time on the water and it could be the other way around: something transcendent might find you. Dr. Steingass recalls communing with a pod of orcas during a seal-counting expedition—literally making meaningful eye contact with one as he swam directly under her inflatable boat. "It fundamentally altered my consciousness," she says.

It is highly likely that we will continue to discover new species of sea life; it is a statistical near certainty that many "charismatic aquatic megafauna" have been around in our lifetime and gone extinct without us ever encountering them. But whether or not we prove there's a real animal behind a given legend, we should not overlook the deep meaning and spiritual fulfillment these creatures—both real and imagined—provide. Dr. Steingass said it best: "If we look at a clip of lake monster footage and it turns out to be a wave . . . that doesn't mean that it's not Ogopogo."

Status check. So far we've considered mysteries of faith, outer space, the woods, and the water. Next we turn to unexplained anomalies from a place that's often just as alien and inscrutable as the distant galaxies or the ocean floor: our own ancient past.

Chapter 8

STRANGE STRUCTURES

THE DREAM OF CRESCENTIS

The purpose of George Gelé's life came to him in a dream. Gelé, an architect and contractor, had harbored an intense fascination with lost civilizations ever since he'd first seen Chichén Itzá as an archaeology student at LSU in 1966, but that fascination metastasized into an obsession after a vision came to him in his sleep one night in 1974. "The dream was what I call the Star of David Diagram," he says. This diagram came to him as a series of mathematical equations. He quickly graphed it out and placed it over a map of the world. "It showed that if you start off at Giza and the Great Pyramid, that there were six cities at that same latitude. These are major spiritual centers, regardless of when they were built. They are organized on the earth in a special pattern." One of those other cities was the Potala Palace in Tibet, the winter home of the Dalai Lamas for centuries. But, according to Gelé's "David Diagram," one of these spiritual hot spots was located—if not now, then at some point in history—off the coast of Louisiana in Chandeleur Sound, about sixty miles east of New Orleans.

Weeks later Gelé came across a Landsat photograph of that same area. It showed an "unusual pixelation" right where he'd figured his sunken city to be. "The dream had shown there was a mathematical possibility of something existing there. It was enough for me to say, 'We got to go out there.'"

Gelé received official permission to conduct exploration dives in the area. Dozens of expeditions ensued, and in 2011 he says he hit pay dirt: "I put a remote-operated vehicle over the side of the boat and my God. Boom!" The ROV's video camera reveals, scattered on the seafloor, piles of large granite blocks. The cubic stones don't seem to be natural at all, since they have ninety-degree square edges. Some have carvings and cuts.

Gelé is positive he's found the remains of a lost civilization roughly twelve thousand years old.

"I'm an architect," he says. "I do know what buildings look like, even if they're underwater and covered up somewhat with sand." He's convinced this is one of the spiritual centers delineated by his "David Diagram." He's even given it a name: Crescentis.

A TECHNIQUE, NOT A SCIENCE

Perhaps more than any other academically recognized field with which our show engages, archeology's border with rogue theories and pseudoscience is the most porous. Artifact evidence is the gold standard by which archaeology's theories are evaluated. But it's not some free-for-all where any idea is just as valid as the next, but not chemistry or physics either. Its conclusions can't be independently verified with repeatable experiments. Our primary in-house archaeologist, Dr. Ed Barnhart, admits that his field "falls a little short of what we call a science. It's a technique, but it's compromised because every site we dig we destroy. So we unearth things and then we theorize."

That means many mainstream archaeological theories are built upon inherently loose foundations. The pillars of the faith are commonly challenged, even upended. In the course of Dr. Banhart's career alone, there have been at least two such upheavals.

- The discovery and excavation of the Göbekli Tepe site in Turkey (which includes what's widely referred to now as the world's oldest temple) pushed back the timeline of the first ritualistic buildings and possible sedentary residences by three thousand years, reshaping the discussion about the origins of the cradle of civilization.
- Rapidly evolving LIDAR technology has recently uncovered large cities in parts of the Amazon where nobody ever thought they could exist. "We've been talking forever about myths of El Dorado," says Barnhart. "Everyone thought there was no way to have a major civilization in the Amazon. Now that's been shot out the window as we're finding major geoglyphs and artifacts there." In Bolivia, LIDAR has revealed a network of interconnected cities, roads, and canals. And the evidence suggests those civilizations were there for a long time. Some of the pottery dates back to 6000 BC, the oldest found in the Americas by a couple thousand years.

In other words, archaeology is perennially primed for big surprises, even more so than natural history as it assimilates shocks like the sudden reemergence of Lazarus species. With the "settled science" so unsettled, and every prevailing theory just one game-changing dig away from defenestration, there's an inherent "permission structure" that enables wilder "secret histories" to gain traction. Graham Hancock, for instance, has made a living advocating his "ancient apocalypse" theory, positing that a highly advanced civilization existed during the last ice age, only to be almost entirely wiped out by a comet. The survivors managed to pass on shreds of their knowledge and culture to the hunter-gatherers that followed, which facilitated the founding of what we consider the earliest civilizations like those in Sumer and Mesoamerica.

There's another factor at play here that has nothing to do with academia. It stems from the common cultural bias often referred to as "Presentism." This is the assumption that we here in the present are currently standing atop the peak of human civilization. Everything has always been getting better; nothing has ever gotten worse. Therefore, whatever and whoever came before must have been more primitive and backward, technologically, intellectually, and morally. Faced with the imposing reality of amazing ancient monuments and structures, the Presentist sensibility produces a cognitive dissonance in the modern mind. Upon first seeing the Mexican Pyramids or the Great Wall of China, one can't help but ask, "How did *they* make *that*?" (I'm not immune to this, by the way. In fact, I'm still puzzled how anyone ever practiced journalism without a cell phone.) And one of the most seductive answers to that question is at once profoundly radical and smoothly simple: "They didn't."

This is how we arrive at the "Ancient Aliens" theory. First elaborated by Swiss writer (and convicted fraudster) Erich von Däniken in his 1968 book *Chariots of the Gods*, the crux of the theory is that aliens have been visiting Earth since the dawn of civilization, bestowing the planet's earliest human civilizations with the expertise and technology required to create many of the structures we regard with such amazement today. Stonehenge, the Egyptian Pyramids, the Nazca Lines, you name it: if it's really old and really impressive, there's a good chance Ancient Alien theorists have claimed at one point or another that extraterrestrials deserve the credit.

It's certainly fun to look at a carving of a Maya chieftain sitting in what looks like the cockpit of a spaceship, his hands at the controls, and wonder whether aliens may have lent the Mesoamericans some of their tech; or to contemplate what looks like a helicopter and a *Star Wars*–like land speeder carved into the walls of an Egyptian tomb alongside floor-to-ceiling hieroglyphic inscriptions. The HISTORY® network's *Ancient Aliens*® has been exploring these oddities for twenty seasons, and on *our* show we've investigated (and debunked) claims that the Teotihuacan Pyramid was constructed by a now-extinct "Cydonian" civilization on Mars, and that the depictions of the Wandjina Sky People in Australian aboriginal cave art are really portraits of extraterrestrial visitors.

Fun, yes, but also controversial. Among many in the academic community, such speculation "platforms" the offensive argument that the indigenous cultures of those early periods were too primitive or dumb to have created their own monuments. It was no easy thing to find a legitimate archaeologist with a university affiliation and a Ph.D. willing to commit to our show.

That's why I've always been grateful for Dr. Barnhart, an instructor at Texas State University, the director of the Maya Exploration Center, and the explorer who discovered the ancient city of Ma'ax Na in northwestern Belize. He does our show, knowing full well that it entertains theories many of his colleagues dismiss because he considers his role as an educator as much a calling as a job:

"I'll always show up when there's an opportunity to be part of the conversation. My attitude is that education is for everybody. And anyway, if you ask what inspired most 'legitimate' archaeologists to devote their lives to it, it's often fanciful and fantastic things like *The Lord of the Rings* anyway."

We've been equally fortunate to have planetary geologist Dr. Robert Anderson, a core member of the Mars Science Laboratory team at Caltech's Jet Propulsion Laboratory. Since the *Curiosity* rover landed on the Martian surface in 2012, Dr. Anderson's primary project has been collecting and analyzing the data it's sent back. On a daily basis, he's seeing images of the red planet no human being has ever seen before, one of the few thrills *Homo sapiens* can experience that never get old.

In other words, Dr. Anderson has other things he could be doing with his time than analyzing the images we send him. So why does he bother? "Frankly, because it gives me the opportunity to talk about what I do with people who aren't scientists," he says. "Plus, some of the anomalies I have to explain are really fun challenges. And the show gives me an opportunity to speak the truth and push back on the conspiracy theories that are so rampant. If I can even get through to ten or fifteen percent of those folks, it's worth it."

LOST WORLDS, FOUND FOOTAGE

There is no more magnetic legend in this space than Atlantis. The theory of the ancient sunken city continues to hold sway, and with good reason. We know of many lost civilizations that exist not only in surviving legends, but in artifact-strewn sites on the ocean floor. Their precise locations have been pinpointed and studied.

- The ancient Roman city of Baia, known as the Las Vegas of its time, was located on the flanks of a supervolcano called Campi Flegrei. Most of it is now located in the Gulf of Pozzuoli, just off the coast of Naples; what remained was abandoned by 1500. The first significant excavations of the sunken site took place in the 1940s, and discoveries continue to this day. An impressive mosaic bathhouse floor was uncovered in 2023.
- Doggerland is a forty-six-thousand-square-mile area of the North Sea, almost equidistant to England, the Netherlands, and Denmark. It was a hilly, forested marshland quite popular with the hunter-gatherers of the Mesolithic period until rising ocean waters caused by glacial melt and a tsunami submerged it about 6000 BC. (Yes, there were periods of drastic climate change before the Industrial Revolution.) The first clue that it was once inhabited by humans occurred in 1931 when a fishing trawler happened to drag up a harpoon carved out of an antler. That was quite a catch! Since then Doggerland has become a hot spot for cutting-edge geophysical mapping techniques, pioneered by the oil exploration industry and since adopted by underwater archaeologists.

"That's why there is some believability to the Atlantis legend," says our anthropologist Kathy Strain. "We know places like Doggerland existed; and we know other sophisticated societies like Pompeii were wiped out and buried by sudden cataclysms like volcanoes. We have lots of civilizations that have been destroyed or abandoned, so there's no reason Atlantis can't be at least partly true.

It's just not going to be as easy as diving to the ocean floor and finding it. It could very much be the case that there's so much silt on top of it now, you'd need to excavate before you see anything."

The real problem with the Atlantis legend isn't that it can't possibly exist. In Strain's words, it's that "we have lots of people looking, but they're looking in crazy places." Here's the thing: Atlantis was originally described by Plato in his dialogues the *Timaeus* and the *Critias* as a large, sophisticated, and powerful city-state in the Mediterranean Sea or possibly just past the "pillars of Hercules," commonly understood to be the Straits of Gibraltar. The Atlanteans were gifted and virtuous, until the corruption of their civic character prompted Zeus to annihilate them with a plague of earthquakes. The story is often read as an allegory of the wages of vice, while those who take it literally have placed the island anywhere from off the coast of Egypt to the city of Akrotiri on the present-day Greek island of Santorini. Akrotiri was destroyed by natural disasters in the sixteenth century BC and may have inspired Plato's tale centuries later.

Nevertheless, candidate locations for Atlantis continue to pop up in exotic spots thousands of miles away in the western hemisphere. One that caught our attention emerged in 2022, when the crew of an exploration vessel combing the ocean floor near the Papahānaumokuākea Marine National Monument in Hawaii live streamed a startling moment. At a depth of 3,375 feet they come upon what looks like a large assemblage of perfectly arranged, yellowish bricks. On the video, you can hear one of the crew exclaim that they've just found "the road to Atlantis." The blocks are nearly identical in size and their grouping looks everything like an ancient brick road. If it isn't Atlantis proper, it could be another ancient civilization that sank beneath the waves.

But Strain didn't see enough to convince her this site was created by human hands. "Ancient cities that had these kinds of thoroughfares always had lots of elaborate other artifacts along the pathway," she says. "You wanted to show off your wealth, so you would have foundations of structures, pillars, statues, archways. And some of those things would be very heavy. Even over time, you'd expect to see some remnants like that."

Again we ask: So what was it? It took our geologist Dr. Bob Anderson quite a while to come up with an answer. Ultimately, his experience studying the Martian surface triggered his eureka moment. He'd seen similar "yellow brick roads" there, specifically in sulfur deposits near dormant volcanoes. The coloring happens when the yellow sulfur comes out of a thermal vent. As for the curious "bricks," they are formed by the weight of the water column on top and the uneven topography underneath. "That's common in these areas where you have a very thin layer of sulfur," says Anderson. "It breaks into these very nice patterns." So no lost civilization off the coast of Hawaii, I'm afraid.

Another Atlantis wannabe, the popular "Bimini Road" in the Bahamas, is a linear cluster of block-shaped rocks on the ocean floor. Not only does it look like the thoroughfare of a sunken city; it allegedly emits a paranormal force. We spoke to a passionate snorkeler named Robbyn LaPlant whose account squares with the popular speculation that Atlantis may have been populated by extraterrestrials, or benefitted from alien tech. "Every time I've swum across the road, it has been a completely different experience," she says. "It's almost like electrical frequency amplifies from the stones. Many people have incredible visions. It's a truly magical place."

Again, our experts were not persuaded. For one thing, just as with the "yellow brick road" near Hawaii, there are no man-made artifacts discovered anywhere nearby. So what made the Bimini Road? "I believe that it's an ancient shoreline of where the water was about somewhere between twelve to fourteen thousand years ago," explained Dr. Barnhart. "And what happened is that as the water has risen, the shoreline has become submerged and all the shells and everything that washed up on the shoreline became cemented together to form limestone. Because of limestone's chemical composition and structure, it breaks off in very blocklike formations." We end up with rock formations that look very much like giant man-made blocks.

Europe has no monopoly on legendary lost civilizations. Easily the most curious in my book—and this is, after all, my book—is the Japanese kingdom known as Yamatai. Its legend comes with a generous serving of fantasy: Yamatai was said to have been ruled by a secretive sorceress named Himiko. Its location has never been determined, much less the reasons for its disappearance.

One intriguing theory originates from eighty-five feet beneath the waves off the coast of Yonaguni, one of the chain of Japanese islands called the Ryukyu. Yonaguni sits so far south of Okinawa it's much closer to Taiwan, and the wonders to be seen off its coast attract divers worldwide. There are two main attractions: a thriving population of hammerhead sharks, and a set of massive, mesmerizing sandstone rock formations with such straight lines and sharp edges they strongly resemble man-made monoliths.

Aside from their sculpted shape and near-perfect right angles, the arrangement of the rocks looks anything but accidental. They appear to form structures, which in turn form something that resembles a sunken city. Divers who've made the trek describe it as "like stepping back in time." Marine geologist Masaaki Kimura has argued that the Yonaguni ruins were aboveground about three thousand years ago, and that they contain a pyramid and monuments. He has argued this site was part of Yamatai.

Dr. Anderson admits the area could have once been on dry land, much like the Bimini Road. "Shorelines have been changing," he says. "If you go back twenty thousand years ago, the shorelines moved around to different places. So you can't rule out that it was above-water." But were the stone structures man-made? That's another story. "These are the sorts of things that geologic formations can break into because of earthquakes or tsunamis," explains Dr. Barnhart. "As they move, those plates break into very geometric forms. There's no reason to believe that they had to be cut by man. If they were, they are larger than anything any civilization, ancient or modern, has ever attempted." Then why, if these rocks are natural, don't we see similar formations elsewhere in the world where there are frequent earthquakes and tsunamis? The answer traces back to the aspects of this location that make it unique—the currents, the abundance of sandstone, and so on.

So we're prepared to conclude that Yonaguni is not Yamatai, but we're *not* prepared to say Yamatai is merely a myth or allegory. Unlike Atlantis, which has no corroborative documentation to back up Plato, *Yamatai turns up in official Chinese histories* from the first, second, and third centuries. One such account describes the kingdom as consisting of roughly seventy thousand households. Another records Queen Himiko dispatching an envoy to the Chinese emperor. And while we should acknowledge that "serious" ancient Western historians like Herodotus and Pliny included fantastic tales in their accounts—Herodotus characterized ancient Libya as populated by men with heads of dogs—the multiple mentions of Yamatai in independent accounts spaced out by hundreds of years suggest there was something more to this lost kingdom than an enduring fable. So where did it go?

Accounts of Yamatai and strange sites like Yonaguni fuel the controversial (and lucrative!) aforementioned "ancient apocalypse" theory advanced by British author Graham Hancock, who believes an advanced ice-age civilization spread its wisdom around the globe after being almost entirely wiped out by a massive flood. It is certainly both true and thought-provoking that great flood narratives are deeply embedded in the origin stories of dozens of disparate cultures from the ancient Hebrews (Noah), Sumerians (Gilgamesh), Hindus (Manu), and even the Cheyenne. But Hancock's theory has been debunked if for no other reason than he claims the "ancient apocalypse" flood happened near the end of the last ice age, while almost every ancient site he visits to prove his theory is widely acknowledged to have been constructed thousands of years later. In order to go along with Hancock, you don't just have to accept a new interpretation of the existing facts; you have to accept that most of the existing facts are wrong. Still, the guy's sold many more books than I ever will and landed his own Netflix series, so I tip my hat to the hustle.

The people I truly admire are those like George Gelé, who don't just write about well-known archaeological discoveries but devote their lives to making new ones. There may in fact be nothing more commendable in the human species than its innate desire to explore. So what of Gelé's great discovery, the lost city of Crescentis that first appeared to him in a dream?

First let us take a moment to praise the many great things that were inspired, directly or indirectly, by dreams: Caedmon's hymn, Kekulé's model of the benzene ring, Paul McCartney's melody for "Yesterday." This stuff happens.

So is there some way to explain away the sculpted stones Gelé found in Chandeleur Sound? One proposed theory was that he'd just stumbled upon an artificial reef, which are frequently created to improve local marine ecosystems. But Dr. Barnhart pointed out that "typically, when we make reefs, we don't make them out of stone. We use things like tires and other lighter materials that work just as well." Plus, Gelé's stones were found in an area where the currents are relatively strong—not a good place to locate an artificial fish habitat.

Another explanation was that the granite blocks could have been ballast jettisoned from the European ships that were colonizing and trading in the area centuries ago. It is true that ballast blocks were needed on ships to lower their center of mass and increase the stability, and that such blocks were sometimes thrown overboard when not needed. But the sheer number of blocks found at the site implies that at least three dozen ships would have dumped ballast stones of identical design—in that one location. Seems unlikely.

If, as Gelé says, the site is twelve thousand years old, it would date to the early stages of the Clovis civilization, thought to be some of the earliest human inhabitants of the Americas. But the Clovis culture was a hunter-gatherer society, not a sedentary people who built cities with stones. Ultimately, we concluded that there was no mundane explanation for how those blocks got to the site. (Gelé believes the stone was transported from the head of the Mississippi River in Minnesota, where granite is plentiful.) And given that sea levels change over time, it makes sense there could have been a city that was once along the shore but is now submerged miles from the current coastline. Until more conclusive evidence comes forward to defeat Gelé's theory, we're sticking with our verdict that this was "possible city ruins."

BIG ROCKS, BIG RIDDLES

So—aside from Crescentis—we've spoiled all the fun, haven't we? Whenever we debunk some rogue theory, in my head I hear the classic tuba riff from *The Price Is Right* that's played when a contestant is eliminated. They call it the Losing Horn—*bwah bah bu bwaaaaahhh.*

But take heart. You can still tweak out on plenty of unsolved mysteries even sticking to plain old regular, vanilla-flavored mainstream archaeology. Consider the Longyou Caves of eastern China. Only recently discovered in 1992 by local farmers, this set of twenty-four cavernous excavations has been called the ninth Wonder of the Ancient World. The largest five caves are supported by huge stone pillars buttressing sloped ceilings between sixty and one hundred feet high. The average size of the caverns is eleven thousand square feet, seven times bigger than the average American house. The walls are covered in a series of parallel chiseled lines and symbols, including stone carvings of animals. Visitors find it hard to believe the caves weren't made with modern machinery, but they are anything but modern. Pottery found on the cave floor dates back more than two thousand years, and archaeologists believe the underground grottoes were carved by hand during the Han Dynasty. Even more remarkable, the walls and columns supporting the cave ceilings are relatively thin, yet they've remained intact for millennia, despite chronic seismic activity in the area.

What was the purpose of this gargantuan project? Every archaeologist and their mother has a theory: an emperor's tomb, a storm shelter, a reservoir. Dr. Barnhart's pet hypothesis is that the caves were factories for silk weaving, a craft for which the Han Dynasty was famous. Since that process is ideally done in very humid environments, the caves and their lined walls would create a space conducive to condensation, making for optimal weaving conditions.

That makes sense, but as I've said a few times already, one expects to find artifacts consistent with a location's function at or near that location. No looms, silkworm cocoons, or minerals for dyes have been found in the caves. Nor is there any surviving documentation in the written record explaining how the caves were built or why. That's especially strange since the project was insanely labor-intensive—experts have estimated it would have taken one thousand people working twenty-four hours a day for *six years straight* to complete it with contemporaneous tools and methods. A project that colossal would merit a mention in some official ledger, no?

Still, the most nagging mystery of the Longyou Caves is that no one has ever found the final resting place of all the excavated rock, thousands of tons of it. These guys didn't have Caterpillar mining dump trucks. The cost of hauling that much rock off to who knows where would have been staggering. It would have been much easier to leave it all in some massive pile nearby.

In short, the how and why of the Longyou Caves qualify as bona fide mysteries, and that last puzzle of the transported excavated rock contributes to a pattern connecting archaeological wonders all over the world.

That's because transporting large objects, an activity that barely attracts our notice when we see a freight train in the distance, or a container ship on the horizon, was a Herculean labor for people living before the Industrial Age, the excavators of the Longyou Caves among them. And imagine what it was like for those forced to tackle such tasks before the invention of the wheel, which is generally believed to have been first put to use on a vehicle in Mesopotamia sometime around 3500 BC at the earliest.

What then to make of the Almendres Cromlech, an arrangement of ninety-three massive boulders outside the Portuguese city of Évora? Informally known as "The Portuguese Stonehenge," the site was likely completed around 5000 BC. That means it predates Stonehenge by about two thousand years, the Great Pyramids of Giza by about one thousand years, and the wheel by about fifteen hundred. The stones are clearly arranged intentionally in several rows, forming an oblong oval shape. And on the winter solstice, the shadows cast by the standing stones each point directly to another standing stone some two kilometers away. On the autumnal and vernal equinoxes, the sun and moon rise and set over exactly the same points on the monument's axis.

How the stones got there is a matter of pure conjecture. Here was Kathy Strain's best shot: "It is theorized that they would take logs, grease them up slightly, and use rope tied to their cattle to help pull the stones along. After a stone moves off one log, you run that log up to the front and so on." Dr. Barnhart likes that theory as much as any, but he urges caution: "This is one of the perennial 'biggies' when it comes to archaeological mysteries: How did ancient peoples move their giant megaliths? They're found all over the world, in different ecological zones—from Stonehenge to the Olmec heads. Many of these stones weigh more than ten tons, some ridiculously more. Archaeology has not been able to say, 'There it is; that's how it's done.' We have a bunch of theories, but no proof."

There are no extant records to explain the site's function, and adding to the mystery, the Almendres Cromlech lay abandoned and forgotten for centuries. It was only discovered in 1964, and since then theories have blossomed about its purpose. Since some of the stones bear unusual carvings, some have suggested it had a religious function—the ancients filling Pascal's God-shaped hole with massive rocks. Others say the astronomical precision may have had a more practical purpose, such as determining the start of agricultural planting and harvesting seasons, though that would assume the neolithic civilization that made the Almendres Cromlech had transitioned from a nomadic lifestyle to sedentary farming.

The civilization that built the site is unknown. Sure, they may have had alien assistance getting those stones in place, but I'm more easily seduced by Dr. Barnhart's hypothesis—that the Almendres Cromlech, like many other megalithic sites, has less to do with gods or crops than it does with that most fundamental of human desires: the drive to create something bigger than ourselves, something that lasts. Was that drive strong enough to inspire our ancestors to drag those huge stones into place? We may never know their names, but we can simultaneously revel in the mystery of the unknown and recognize ourselves in their need to leave a mark. "These stones are early man's attempts at immortality," Barnhart concludes. "People said, 'Let's do something so amazing that people will remember it and admire it well after we're dead.' But whatever they called themselves, it's hidden to history."

Chapter 9

PHREAKS OF PHYSICS

SPRINGTIME AT SKINWALKER RANCH

Do not come to Skinwalker Ranch uninvited. Surprise guests are not welcome.

Stepping on the property could be bad for your health anyway, even if they were to roll out the red carpet. The ranch is easily the hottest paranormal hot spot in the United States, and a big part of its lore derives from abundant reports of visitors suddenly afflicted with mysterious ailments. Nausea, disorientation, dizziness, even temporary paralysis. Some people get better as soon as they leave. Some get hospitalized. Everyone who works there has his own story involving nasty physical symptoms that converted them into Believers, literally on a visceral level.

Like everyone allowed onto the property, I entered through a steel gate and drove past the giant NO TRESPASSING signs. I'd come here with a crew and our host, Tony Harris, to shoot elements for a series of special episodes that would air immediately after new episodes of another series, *The Secret of Skinwalker Ranch®*. I was thrilled at the opportunity to visit the place and meet the SWR team who'd become household names to the show's fans: physicist

Erik Bard, superintendent Thomas Winterton, security chief Bryant "Dragon" Arnold, and his lieutenant, a hulking former Marine named Kaleb Bench.

We'd heard the stories. They go back to the time when the Navajo allegedly dispatched a shape-shifting monster called a Skinwalker to terrorize their enemies the Utes. Since then, frequent and varied anomalous incidents have made the 512-acre ranch the subject of local legend and government-funded research. Now, under the ownership of real estate mogul Brandon Fugal, it is a "living lab" for ongoing scientific experiments documented on the TV series, designed to ascertain the source of all the "high strangeness."

The diversity of the incidents is noteworthy—everything from UFO sightings, odd lights and sounds, sudden changes in temperature, perplexing episodes of electromagnetic interference, and poltergeist stuff like doors slamming by themselves. Almost every square foot of the property is now under continuous security camera surveillance to document these anomalies, and to alert the team to the deranged trespassers who occasionally step on the property with the piety of pilgrims, certain that the forces there have summoned them.

What weird stuff went down during the days we were there? Nothing. We completed our shoot, enjoyed a hearty steak dinner, and the SWR guys could not have been more hospitable.

Why were they nice to us? Because they sensed we took their work seriously. We weren't just showing respect; we genuinely felt it. That respect came naturally for me and Tony, since after all we're in the anomaly business too. *The Proof Is Out There*® series is a different show from *The Secret of Skinwalker Ranch*®: we don't do experiments, we analyze other people's videos; and our "living laboratory" is the whole observable universe, not just one especially active location.

The author (right) on set with host Tony Harris (center) and director Joe Gabriel
Photo courtesy of the author

Bigfoot experiencer Claudia Ackley

The mysterious "Wichita Triangle"
Jeffre L. Templin

"The Dress"

Cory Hearon's Cloud Angel
ViralHog

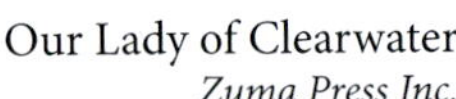

Our Lady of Clearwater
Zuma Press Inc.

The Blood of St. Januarius
Michael O'Neill

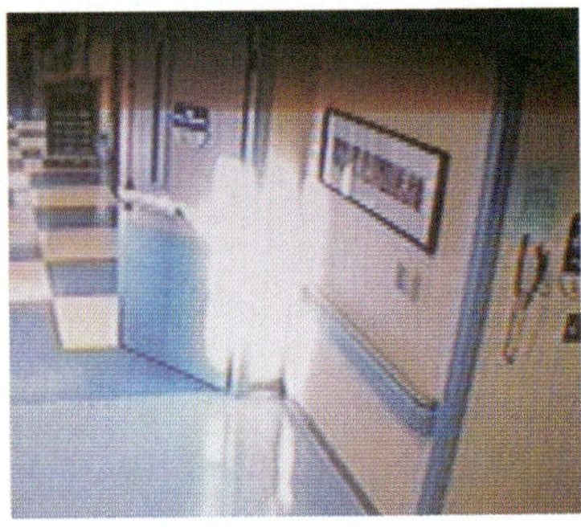

Chelsea Banton's ICU Angel
Colleen Lands Banton

A miraculous near miss
Charles E. Evans

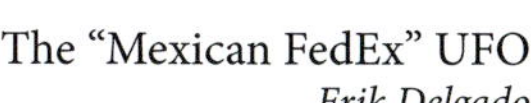

The "Mexican FedEx" UFO
Erik Delgado

Major Marcel and the Roswell debris
The University of Texas at Arlington Library Special Collections

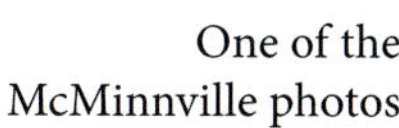

One of the McMinnville photos

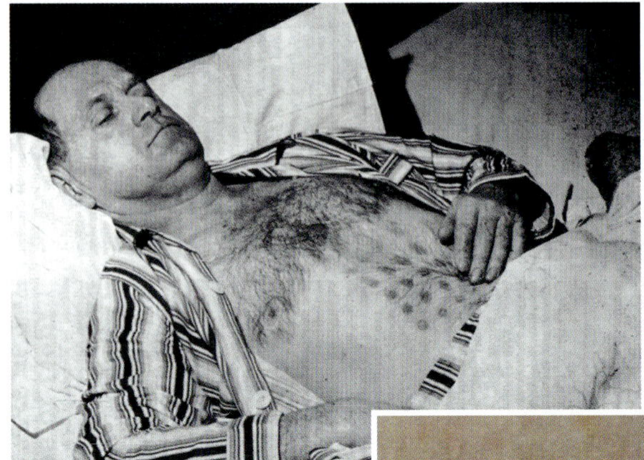

Stefan Michalak's anomalous injuries
Chris Rutkowski

Sev Tok's marks
Sev Tok

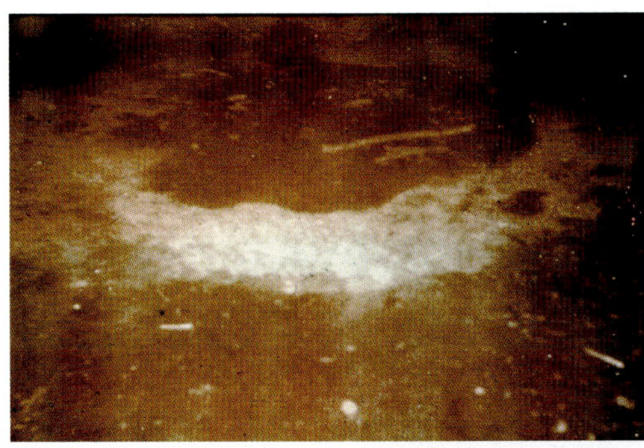

Discolored soil from the Delphos UFO incident
Ginger Phillips

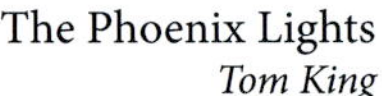

The Phoenix Lights
Tom King

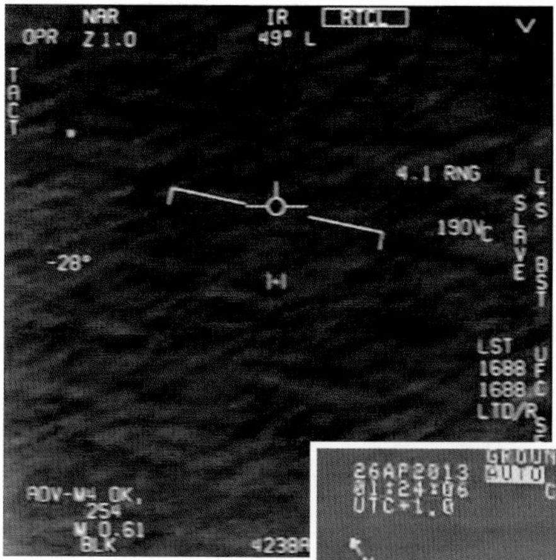

The game-changing Pentagon video, GOFAST

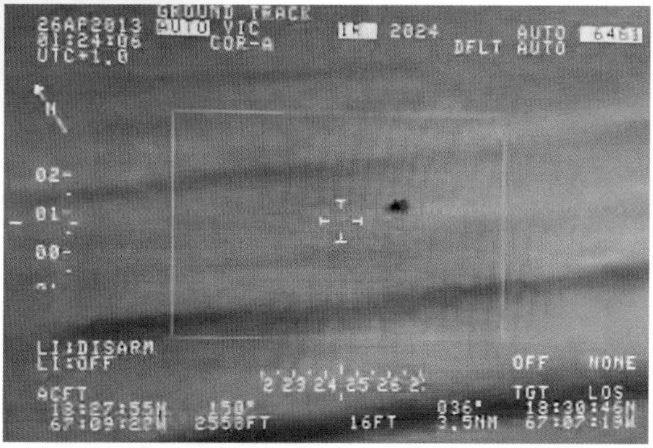

The Aguadilla UFO

The Rubber Duck UFO
Andy Marcial

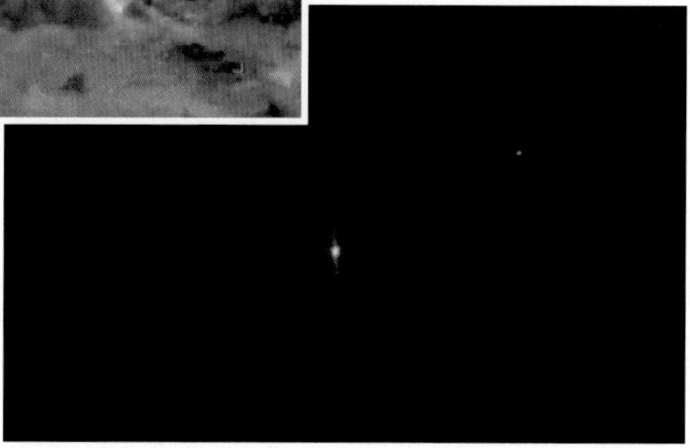

The Wisconsin Orb
Jon Kelly

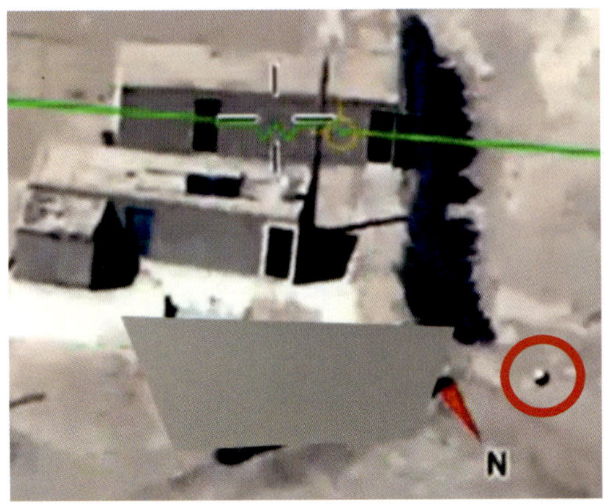

The Mideastern Orb

A Jeremy Corbell scoop:
The Mosul Orb
Images and video obtained and released by journalists Jeremy Corbell and George Knapp on their Weaponized *podcast*

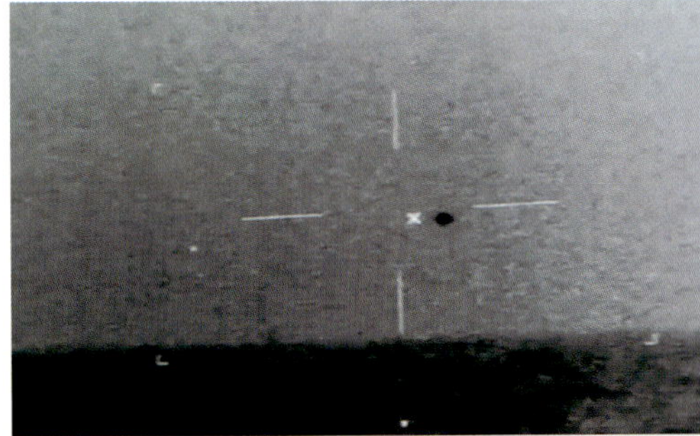

Another Corbell newsmaker:
The Omaha USO
Images and video obtained and released by journalists Jeremy Corbell and George Knapp on their Weaponized *podcast*

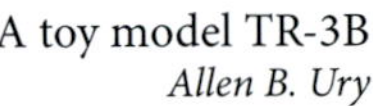
A toy model TR-3B
Allen B. Ury

The author at the
Very Large Array
Photo courtesy of the author

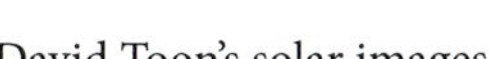

David Toon's solar images

The "cosmic question mark"

Illustration of a Dyson Sphere

The White Sands UFO crash

A preview of
the "EMPCOE"?
Photo by Lennart Bourin

Mars Truthers' "bones"

Trees remain
standing after a
California wildfire
*Matt Dutcher/Moment
Video RF via Getty Images*

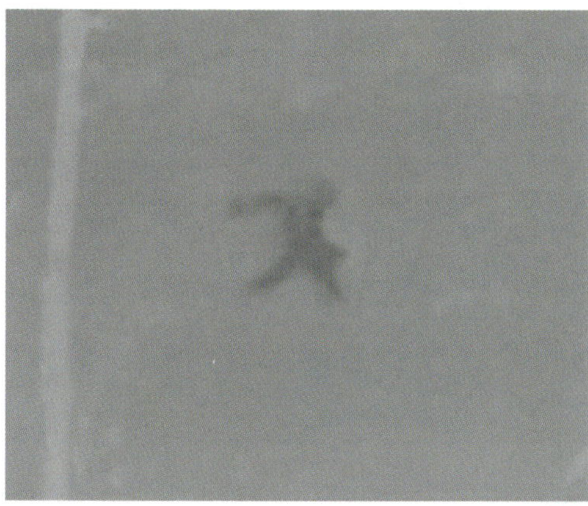

The Brown Bigfoot footage
Stacy Brown Jr.

The fabled “Orang Pendek”?

Patty

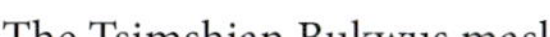

The Tsimshian Bukwus mask

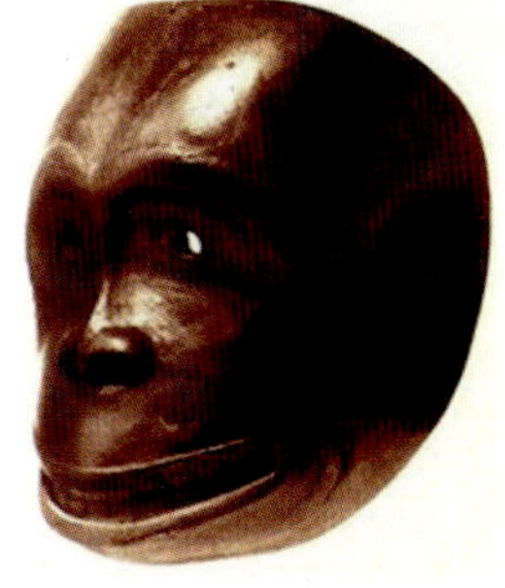

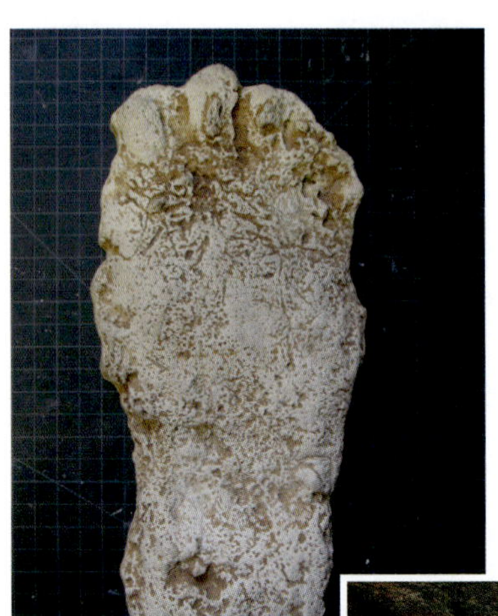

One of the Freeman footprints
Cliff Barackman

The "Hairy Man" pictograph
Kathy Strain

An alleged Australian Yowie
Dean Harrison

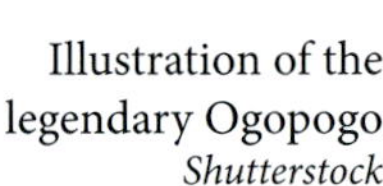

Illustration of the legendary Ogopogo
Shutterstock

The Lake Van Monster
Associated Press

A human-faced shark
ViralPress

The Challice Loch Ness photo
© Steve Challice

Afri Gregory's curious beach find
Afri Gregory

The "Alien Golden Egg"

The "Road to Atlantis"
Ocean Exploration Trust/ Nautilus Live, NOAA

The Almendres Cromlech
Jeff Lopes

The Longyou Caves
Andrew Kuznetsov

The Yonaguni "ruins"
diveplanit.com

An alleged pyramid on Mars

Illustration of a wormhole

Alleged UFOs exiting "El Popo"
H. Miller

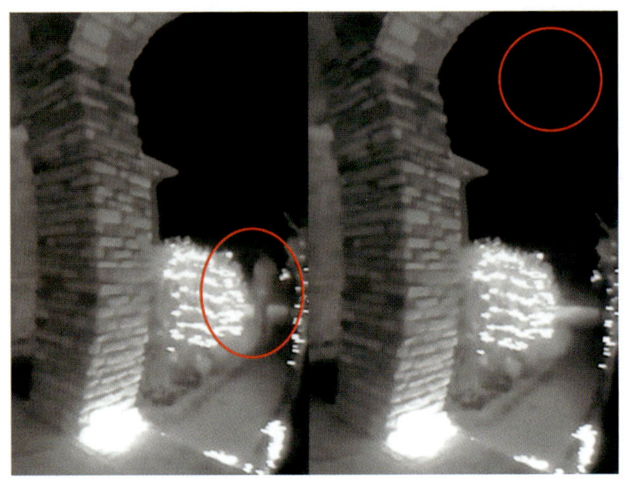

A teleported Texas man?
Brent Maggio

Knuth Road, Boynton Beach, Florida
Photo courtesy of the author

The "Simulation Theory" selfie
Amy Celeste Dye Millett

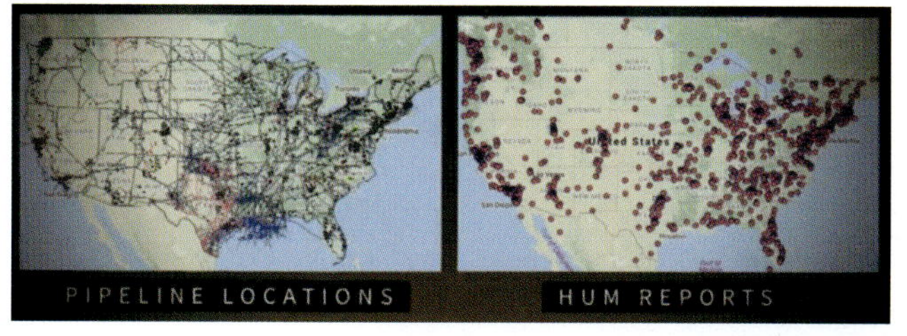

Steve Kohlhase's maps
Steve Kohlhase

HAARP antennae

The US Embassy in Havana, Cuba

The "Gettysburg Ghost"
Safia Azizi

The Barmby Place shadow
Adam Mawson

Alec Baldwin
Jim Spellman/WireImage via Getty Images

President Millard Fillmore

A North Korean "supersoldier"?
Associated Press

Jetpack Man
Sling Pilot Academy

But like the SWR crew, we're keenly interested in head-scratching incidents that seem to defy the common scientific understanding of how the world works—what we call "Phreaks of Physics."

A PHREAKY UNIVERSE

Let it be said at once that physics is freaky enough already, thanks to a series of revolutionary discoveries that began in the twentieth century. Start with the fact that time is relative (thank you, Einstein); that matter on a subatomic level operates by completely different and contradictory rules than the world we see with the naked eye (Schrödinger); that a degree of uncertainty is, in many cases, insurmountable (Heisenberg). Add to that the theory that there are multiple universes, and that matter is ultimately composed of tiny strings vibrating in as many as eleven dimensions. Physics, in other words, has convincingly established that the everyday reality we inhabit is not telling us the whole story.

The Believers take that as license to assert that the mind-bending theoretical possibilities physics accommodates are more than possibilities—they're real; they're happening around us; they are the scientific grounding for many phenomena we've traditionally dismissed as paranormal bunk and superstition. Anomalous events like those dissected on shows like ours prove it.

Do they?

We're proud to have had a rotating tag team of physics heavy hitters around to make those calls. You heard from some of them earlier: Prof. Michio Kaku, world renowned theoretical physicist and author; Prof. Matthew Szydagis; and Prof. Hakeem Oluseyi, cosmologist. They're not just excellent thinkers; they're excellent communicators. If you want to know more about anything mentioned in this chapter, please read their books, watch their lectures, and enjoy.

This is how they've addressed some of the most common concepts of physics, and the attendant misconceptions about them, that we tackle on the show.

WORMHOLES AND PORTALS

One of the most shamelessly prostituted ideas of Einstein's is the concept of wormholes (or, if you want to sound snootier, Einstein-Rosen bridges). Derived from Einstein's initial work on general relativity and its key discovery that space-time is curved by gravity, wormholes are theoretical tunnels or "shortcuts" between two different points in space-time that might conceivably make the impossible possible—things like teleportation and time travel. They've been a common trope in science fiction novels and movies for years, though it was blockbusters like *Contact* and *Interstellar* that really implanted them into pop culture.

Wormholes are "theoretical" in the sense that we have never observed one through our telescopes. Their existence has not been confirmed. Professor Kaku actually credits Lewis Carroll with first introducing the concept in *Through the Looking Glass*. But a lot more has gone into this idea than imagination. Wormholes *do* exist mathematically (or a priori). Any illustration or animation of one is the graphic representation of a solution to what's now called the Wormhole Equation. And bear in mind, modern astronomy *has* confirmed the existence of several phenomena that started out as theories of Einstein's, from black holes and gravitational waves to the expansion of the universe. If Einstein said something *could* exist, there's a strong chance it *does* exist, but we just haven't found it yet. Dismiss the man's speculation at your own peril.

Because the concept has legitimate scientific endorsement (from the greatest physicist in history, no less), and because it's now more widely known thanks to the movies, wormholes have been put to use as explanations for various caught-on-camera phenomena we've examined. In the paranormal community, the term is often used interchangeably with the concept of "portals" said to exist between different dimensions or universes. Wormholes are even invoked occasionally to explain UFO or Bigfoot sightings.

Take, for example, a recent story we did into a video clip publicized by Jaime Maussan, probably the most popular UFO investigator in Latin America. Despite the fact that he's tried to pass off hoaxed "alien mummies" as legit, Maussan is still taken seriously enough to present his work to the Mexican legislature.

This video, a night vision shot of the Mexican volcano Popocatepetl, shows a string of luminous, cigar-shaped objects apparently taking off from the volcano's mouth. "El Popo," as it's commonly known, is notorious for frequent UFO sightings, leading Maussan to assert that the volcano is a portal through which UFOs can enter and exit. More specifically, the claim is that the intense magnetic forces inside an active volcano would make it possible to open up a wormhole that would tunnel to a distant part of the universe, another dimension, or the future (or past).

Other alleged portals do not involve aliens. In September 2019 a woman in the coastal English town of Weston-super-Mare awoke to find an image of her neighborhood being projected onto her bedroom wall, upside down. While some dismissed the footage as a CGI hoax, others suggested we were witnessing proof of an interdimensional portal that had opened up into a mirror universe.

The trouble is, we're not allowed to pick what we like out of Einstein-Rosen Bridge theory and forget the inconvenient portions. To begin with, as Professor Kaku has pointed out on air repeatedly (with remarkable patience and good humor each time), wormholes, much like black holes, would require the energy of at least ten of our suns to form. "If a wormhole were to open in someone's bedroom, the energy would be so great that the person, the bedroom, and everything else nearby would be sucked inside and never seen again." There goes that theory.

Even if we somehow allow the possibility that a "mini-wormhole" might somehow exist someplace on earth, say in the bowels of El Popo, that explanation for the line of mystery objects shooting out of the volcano's mouth falls flat. Professor Szydagis notes that, per Einstein, a wormhole would exhibit evidence of what's called microlensing, a bend in space-time caused by the gravity of its extremely compact mass that would create major distortions of the light around it. He says we don't see anything like that in the El Popo video. And in any case, "I have no idea why, if I were an advanced civilization, I would put my wormhole next to something as extremely dangerous as a volcano. Some have speculated that advanced civilizations need volcanoes to refuel, but I don't understand why you would need to refuel from something producing energy in a very unusable form—kinetic energy and heat in the eruption of magma and lava."

What were we really looking at then? Well, the case of the inverted mirror world was genuinely strange, but not that hard to explain. It wasn't a CGI trick. What we were seeing was an optical effect triggered by a random gap between the closed curtains in front of the woman's window—a gap in the shape of a small, thin rectangle. That being the only way light could get into the room, it created what's called a pinhole camera. The effect of the inverted projection created by light passing through the small aperture is a phenomenon of optics known as camera obscura.

As for the string of UFOs shooting out of that mysterious Mexican volcano? Many other El Popo UFO sightings have been explained by the coincidence that if one films the volcano looking west to east, El Popo will be positioned directly between the camera and Puebla International Airport, about twenty miles east of the peak. On a good night, depending on wind direction and visibility, you can record "UFOs" taking off and landing every few minutes.

But they never look like this straight string of cigar-shaped, illuminated objects. Nor do Starlink satellites. Those do move in straight lines, but they look like a series of points or dots, not elongated streaks. Szydagis' best guess is that we're seeing some variant of "earthquake lights," ionization of the air caused by seismic activity: "I can't explain, though, why that would create a series of lights in a line." Without an explanation that fit all the facts—we concluded that was an unexplained natural phenomenon. This was a remarkable piece of footage we couldn't debunk, but it had nothing to do with a wormhole portal. Like most of Einstein's theoretical entities, the existence of wormholes, when it happens, will be confirmed with telescopes of one kind or another, not consumer smartphones or security cameras.

SIMULATION THEORY AND THE PARABLE OF PONG

For a found footage show like ours, simulation theory offers a bountiful harvest of food for thought and a steady stream of challenging videos to explain. We've been chewing on this type of content for five years now. It never gets old.

The central concept is easy to grasp—what if the world we're living in is not reality, but a vast and highly sophisticated computer simulation? Everything from the external world to our physical bodies to our fundamental sensory perceptions is generated by lines of computer code. Our "selves" are but one of any number of potential entities—human brains jacked into the simulation, or life-forms incubated within the virtual terrarium designed to play the role of humans.

While the general framework of simulation theory was spelled out masterfully in the 1999 movie *The Matrix*, it's been a topic for philosophers for millennia. As mentioned in the first chapter, Plato indicts the credibility of sensory perception in his dialog the *Theaetetus*, and he makes a similar point in the broader allegory of the cave in *The Republic*. In that dialogue reality is compared to shadows on the wall of a cave, an incomplete and impoverished version of the deeper, truer world of the Platonic ideal.

But Plato has no monopoly on this line of thinking. Around the same time he was writing in Athens, Chinese philosopher Zhuangzi was expressing similar thoughts quite elegantly, when he described waking from a dream in which he was a butterfly; then he started questioning if in fact he was really a butterfly dreaming he was a Chinese philosopher named Zhuangzi.

Roughly two thousand years later, René Descartes would take a similar swipe at our perceived reality in his *First Meditation*, in which he admits the possibility of an "evil demon" that has deceived him about all his sensory perceptions, forcing him to doubt everything, except his ability to doubt.

Among postmodern philosophers, Jean Baudrillard's fascinating and frequently impenetrable work *Simulacra and Simulation* is the go-to text, and the Wachowski siblings, who wrote and directed *The Matrix*, went to it at least twice: one shot reveals that the protagonist, Neo, stores his contraband computer files in a carved-out copy of *S&S*; and the book itself contributed one of the film's most memorable lines: "Welcome. . . . To the desert of the real."

For most of human history these musings could be dismissed as mental experiments and provocative hypotheticals, but a couple of twentieth-century innovations changed the conversation, and changed the game. The first was quantum mechanics, many principles of which support, at least theoretically, the simulation hypothesis. A prime example is the "observer effect," demonstrated in the famous double-slit experiment, in which it was proved that only when a particle is observed does it exit a state of probability and resolve into a definite state. This "observer effect" is highly akin to the behavior of a computer game, which only renders the portions of a game's world the players are operating in at any given moment.

The other innovation was the computer itself, which even in its infancy inspired imaginative people to envision a future in which computers are able to create entire worlds and intelligent beings to inhabit them. The brilliant Polish writer Stanisław Lem wrote a profound and, I submit, very important short story on the topic and the role of free will in such simulations called "Non Serviam" back in 1971.

But for my money, the real breakthrough came with futurist Ray Kurzweil's 2005 magnum opus, *The Singularity Is Near*. Its central thesis is so powerful and so simple, I found myself completely entranced by it before I got to the end of the first chapter:

human technological progress advances not as a linear function, but as an exponential one. For a long time, very little happens. Then things start to accelerate, then the rate of acceleration itself accelerates, and when you hit the inflection point in the curve—the Singularity—things start happening so rapidly that it would be impossible for people living prior to the singularity to even get their heads around it.

Kurzweil presents an abundance of graphs to underscore his hypothesis that humanity is approaching its own singularity. They include a visualization showing how Moore's Law—the prediction by former Intel CEO Gordon Moore that the number of transistors in an integrated circuit doubles every two years—has held true since 1975.

You shouldn't require graphs to feel the pull of singularity theory. Just pick up your smartphone for a moment and ponder the massive computing power you're wielding in your hand. A modern iPhone's processor runs fifty thousand times faster than the guidance computer on the Apollo 11 mission. The device can perform 11 trillion operations per second, running five thousand times faster than the CRAY-2 supercomputer, which was the world's fastest in 1985. It is also much easier to tote—the CRAY-2 was as big as a refrigerator and weighed five thousand pounds.

The true nexus of simulation theory and singularity theory happens when we consider human progress in video game design. It was just 1972, a mere fifty-three years before this book was written, that some guys from a new company called Atari rolled a machine made with a black-and-white Hitachi TV monitor and a four-foot wooden cabinet into a Sunnyvale, California, bar called Andy Capp's Tavern. It was an arcade game called *Pong*, a simulation—

there's your S-word—of table tennis. It would be hard to imagine graphics more primitive: a black screen split down the middle by a dotted line representing the net, two small white rectangles representing the paddles, and a bouncing square representing the ball.

Fast-forward to the present, where today's "AAA video games" like Red Dead Redemption and Assassin's Creed bring players into fully immersive worlds where the humans and animals move in perfect biomechanical accordance with gravity; environmental elements like grass and mud are textured down to the individual blade or clump, the trees and smoke move just as the wind would dictate, and the shadows are all precisely in proportion to their angle with the primary light source.

Try to imagine where our video games will be in a thousand years. Then try to imagine what an alien species' video games would be like if they invented their *Pong* not fifty-three years ago, but a million years ago; and if—big if—they'd ascended up the exponential curve of progress without destroying themselves in the interim.

What does it all mean? It means that simulation theory might not just be a theory; it might be the case. How small should epsilon be in this particular probability function? According to philosopher Nick Bostrom and astronomer David Kipping, not small at all. Using Bayesian reasoning, they put the odds of us currently living in a simulation at about fifty-fifty.

Just as in *The Matrix*, if our reality is a computer simulation, there are bound to be flaws in the code, malfunctions in the machinery, and "glitches" that would likely appear as anomalies of physics to us.

We often receive "glitch in the matrix" videos submitted as evidence for simulation theory, like one from Port Colborne, Ontario, near the coast of Lake Erie. A woman and her young daughter were driving down tree-lined Lakeshore Road and recording through their windshield. In the distance, straight ahead and across the water, an old mill looms in front of them. But as they drive closer, moving past the trees and toward the shoreline, the big building seems to shrink right before their eyes, when we'd expect it to be getting bigger.

We had our forensic video analyst Michael Primeau confirm that no CGI was involved here, so what was going on? Professor Kaku did not warm to the simulation hypothesis: "The whole idea that physical reality itself is an illusion created by a computer program is so fantastic. Think of what it would cost to maintain such a matrix. Not just one person, but all of reality, all of space-time, all the universe, would have to be simulated in the memory of the matrix. Not possible." (Not possible for us, maybe, but aliens with a million-year head start?)

Kaku instead pointed out another optical illusion that explains what happened. When the observer is moving and does not have the ability to see the horizon, the eye is tricked by the surrounding information—in this case, the trees lining the street, which make the object look bigger than it actually is. Remove the trees from the view and add the horizon, as the driver did as she reached the shoreline, and the mill across the water gradually reverts to its proper size. This was a "glitch" in our brains, not in a simulation. (Unless the simulation designer was just sloppy writing the code for our optical perception!)

So have any purported "glitch" videos survived scrutiny? The short answer is yes. One was shot by an unbearably sweet British couple, Meg Oxtoby and Jeff Parlett, who were hiking with their trio of Hungarian vizslas on a sweltering day in 2020. "We were walking along, just having a chat like we normally do," says Meg. "And then we noticed that the dogs weren't moving." Their smartphone video confirms it—the footage looks like a still photograph of three dogs immobilized mid-stride. One has his leg raised and his tail curved; another is frozen at such an odd angle it seems impossible for it to maintain balance for ten seconds, and the dogs remain in that exact state of suspended animation for a full four minutes. You'd think you're looking at a still photo, except the shrubbery is clearly oscillating from the wind. "We were completely gobsmacked," Jeff recalls. It would be odd enough if just one dog were doing this, but three? At the same time?

As our experts analyzed the footage, they considered whether the dogs had been frightened into freezing. That happens with some dogs, but there was nothing in their body language to indicate fear—their ears and tails were up. And while it's true some hunting dogs like vizslas can hold a posture when they lock on prey, they usually do so with all four feet planted, not in these off-balance postures, and they don't do it for four minutes straight. One of our biologists suggested the dogs were merely superbly bred and trained for this, but Meg and Jeff aren't hunters, and they've never trained their dogs to do anything other than sit and go through hoops. "This was something on a completely different scale," Jeff said. "It's something I can't see being taught to them whatsoever."

One of our experts was positive the video had been edited. And when Michael Primeau performed his forensic analysis, he told us there were apps that can animate certain areas of a picture while preserving other areas frozen in time. He can find such frauds using Error Level Analysis tools, but this video passed inspection: "We found no evidence to support that this file was manipulated, slowed down, or frozen in any way." We called this an unexplained animal anomaly, and if you want to consider that evidence supporting the simulation hypothesis, be my guest.

As a matter of full disclosure, I need to mention one "simulation theory" image we got spectacularly wrong. I might be embarrassed about this if I didn't find it so amusing. In our very first season we analyzed a truly strange photo—it shows a pair of girls standing next to a mirror as they pose for the camera. What's nuts is, one of the girls is smiling at the camera, but her reflection in the mirror has a completely different facial expression, with her mouth agape and her eyes looking in another direction. We presumed this had to be a doctored photo, but Primeau found no inconsistencies in the digital information or anything suspicious about the compression blocks. "We would expect to see some sort of pasting of these two faces," he said, "but I did not detect any evidence of tampering."

We declared that image a genuine unexplained mystery. That was, until a viewer emailed us immediately after seeing the show with the solution: the photo was taken on an iPhone in "pano" mode, and while the camera was panning from one side to the other, the girl changed her facial expression. For anyone sufficiently fluent in the full functionalities of modern smartphone camera apps, this was a *no duh*. To our shame, nobody assigned to the piece was sufficiently fluent. To our credit, we interviewed the viewer who solved the mystery, updated the piece, reran it, and properly serviced the audience with integrity . . . and well-earned humility!

In that same spirit of disclosure, I should say that while I find simulation theory attractive, some of our most authoritative experts despise it, Professor Szydagis foremost among them.

"It's not a theory," he chides me. "It's a hypothesis. It's religious belief. It's something you talk about over beers or with some pot with your buddies on the couch at three in the morning. Why do I say that? Because it's not provable or disprovable. Any evidence you bring against it, you can say that's what the designers want you to believe."

His critique is not just epistemological; it's technical. As Professor Kaku mentioned, the computing power required to simulate our entire observable universe would be immense beyond comprehension. "Simulating our universe would require multiple universes of atoms," says Szydagis. "Chaos and quantum mechanics prove that our reality is not simulatable."

I tried to rebut Szydagis by invoking Kurzweil, *Pong*, the exponential curve of progress, and the aliens' million-year head start. He was prepared: "I have a bombshell for you: I vehemently disagree with Kurzweil, and I can disprove singularity theory with one word: airplanes. If technology increases exponentially, why can't I get on a plane to London tomorrow and be there in ten seconds? Plane travel hasn't gotten any faster for decades; in fact, with the retiring of the Concorde, it's gotten slower.

"The reason is technology does *not* increase on an exponential curve; it increases on a sigmoidal [S-shaped] curve. But when you're in the middle of it, you *think* you're in an exponential curve, because you are not aware yet that it's going to flatten out. But look around you: plane speeds have flattened out. And Moore's Law is dead too—progress in processing power has been stagnant for a long time; they just aren't telling you. To get things going again, you need a paradigm shift, like balloon to airplane, and we haven't had one in a long time. You shouldn't be impressed with your fast iPhone; you should be depressed about your slow airplanes. Humanity should be ashamed of itself for its lack of progress!"

Professor Szydagis insists that his skepticism about simulation theory—sorry, the simulation hypothesis—is purely a matter of scientific reasoning; but his visceral loathing for it comes from what he believes to be its moral and social implications. "If we're just living in a simulation and nothing's real, why help your neighbor? Why strive to fulfill your potential? Why do anything?"

I might retort that video game players frequently care intensely about the quality of their play, even when they know the world of "Call of Duty" isn't real. Still, I don't have the physics chops to go toe-to-toe with him on this, so my standard inclination would be to defer to his expertise.

But that's not so easy and the reason has nothing to do with my reading of Kurzweil, Bostrom, or Baudrillard. Here I find myself aligned, somewhat uncomfortably, with the Bigfoot and UFO experiencers. I can't just reject simulation theory outright because something happened to me. I firmly believe it was real and yet can't explain it. It was nothing spectacular or cinematic, but it was profound. It is "my truth."

It happened in late 2024 as I was driving to a state park in Florida I'd never visited before. As my bike bounced up and down on the rack attached to my car's trailer hitch, my mind gravitated to one of its biggest concerns of the past two years: the challenge of writing this book. I'd recently attended the SCU conference in Huntsville, Alabama, where I'd heard Prof. Kevin Knuth give his presentation about extraordinary events and the chronic undervaluing of the epsilon variable in probability models. While I was wrestling over what chapter I'd put that tidbit in, I realized I was driving through a town I didn't know. While I trust the GPS directions, I told myself to pay more attention to my surroundings. So

I looked up at a passing residential street sign, and noticed that at that very moment, I was passing by . . . Knuth Road.

A tingling feeling came over me. I had just been thinking about a man who speaks about exceedingly rare occurrences, who has an exceedingly rare last name (it indexes only around 3,000 in the United States on Gennet, compared to 1.1 million for Williams), and at that exact moment I passed by a street with that same exceedingly rare name. Was that really just a random coincidence, or might it qualify as a phenomenon known as "paranormal synchronicity"? Were my thoughts somehow connected to that location by some quirk of the simulation's code? Had the supercomputer's algorithms directed me to that physical location because of that specific thought, or maybe directed my mind to that specific thought because of my physical location? Was my understanding of reality missing something fundamental? So, sue me. I'm not giving up on simulation theory . . . or perhaps another strange principle of quantum mechanics is at play.

QUANTUM ENTANGLEMENT, TELEPORTATION, AND TIME TRAVEL

If simulation theory helps explain reality's breakdowns, quantum entanglement helps explain its magic tricks. It occurs on the subatomic level when two particles become correlated so that their states match instantaneously, even though they may be very far apart. A change in state of one entangled particle will be reflected in the other, instantly. Einstein famously referred to the phenomenon as "spooky action at a distance."

Alleged cases of time travel and teleportation find a measure of scientific support in some of the recent breakthroughs in this field. As always, it's risky to go too far too fast, but regardless, many Believers are fond of incanting the word "quantum" not merely to muse on the mind-bending things happening at a subatomic level, but to validate highly dubious claims about events in the macro-atomic world. We're seeing this with greater frequency as quantum mechanics evolves out of the lab and into real-world applications, quantum computing foremost among them.

Caught-on-camera teleportation cases are among the most eye-popping videos we've ever investigated. Take, for example, a video from a motion-activated doorbell camera shot in Porter, Texas, shortly after Christmas in 2019. The footage shows a man heading out alone on what seems like a normal walk, but as he reaches the sidewalk and turns toward the driveway, he freezes for a moment and then simply vanishes, right as a halolike ring of light appears just above his head. It's the closest thing you'll see to a real-world "Beam me up, Scotty" moment.

Another famous video has become such an internet classic we knew we'd be giving it the *Proof* treatment the moment the show was green-lit. It's police dashcam footage out of Georgia from all the way back in 1997, documenting a high-speed pursuit. Officer Wayne Daniels is chasing the driver of a stolen vehicle. The thief performs a series of impressive evasive maneuvers on the road, then takes a left turn into a residential neighborhood and heads straight for the tall chain-link fence surrounding someone's backyard at high speed. But as Officer Daniels' cruiser approaches the same fence just seconds later, braking just in time to avoid hitting it, the car has disappeared in a cloud of dust and the fence is standing, intact and undamaged. Daniels recounted the incident like this: "When it all occurred, it happened so fast. I figured the fence would wrap him up; he'd be in a big old cocoon, But yet the fence was still standing in front of me, keeping me closed off from getting inside the yard. So I had no idea how a car could get through."

Did the doorbell camera capture a moment of genuine human teleportation? Did Officer Daniels' dashcam record the same phenomenon happening with a hot car? As far-fetched as the notion might be, it has gained contemporary traction due to the fact that quantum entanglement makes certain kinds of teleportation possible. The first successful teleportation of a quantum state occurred in 1997, when an Austrian team led by Anton Zeilinger entangled two photons and transferred the state of one to the other. Zeilinger would win a Nobel Prize for his work. More recently, in 2015 the National Institute of Standards and Technology teleported quantum information over one hundred kilometers of optical fiber, only to be surpassed two years later by a Chinese team that beamed entangled pairs of photons from an experimental satellite to three ground stations, each separated by more than twelve hundred kilometers. And just a month prior to this writing, Oxford researchers made another breakthrough, teleporting quantum data between two separate computer chips. These rapid advances—which have left luminous influencers like Joe Rogan agog—suggest that the age of quantum communication and encryption may be dawning already.

Teleporting people and cars, however, would require an entirely different order of technology. "You would need to know what we call the distribution function for every particle that makes up your human body; every electron, neutron, proton, needs to be disassembled and then put back together somewhere else," says Professor Oluseyi. "And that just can't be done by any means that we know of currently." Such deconstruction and reconstruction would require the transmission of vast amounts of information. And that's just getting the atoms from one place to another in the right arrangement.

Another problem: entanglement, for all its wonders, is extremely fragile. "People forget that entanglement is very unstable," says Professor Szydagis, "and that's only with a subatomic particle. It's always a stretch. Any force—gravity, electromagnetism, radiation—will ruin it. That's why we don't have quantum computers yet."

Yes, that's us humans. But what about an advanced alien civilization? Could they not have mastered quantum teleportation to the point where they can snatch pedestrians in Texas or stolen cars in Georgia? Might alien quantum teleportation tech in fact account for some of the common traits recurring in alien abduction testimonies? "Yeah, maybe an advanced civilization could do it, maybe to send a probe, but even quantum teleportation doesn't transcend the speed of light," says Szydagis, "so intergalactic travel of ships and beings wouldn't work. Once again, Einstein gets the last laugh."

So what was captured on those "teleportation" videos? In the case of our beamed-up Texas stroller, Michael Primeau solved the riddle. Having analyzed Ring camera video countless times for criminal cases, he knows those cameras always use a high level of compression to encode and then transmit the video frames through the internet to the server where they are recorded. Through his video forensic analysis, Primeau determined that the encoder was not documenting pixel information at all for thirty frames, right as the "teleportation" occurred. Whether that pause was the result of a camera malfunction or a momentary drop in internet connectivity, it meant that the video transmission cut out for a moment, freezing the image. When it resumed our pedestrian had already walked out of frame. The transition between the last frame in which he appeared to the next when he has gone created the "beam me up" effect.

As for the mystery of the Georgia car thief? No need for quantum mechanics on that one; plain old pre-Einstein Newtonian physics will suffice. After working through his initial amazement, Officer Daniels figured it out soon enough. "On most fences, when you set the poles, you put the fence on the outside of the poles so that it protects anyone from going through the fence into a yard," he told us. "This particular fence was set on the back side of the poles so that when the car hit the fence, the aluminum ties that hold the fence to the poles popped loose. The fence swung open like a garage door. And before the dust could settle, the fence had come straight back down in front of me." Case closed, though there are still those online defending the "ghost car" interpretation.

Then there's the question of time travel. We know from Einstein's theory of both special and general relativity that time is plastic. It moves at different rates depending on an object's mass and how fast it's moving through space. This is not just theoretically possible, it has been experimentally demonstrated. Consider Einstein's famous "Twin Effect"—whereby one twin who goes on an interstellar trip close to the speed of light, thereby slowing down his time, would return to Earth and shake hands with a twin who has grown much older much faster. From the traveler's perspective, he has taken a one-way trip to the future. This happens in tiny increments all the time. Going *backward* in time, however, is a much bigger challenge. "This requires what's called negative energy, and we don't know how to harness a sufficient amount of energy in order to allow for time travel to the past," explains Szydagis, who has given TED talks on the subject.

One of our physicists, Dr. Ron Mallett, is perhaps the only serious academic working on the problem of backward time travel. He's even built early models of a laser column device that, in theory, should be able to send a particle back in time. Dr. Szydagis thinks if more people put resources into work like Mallett's, we should be able to perform some rudimentary backward time travel within a hundred years—not with humans, but with particles, allowing us to send information into the past with a kind of Morse code that transmits through time, not space.

Might time travel be happening already though, independent of human technology or intent? A YouTube search will yield several badly faked "time traveler" videos that claim to show a distressed messenger from the future warning of pending cataclysms, but not every case is so silly.

Take the strange but well-documented incident out of Surrey, England. One night in December 2002, several drivers called local police to report a car losing control on the highway and careering off into a ditch. When police responded, they found no signs of a recent crash. Officer Ian Kyle was there. "There was no broken foliage; there were no tire marks; there was no anything to see even if an accident had occurred there at all," he said. "So we done [*sic*] a circuit and come back down the same location again, but this time a little bit slower. And that's when we come across a reflection of some sort of number plate." (That's a license plate to us Americans.)

As police investigated, they discovered the overgrown wreck of a crashed maroon Vauxhall Astra. Lying underneath it was not the body of a recently deceased motorist, but the skeleton of a missing twenty-one-year-old man. "By going on when he was reported missing, he'd been missing five months," said Officer Kyle. "And when the car was found it was covered in dust. It had been there a long time."

That's right, the fatal accident had apparently happened five months earlier, but nobody reported it at the time, while multiple eyewitnesses said they saw it take place right before their eyes five months later. Did the car somehow slip forward in time through some variation of the Twin Effect? Did the eyewitnesses momentarily go back in time like one of Dr. Mallett's particles? Our experts could come to no definitive conclusion about that bizarre accident. Physicists are quite confident that human time slips have never happened, but in Surrey, England, one veteran policeman isn't so sure. "I just find the whole episode very, very, very strange," says Officer Kyle. "In the whole of my thirty-year career in the police, I have never seen anything like it. To this day, I still can't explain it."

Officer, the team at Skinwalker Ranch is right there with you.

Chapter 10

SONIC MYSTERIES: HUMS, HAARP, AND HAVANA

THE WORLDWIDE HUM

Like most of us, Steve Kohlhase was in bed when his nightmare began. Unlike most of us, he wasn't asleep.

"I started hearing a low-frequency disturbance," he said. "A droning sound. And it got progressively worse." It was 2009, and Kohlhase, a mechanical engineer living in Connecticut with his wife and kids, fell down a well of distress and depression when he realized this hum wasn't going away.

Days passed. Steve kept hearing the noise intermittently at home and around town. The hum's intensity varied depending on Steve's location; it never just went entirely away, especially at night. "The irritation and disturbance breaks your sleep pattern," he said. "You get your ear ringing. Your body feels acoustic pressures in the room. It can give you uneasiness, queasiness, irritability. It's impossible to live with."

It wasn't just the irritation; it was the feeling of isolation. Steve's wife heard nothing. Was this all taking place in Steve's head, a psychosomatic condition his mind was inflicting upon itself? To prove that wasn't the case, Steve began searching for the source of the hum, first in his house, then in his town, and of course online.

Years passed. The hum did not. But Steve found a measure of solace when he discovered he was not alone. Tens of thousands of people around the world have joined Facebook groups and other social media platforms to commiserate over their experiences with what's come to be known as the Worldwide Hum, and try to determine what's causing it.

The puzzle is grotesquely complex since, as Steve learned, many people do not hear the Hum at all, even in locations with high concentrations of self-identified sufferers. Moreover, the Hum is not the same to everyone who hears it. Frequency, amplitude, and timbre vary from person to person. In the words of sound ecologist Dr. Ben Gottesman, "The Worldwide Hum is an amazing sonic mystery."

Without any consensus on what the noise even was, and an appalling lack of solid medical research on the topic, conspiracy theories spackled in the knowledge gaps. As we've seen, that's what they do. Some people have suggested there's a breakaway troglodyte civilization underground, and the Hum is the sound of their machines excavating deep below the Earth's surface as they construct vast subterranean cities. Others have claimed the Hum is generated by the U.S. military, which maintains a vast archipelago of underground bases connected by tunnels, using shuttered Wal-Marts as entry points and supply stations.

Steve himself has spent years gathering evidence for his own theory, which is that the Hum is generated by underground natural gas pipelines. They have expanded dramatically since 2009, when his first symptoms hit. His most impressive data is a map of intra- and interstate gas pipelines as reported by the Energy Information Association, which aligns with what he claims is 95 percent accuracy with a map of what he calls "home reports" of Hum experiences. "I now call the condition Gas Pipeline Syndrome," he says. "This is a consequential problem of changing technology and the needs of society that is not well understood."

THE THEATER OF THE MIND

Anomalous auditory events form a special subcategory of our "Phreaks of Physics," and we approach them from a distinct analytical perspective. Usually we're playing a kind of matching game, comparing the recording in question side by side with samples of known noises. Our experts, sound ecologist Dr. Ben Gottesman and electrical engineer Prof. Bob Maher, take the analysis down to the subharmonic level and are, thankfully, able to detect subtle signs of fakery. Reading a spectrogram like radiologists read X-rays, they can spot minutiae like imperfect edits and the rich low frequencies that indicate a sound was recorded close to the microphone. (That's important when the eyewitness claims he heard the sound off in the distance.)

You don't have to be an executive producer to know that sound recordings don't make great television. How sexy can a waveform animation get? Yet strange sounds provide some of our most intriguing cases, precisely because when the source of a bizarre noise is not visible, the imagination steps forward to fill in the blank. This is the "theater of the mind" with which radio and podcasts can engage a listener so mesmerically, whether the format is a scripted drama, live news and sports, or music. Orson Welles' 1938 *War of the Worlds* production would never have triggered its audience to run panicked into the streets had it been a TV show.

The human ear itself also adds a layer of intrigue here, as many of its functions are wonders of biology about which much remains to be discovered. How the ear's hair cells convert minuscule changes in atmospheric pressure (sound waves) into electrical signals the brain interprets as sound is a marvel of nature, allowing us to perceive sound much faster than the eye perceives light, and at a much wider range of frequency. The ear also comes with automatic amplitude adjustment that dials its sensitivity up or down depending on the given acoustic environment. And the ear even emits frequencies of its own, which vary not only person to person, but left ear to right ear.

Today anomalous sounds proliferate and go viral if for no other reason than they are so easy to fake. Anyone with a rudimentary knowledge of software like Pro Tools, Adobe Audition, or even the iPhone's Garage Band app can hoax a convincing Bigfoot howl and dub it over a wide shot of a sylvan landscape just before someone off-camera exclaims, "What the heck was that?" The Sierra Sounds mentioned in the earlier Bigfoot chapter stand out as one of the very few alleged Sasquatch recordings we couldn't explain away as this type of fake, or a misidentified natural call of an animal people aren't used to hearing, such as a lynx or moose.

SKY TRUMPETS

Taking the silver medal for audio fakery are the many alleged recordings of "sky trumpets." In these cases hoaxers are trying to either dupe or inspire fundamentalist Christians who believe, per the book of Revelation, that the Last Judgment will be heralded by seven angels blowing seven trumpets, each with increasingly apocalyptic consequences. The King James Version tells it like this:

> *And the seven angels which had the seven trumpets prepared themselves to sound.*

The first angel sounded, and there followed hail and fire mingled with blood, and they were cast upon the earth: and the third part of trees was burnt up, and all green grass was burnt up.

That's just the first trumpet. Even if you're unfamiliar with the text, you can probably guess things go downhill from there.

Many evangelical Christians take Revelation literally, so there's a built-in audience for sky trumpet videos. And so it came to pass that, in 2017, a young man named Dillon Dickerson posted a video he said he'd shot while taking out the trash from his North Carolina home. As he was in his backyard, he heard a piercing, blaring sound that continued periodically as he unsheathed his smartphone to document the scene. "It sent chills down my spine," he said. "I really didn't know what to think." On the video, there are exactly seven blasts, so naturally many believed it to be the sky trumpets from Revelation.

When Dr. Gottesman put them through the spectrogram, he was able to identify the sound by its harmonics and tonal structure as, most probably, the sound of a semi-truck braking. But it wasn't just one—it was several such sounds, layered together to make the uniquely ominous blare. Dillon swore to us his video hadn't been doctored, but I might recommend another section of the Bible as nightstand reading: the book of Exodus; specifically, the Ten Commandments. Number nine says thou shalt not bear false witness.

SKYQUAKES

Fakes aside, the percentage of odd sounds that remain difficult to explain even when subjected to rigorous analysis remains relatively high compared to, say, UFO footage. Take an incident recorded all over San Diego County in March 2021. Shortly before 5:00 pm, residents reported hearing a disturbing sound that rattled some neighborhoods so violently it set off car alarms. Captured by multiple independent security cameras (and therefore certainly not a hoax), the sound resembles a loud snap—almost like a huge racket in the sky has just smashed a giant tennis ball with the force of a Djokovic ace.

This was but one example of an ongoing phenomenon known as a "skyquake," heard throughout history and all over the world. Historically, they have been attributed to a vexed God (in the Old Testament) or creator spirit (in Iroquois mythology). Today many reported skyquakes can be explained away by human activity—such as Tannerite explosions that somehow became a popular tradition in baby gender "reveal parties" while I wasn't looking.

But when Dr. Gottesman analyzed a recording of the San Diego skyquake, he determined that most of its acoustic energy occurred at a frequency below one kilohertz. Tannerite explosions aren't that low, and their acoustic radius doesn't extend beyond a few miles. This skyquake was heard all across the county.

A sonic boom from a plane was a promising candidate since the frequency was roughly compatible, as was the duration—both last for less than a second. The San Diego area is home to major military facilities for both the Navy and Marines, but our aviation expert Tim McMillan didn't think a plane was responsible. Commercial jets don't fly faster than the speed of sound, and military planes only break the sound barrier under highly regulated circumstances. They're almost never permitted to do so in residential areas precisely because they disturb the peace. In any event, when local police and news stations inquired, none of the local military bases took responsibility.

Could it just have been a thunderclap? Dr. Gottesman didn't think so, because thunder almost always lasts for more than a single second. To this day that San Diego skyquake remains a mystery, and the topic is widespread and puzzling enough to have attracted academic attention. Between 2013 and 2014, scientists from the University of North Carolina attempted to determine the origins of skyquakes with a mobile network of four hundred atmospheric sensors and seismographs. They were able to rule out seismic activity as a cause, but besides that they arrived at no definitive answers. Meanwhile, the quakes keep rumbling.

HAARP

Other peculiar noises are less likely to be confused for explosions, thunder, or tectonic stirrings. They sound too industrial or otherwise man-made, and steadier than anything a passing jet would generate. One head-scratcher came to us from a man named Noel Riggs, an English educator living in Albacete, Spain. Mr. Riggs was awoken in his apartment at 6:30 on a Saturday morning by a thunderous metallic sound that came in waves, growing louder and then fading. There had been construction taking place in the area, but Noel quickly remembered it was the predawn hours on Saturday morning, an unlikely hour for a construction crew to be at work (especially in Europe!), and he didn't see any activity at the site from his balcony. There was a rock quarry ten miles away, but that too was not operating at the time. The sound disappeared within the hour, but Noel had to know: What was it? He turned to the internet soliciting answers.

A vigorous debate ensued. As we see often in cases like this, some were convinced that the sound traced back to a U.S. government program that became a darling of the conspiracy crowd back in the nineties—the High-frequency Active Auroral Research Program, or HAARP. Originally a U.S. Air Force/DARPA project designed to study the ionosphere with an array of massive transmitters and measuring devices, HAARP achieved notoriety because it does indeed blast high-frequency radio waves into the sky to tickle or "excite" a small portion of the ionosphere five hundred miles above the Earth. The ostensible purpose is to generate data helpful for improving radio transmissions. But the fact that the American military was toying with the planet's atmosphere gave the conspiracy theorists all the ammunition they needed to claim that the government was manipulating weather (which, as we know, is relatively commonplace these days), controlling people's minds, and even triggering natural disasters. Venezuelan strongman Hugo Chavez went as far as blaming HAARP for the devastating 2010 Haiti earthquake. HAARP was transferred from the Air Force to the University of Alaska in 2015, but the rumors of malign intentions persist.

What was the source of Noel's Spanish Metal Sound? One of our experts believes it was a hoax—a manipulated recording of the sound of the smoke monster from the hit TV show *Lost*. But Dr. Gottesman thought otherwise (in part because Noel is much more earnest and consistent with his story than most hoaxers). Building on the analysis of our meteorologist Juan Hernandez, Gottesman believed a thermal inversion in the atmosphere was responsible. These inversions occur when the normal atmospheric temperature profile flips, and cold air is near the surface while warmer air is aloft. The higher thermal layer can act as a wall, bouncing back sound waves that may have originated at a distant location. Gottesman compared the mystery sound to noise emanating from an industrial shipyard more than one hundred miles away that operates continuously in round-the-clock shifts. There were significant differences in the two sounds when he did a side-by-side comparison—the impulsive motor noises of the shipyard didn't include the droned-out metallic sounds from Noel's recording. But that could be explained by the distance the sound would have traveled. "As it's bouncing and traveling farther than normal," Dr. Gottesman explained, "its frequency response can change because certain frequencies are able to reflect better than others. And that can lead to what was a very common-sounding sound turning much more bizarre and strange." So—a thermal inversion of sounds from shipyard machinery, or a hoax. We left this as a split decision and let our beloved viewers decide for themselves. In any event, we were positive the evil overlords running HAARP weren't to blame.

THE BUZZER

That said, the world's governments *are* responsible for their share of truly peculiar sounds, and some may have clandestine purposes. An amateur radio enthusiast named Ryan Schaum belongs to a large online community that monitors an enigmatic shortwave broadcast that has been transmitting a monotonous sound virtually nonstop for five decades. It's a buzz of sorts, occasionally interrupted by a voice speaking Russian. Ryan admits he "got hooked" on the transmission and became obsessed with its secrets. "Like, who's broadcasting this?" he wonders. "Where are they, and what possible purpose could this have?"

Over the years it's been theorized that "the Buzzer," also known as UVB-76, was set up by the Russian admiralty to communicate with submarines, but Professor Kaku eliminated that possibility because the frequency was too high. Others thought it was a "dead man switch" that would trigger the launch of Russia's nuclear arsenal if Moscow, the presumed source of the transmission, were attacked first and the signal was interrupted. But Tim McMillan learned that the signal ceased for a good portion of 2010. A nuclear holocaust did not transpire, so that hypothesis was scratched off as well. The best guess our team came up with was that "the Buzzer" was a so-called numbers station used to send coded messages via shortwave radio to overseas spies. The buzz itself is noise meant to saturate that radio channel so no one else will try to use it. Then the Russian voice comes on when there's a coded message to send, usually conveyed in numbers. "And the information that it's sharing, unless you know the code, *is* virtually uncrackable," explained McMillan. "It's fairly unsophisticated, but a brilliant way to communicate with your deep-cover spies who may be all the way across the world." (Shortwave radio, by the way, bounces radio waves off the ionosphere, so you can see why the Air Force built HAARP.) Today, given the advances in internet encryption, it's likely that Russia's spies prefer twenty-first-century modes of communication, so why is "the Buzzer" still buzzing? Good question. We don't know if it's still being used for active espionage operations, if it's been kept running as a disinformation op (*maskirovka*, as the Soviets termed it so aptly) to keep Russia's adversaries guessing, or if it's just serving as a placeholder for the frequency.

SONIC WEAPONRY AND HAVANA SYNDROME

Other state-sponsored strange sounds can be abjectly malevolent. Indeed, they can be weapons. I'm old enough to remember the now-legendary "music torture" story of the U.S. Army surrounding Panamanian strongman Manuel Noriega after he sought refuge at the Vatican embassy during the 1989 U.S. invasion. For days a ring of Humvees blasted a playlist of hard rock featuring Van Halen, Guns N' Roses, and The Clash. Noriega eventually surrendered, while the U.S. Army went on to hone this technique as a means of psychologically breaking detainees during the Global War on Terror.

More sophisticated modern audio weapons include the long-range acoustic device, which can project an alarm signal or bullhorn-style commands at ninety decibels up to two miles away—an ideal tool for crowd dispersal during civil commotions. And more recently, a team of college students in Toronto developed an anti-drone platform that uses ultrasound waves to destabilize enemy drones' navigation systems, causing them to crash or veer off course.

But our business is weirdness, not the stuff that fills the pages of *Popular Mechanics*. So it was only a matter of time before we turned our attention to the most infamous sonic mystery of recent years, "Havana Syndrome." The story began at the U.S. embassy in Havana in late 2016, where several diplomats and other staffers reported feeling ill after hearing a strange, high-pitched noise. The following year, the Associated Press released recordings of the sound allegedly heard by some victims. It is indeed a high-pitched whine, which seems to undulate, even writhe, provoking that nails-on-a-chalkboard reaction among those unfortunate enough to be within earshot.

Similar cases were later reported by other State Department personnel in China and Russia, though the type and degree of symptoms were frustratingly inconsistent. A senior CIA official named Marc Polymeropoulos claimed to have been targeted while on official business in Moscow. He has since become the public face of the Havana Syndrome victims. "This was by far the most terrifying experience," he told us. "The room was spinning. I couldn't stand up without falling down. I felt nauseous, sick to my stomach. I had an incredible case of tinnitus ringing in my ears, a headache. And so I knew something was seriously wrong." He hoped the symptoms would wear off. They didn't. The chronic fatigue and headaches were so crippling they drove him into retirement. Polymeropoulos and other victims believe they were targets of a sonic weaponry campaign, which they claim is still ongoing.

Could that AP recording of the alleged Havana Syndrome be identified? Dr. Gottesman agreed that the sound had a piercing quality but didn't think it was produced at a volume sufficient to induce the wide range of reported symptoms. After comparing it to naturally occurring noises, he concluded the AP recording most resembled the call of the Indies short-tailed cricket. "The frequency range is a perfect overlap and it also has similar harmonic characteristics," he told us. "So I'm saying it's a really clean match."

That might explain the origin of that particular recording, but it doesn't explain the cause of the victims' reported symptoms, which resembled those of a concussion. Where do those come from? Our military expert Tim McMillan suspected that while those crickets were chirping in Havana, the real source of the Syndrome was a directed energy weapon using microwaves. This would have to have been a truly secret weapon designed by one of our rivals, since as of today, those types of weapons are not known to exist. "Frankly, it really is a mystery," McMillan said with resignation. "There's enough physical and medical evidence that it does appear to be a weapon. But what is causing this is truly unknown. It's a real concern."

Other respected experts beg to differ. Neurology professor Robert Baloh of UCLA has written that "the available data on Havana syndrome matches closely with mass psychogenic illness—more commonly known as mass hysteria." Professor Baloh says that the epidemiology of the "illness" aligns with other known cases of mass hysteria, like the "dancing plagues" documented in the Middle Ages. "It started from a single undercover agent in Cuba—a person in what I imagine is a very stressful situation," he wrote. "This person had real symptoms, but blamed them on something mysterious—the strange sound he heard. He then told his colleagues at the embassy, and the idea spread. With the help of the media and medical community, the idea solidified and spread around the world. It checks all the boxes." The FBI's famed Behavior Analysis Unit reached the same conclusion, and Baloh's thesis is buttressed by the fact that in the ten years since Havana Syndrome was first reported, neither any uniform physical cause nor any secret directed energy weapon has been identified, despite multiple congressional and CIA investigations, NIH studies, and even an alleged DARPA attempt to reverse engineer such a weapon. In 2025, a revised intelligence community assessment didn't "rule out" the possibility that a directed energy weapon may have been involved in some cases, reigniting the debate. But the majority opinion is with the Skeptics: the evidence is just not there.

Marc Polymeropoulos considers such talk not only offensive but harmful. And he's been hearing versions of it ever since he first reported his symptoms. "So many of us were dismissed by the senior medical staff at the CIA or the Department of State," he said. "And that to me was very challenging, particularly from a mental health perspective. There's a moral injury aspect when you come back and you're dismissed by the medical staff of your parent organization. That's a really serious component of what has happened to us." That's why Havana Syndrome victims often say they would have preferred to have been shot.

Steve Kohlhase had a similar reaction to our conclusions about the Worldwide Hum. We didn't discount his gas pipeline theory, but we did note that many self-identifying Hum experiencers live far from such infrastructure; and some are hearing normal sounds of the modern environment. One woman in Rochester, New York, sent us a recording of what she described as the Hum, which Dr. Gottesman successfully matched with the sound of a ventilation fan one finds on the rear alley–facing walls of restaurants or laundromats.

The reason this woman and others find such noises particularly disturbing while others don't, we concluded, ties back to another fascinating quirk of the human ear: a condition called hyperacusis, which entails extreme sensitivity to certain frequencies. For those with the condition, some sounds that most people wouldn't notice or find troubling cause extreme annoyance and even pain.

When I spoke to Kohlhase for this book, he was happy he did the show to get his story out there, but he thought our conclusion minimized what was really going on and our mention of hyperacusis muddied the waters about the gas line issue. For him that was a bummer because, he claimed, our verdict essentially allowed the public to adopt the same posture as Havana Syndrome Skeptics, namely: It's all in your head. Deal with it.

I will admit I was in that camp regarding both Havana Syndrome and the Hum. Worse, I made the assumption that many people who had psychosomatic symptoms actually felt no symptoms at all—they were faking it for attention, sympathy, credit in our decadent society's economy of victimhood, whatever. A classic materialist stance: if I can't see, touch, or in this case hear concrete proof of something, it's probably nonsense. And yes, I thought of Pascal's God-shaped hole once again. In these cases it was neither aliens nor the government but the individuals' own suffering that provided the longed-for meaning and fed the need for there to be "something more" to the world. Their sonic afflictions confer dual status of both Cassandra and martyr, the mysterious sounds standing in for the Holy Spirit.

Then a curious thing happened. It was January 2024, and I was in New York, shooting Tony's on-camera intros and outros for that season's segments. We traditionally shoot those in a large studio in the Bushwick section of Brooklyn. I was in my usual chair next to our director, my eyes moving back and forth between the set and the quad-screen monitors in front of me displaying the feeds from our four studio cameras. Then I heard something. Or rather, I heard more of something—the tinnitus I've lived with ever since I played bass in several overly loud and underly talented rock bands in my teens and twenties. The ringing suddenly grew louder, making it harder to hear the audio from the microphones coming through my headphones. Then I began feeling woozy, as one might an hour after taking a second cannabis gummy when a single dose would have done just fine. Then the periphery of my vision began to fade out, like the common vignetting effect traditionally used by film editors to represent flashbacks or dream sequences in low-budget movies.

I began to suspect I might soon pass out. Concerned that I was experiencing early symptoms of a stroke or an aneurysm, I asked our director to call for a five-minute break and called over our line producer. Shortly after I told her how I was feeling, she insisted that I go with her to an urgent care clinic and get checked out.

I did not pass out, and by the time we got to urgent care I was beginning to feel better. The doctor on call confirmed I was not having any kind of vascular or neurological episode and sent me home. I went to bed and felt better the next day. The tinnitus had subsided back into a constant but tolerable background ringing.

Two weeks later, the symptoms returned on a Saturday morning as I was preparing to run a 5k with my son. Again, the raging tinnitus led the charge with the light-headedness and compromised peripheral vision trailing close behind. My boy Sebastian finished the race in record time. I watched, trying to stay in character as a supportive dad while struggling to maintain consciousness and now also fighting back panic. After we made it home I called my shrink, inquiring if the low daily dose of Wellbutrin she had me on might be to blame. She scoffed at the notion and told me to get to my primary care physician as soon as possible and get tested.

When the symptoms disappeared again, I blew off her advice. A week later, they came back. This time they stayed. I scrambled to book appointments with every specialist who'd see me. An MRI confirmed I didn't have brain cancer; a battery of tests from an ENT confirmed my hearing was actually pretty good. The best advice they could give for the crippling tinnitus was to try to focus on other soft background sounds—a fan, quiet music, the hum of an HVAC system. A true mountebank of a chiropractor—who shall remain nameless to prevent me from enduring an unjustified libel lawsuit and him from enduring an entirely justified incineration of his reputation and business—insisted it was all due to a "subluxation" of my cervical vertebrae. If I paid him $1,700 I could get a major discount for six months of worthless spinal adjustments.

As weeks passed, the symptoms never got worse, but they didn't get better either. I struggled to maintain focus while working, I was too exhausted to exercise, and even reading in bed could exacerbate the light-headedness. For a good month I spent most of my leisure time binging Netflix. To the degree I did any thinking at all, I thought about whether this was going to be how the rest of my life would play out, in a state of quasi-disability and unalloyed fear.

It was about a month before I recalled the ordeals of Steve Kohlhase and Marc Polymeropoulos. Is this what it's like to be a Hum experiencer or a Havana Syndrome patient? Perhaps, except that my symptoms eventually did go away for good, leaving me relieved but still deeply perplexed about what had triggered all of this in the first place. Stress? Proximity to a gas pipeline? A directed energy weapon? In any event, call it a conversion experience, albeit one lacking the pyrotechnics of Apostle Paul's. The moral of the story: just because a strange sound might be "only in your head," it can still be real. Indeed, it can be the most dominating force in your little world. You can go anywhere you please—you will always be living within the walls of your own consciousness. That's reality for you.

And what does our reality look like after we die? Does consciousness shut off like a light bulb? Are we transported to heaven or hell? Or do our spirits somehow persist in this world? People all over the world have been telling ghost stories for millennia. Are they merely stories . . . or is there proof?

Chapter 11

SPIRITS IN THE MATERIAL WORLD

LITTLE EVIE AND UNCLE TIM

Tim Whitt died young. He was only twenty-six when he succumbed to an opioid addiction in 2021. His premature passing devastated his large family in Green, Ohio, a classic midwestern town of 27,000 just south of Akron. Tim had been living with his mother, Debra, and spent countless hours helping her care for his sister Tara's new daughter, Evelyn, better known as "Little Evie." "When I'd go to the park with Evie, he'd come with us and take her on the swing and the slide," a heartbroken Debra recalls. "He was just a big part of her life."

A few weeks after Tim's funeral, Tara started noticing something a wee bit off with Evie. She'd be in the corner, having an intense conversation with an invisible friend. When Tara asked her daughter to identify her interlocutor, she'd immediately respond, "Tim" (although, emanating from her twenty-month-old mouth, it sounded more like "Pam").

These conversations began happening so often, at such length, and with such uncanny seriousness, that Tara decided to document them. A few days later, as Evie was in her high chair, Tara recorded footage of her daughter staring intently into the vacant air a few feet in front of her. Then Evie says something that sounds awfully like the word "Uncle," repeating it over and over. "Who are you talking to?" asks Tara. To which Evie replies again, "Uncle!" while putting her finger over her mouth and telling her mother to shush.

Turning back to the empty space, she says, "Tim. Tim happy."

"Tim's happy?" asks Tara.

"Yeah."

Debra saw the video shortly thereafter and was convinced her son's spirit was in the house, talking to her granddaughter. "I was a little concerned that she was seeing Tim and interacting with him, since he's no longer here. But I feel that it's in a good way because I really feel that he's watching over her. I believe it wholeheartedly."

It's been a few years since that video was made, and Evie has since stopped having conversations out loud with her deceased uncle. But Debra remains convinced not only that the spirits of the departed remain with us, but that some young children have a preternatural ability to communicate with them. "I still think she has a connection with Tim even today. It just came out more back then because she was so young. But I think he'll be with her probably her whole life."

The Little Evie video is far from the only proffered proof of revenant spirits we've seen. A remarkable 2016 video shot at the funeral of seven-year-old Trebby Alamares in Legazpi City, the Philippines, shows one of the white balloons placed near his coffin float toward his grieving mother, Joy, seated in the center of the room. The balloon comes all the way over to her and then, rather than moving past her, it abruptly stops, rubbing up against her as if caressing her face, attempting to soothe her. Joy took it to be nothing less than the spirit of her son. "I felt that he was there to comfort me because I was really crying that night. It's like he hugged me. That's what I felt. I had goose bumps and I kept on crying out loud because I felt him, and I know that was him because he was like that when he was alive."

According to *Psychology Today*, a majority of people grieving a loss report some form of "After Death Communication" or ADC. Around a fifth of those ADCs are backed up by uncanny evidence such as sensing a death before knowing it's happened, or multiple people sharing the same experience independently.

"People believe in ghosts because ghosts are real," says author and paranormal expert Mitch Horowitz, one of our most encyclopedically informed experts on the subject: "Twenty-first-century science is reaching the conclusion that various intersections of time are almost a theoretical necessity." Horowitz is among those who point to the advancements in quantum physics and computing as the game changers here. "We're starting to gather bits of empirical evidence that things *have* to happen outside of the standard arrow of time. The data blows apart common observations of the world. We're amassing data that makes the materialist philosophy almost a fallacy. Just like Darwinism unified the fossil evidence, quantum computing will unify the paranormal." Is Horowitz's position widely accepted? Not yet, but he notes that the most vociferous resistance and "polemical skepticism" comes from social scientists, not the physicists and engineers. That suggests to him that the struggle is more cultural than intellectual, and that it's only a matter of time before general sentiment shifts. "Things are opening up in ways we couldn't have foreseen even five years ago."

Author and podcaster Alexis Brooks, another specialist in the spiritual and metaphysical who was with us at the start, was particularly moved by the Little Evie video. She believes children have a "sixth sense" and may even be able to see a spirit world that exists outside the visual spectrum. This traces to the pineal gland, a small, pinecone-shaped organ in the brain that secretes melatonin, and according to New Agers, is the biological locus of the "Third Eye" or "Alpha Chakra."

"Evie is clearly communicating with some form of intelligence," she concluded. "Babies and infants may have a broader spectrum into the invisible world." As the pineal gland atrophies with age, she says, this ability also dwindles for most people. A lucky few develop into clairvoyants.

ER physician Ed Hope doesn't think so. He points out that babies actually have worse vision than adults, seeing only black and white at first. And he believes Evie's behavior is attributable to her young age, when small kids are still developing their understanding of object permanence: "I think the most likely situation here is that Evelyn is mimicking behaviors of the family members around her going through bereavement. This is a way of Evelyn dealing with that situation." But Prof. Michio Kaku was less dismissive: "The danger here is that we impose our understanding of life and death on children. Maybe children can see another aspect of reality we cannot." We ultimately decided that while it's likely Evie was just imagining Uncle Tim there, we couldn't eliminate the possibility, however remote, that something more was going on. The family certainly believes so.

As for the Filipino balloon? Initially we were sure it was a hoax. Our miracle hunter, mechanical engineer Michael O'Neill, looked to see if there were any surface or edge effects on the balloon indicating it had been inserted digitally, but there were none, and the light source was consistent with the rest of the scene. It could have been physically manipulated, but there were no signs of any strings or wires. Wind was not a viable explanation, because Joy's hair and other objects in the room that would have also been moved by a gust of air remain motionless. And physicist Dr. Hakeem Oluseyi noted that the distance between the balloon and Joy was too great for static electricity to explain what we see. We deemed this an unexplained phenomenon. "My natural explanation would be, of course it's a fake," concluded O'Neill. "But I can't prove it. Is it somehow the soul hanging on for some extra time before going to heaven? Anything's possible."

A FRAUD IN PHOENIX

My own opinions on the matter of spirits and ghosts trend toward the skeptical, largely because of an intense experience I had in 1999. I'd come to Phoenix, Arizona, for an appointment with a well-known psychic/medium I'm going to call Roger Macedo, who claimed to be able to communicate with his clients' dead loved ones. His forty-five-minute sessions cost ninety dollars, and as I had some pressing questions only someone with Roger's gift could answer, I gladly paid. After introducing myself and taking a seat across his desk in a dimly lit, heavily cushioned office, I passed him a photo of my sister Claire and told him why I'd come.

Claire had disappeared from our family's home in Kansas City, Missouri, ten months prior. She'd stormed out after getting in a silly argument with our mother, slammed the front door, and tore out of our driveway in her Volkswagen Scirocco. She was never seen again.

I told Roger we'd done what families of the missing always do—called the police, put up posters with her picture all over town, and organized searches of nearby parks and vacant lots. Neither Claire nor the Scirocco ever turned up, despite the best efforts of the Jackson County Sheriff's scent dogs.

I'd come here because Roger had a national reputation as a spiritualist who could help desperate families locate the bodies of missing and murdered children. His first few sessions were billed at the normal rate, but he'd eventually need to go into the field to allow the spirit to guide him to the precise location, which could take days. That kind of labor-intensive endeavor would run about $500 a day, but certainly the closure it would yield was worth at least that much, was it not?

Roger listened to my story, eyes half-closed as he gently rubbed the photo of Claire lying on his desk. Then it was his turn to speak. "Miguel, I'm so glad you came to me," he intoned in a silken, effeminate voice that reminded me a bit of Paul Lynde from the original *Hollywood Squares*. "And I can tell you Claire is too. I think that for a long time you've suspected what I'm about to say to you. Miguel, your sister is no longer with us."

I choked up, putting my hands on my face. After ten seconds of silence, I gathered myself enough to inquire, "Can you tell me where she is?"

Roger's eyebrows came together. "All I see right now is that she's near water," he said. "But I can tell you she wants you to find her. And if you come back, we can reach out to her again. If she's willing to speak to me, I'll have a better sense of how we can find her together."

I left his office profoundly moved. Not because I was any closer to finding my missing sister, but because I'd gotten what I'd really come for: hidden-camera footage of a con artist plying his unholy trade.

My sister wasn't missing. She was wrapping up her senior year at Yale. And her name isn't Claire; it's Victoria. She also wasn't the girl in the picture. That person's name really *was* Claire, but she was also not missing. Claire was back in her cubicle in the New York offices of the tabloid TV show *Inside Edition*, where she was interning, and where I was spending the late nineties working as an investigative producer during the golden age of the undercover hidden camera sting. The only true thing about my story was that I really am from Kansas City, which I always said on these operations in case anyone decided to pepper me with questions about my hometown.

I'd come to Phoenix with a pair of hidden camera glasses to help out a colleague who was producing a segment on shady psychics who prey on families of missing kids, often racking up thousands of dollars in billable hours by orchestrating tantalizing but ultimately fruitless searches for their kids' corpses. This was all disclosed to Roger three weeks later, when, after scheduling a sit-down interview ostensibly to discuss his "gift," our correspondent played him the video I'd shot, held up the picture of Claire, then invited Claire to walk on set from an adjoining room and shake Roger's hand. It was a beautiful thing.

My little tale does not prove that every alleged encounter with a ghost or spirit is phony. But we need to be extremely careful with this kind of incident because so many of us who've lost loved ones are so hungry for some kind of contact with the deceased that we become highly vulnerable to professional charlatans like Roger, or just the seductions of wishful thinking. When someone close to us dies, the brutal, nonnegotiable finality of the loss can feel like an amputation. Who doesn't yearn to shoplift something out of the past, when our own Tim, Trebby, or "Claire" was alive, and take it with us as we navigate a colorless new reality in which their absence is constantly blaring like an unattended car alarm? Anyone who can feel the sorrow of mourning can feel the pull of the belief in the afterlife, and the possibility of communication between the worlds of the living and dead. That might explain some of those reported "ADCs." My point here is that ghost and spirit stories can be deep and personal and painful in a way that seeing a strange light in the sky is not. So let's proceed with caution.

A GHOST IN GETTYSBURG

The enduring and immense popularity of spiritualism in its many forms is reflected in the sprawling dimensions of the industry that has been built up around it. We've all seen psychics' storefronts in every major city offering a quick reading for a modest fee; others engage clients more like therapists, seeing them regularly over months or years. There have been countless medium TV shows, and entire cable networks have built their programming around ghost hunting content. Ghost tourism is a thriving segment of many historical landmarks where people died. To boost the industry, the National Archives Foundation even puts out its *America's Most Haunted* newsletter.

One of my favorite ghost videos was shot at America's most notoriously haunted battlefield: Gettysburg, Pennsylvania. It was the evening of September 2, 2020, and a family of tourists was driving through the historic Civil War site. As one of the kids shoots video through the car's windshield, you can hear some strange noises. Then history appears to come to life. Just as the road curves past two historic cannons a couple of humanlike silhouettes flash into the frame. One vanishes just as quickly, but the other stays in view for a full three seconds before disappearing.

The family joins a long list of witnesses who claim to have had a ghostly experience while visiting Gettysburg. An eerie energy is said to permeate the entire town as well as the battlefield itself, and accounts of apparitions are frequent at sites like the Baladerry Inn, which served as a Union Field Hospital. Strange footprints are alleged to have marked the floor of the inn, and similar paranormal encounters have been reported at the Daniel Lady Farm, where bona fide Confederate blood can be found throughout the site's buildings, and where apparitions of fallen soldiers have allegedly been seen patrolling the grounds, much like the ghostly figures by the cannons in our video.

Haunted battlefields are so common worldwide that there was a pilot for a show about the concept once, during which a decorated Afghanistan vet turned TV talent agreed to be buried alive at Picacho Peak in Arizona, the site of the westernmost engagement of the Civil War. The show did not get picked up for a series (shame, that), but it would not have lacked for material. To this day, in Japan, people still pray in a cave said to be haunted by villagers who were instructed by the Imperial Army to commit mass suicide during the battle of Okinawa. There's plenty to work with.

But our Gettysburg ghosts? They did not survive their first hostile encounter with our experts. At first, we thought the figures might be swirling columns of dirt known as dust devils, but it is a grassy area and there is no evidence of the requisite winds in the video. The tree branches and foliage aren't moving at all. Plus, the figures weren't as amorphous as your average dust devil—at one point you can make out what looks like a head and torso on the main figure. So we were willing to entertain the ghost theory enough to put our ace forensic video analyst Michael Primeau on the case. Primeau didn't find any issues with the authenticity of the recording; but using an image-processing tool called a Sobel filter that detects and enhances the edges of shapes within an image, he was able to determine that the images were recorded in front of the camera, but they were not as distant as the cannon.

What could be in the space between a camera inside a moving car and the scenery outside? The windshield of course. After adjusting the light and contrast levels, Primeau concluded that our ghosts were the remains of a dead bug, a water droplet, or a bit of tree sap. The "ghosts" were brought to life by a triple coincidence: the size of the windshield smudge against the cannon outside making them look perfectly human sized; the timing of the car being in that particular position, which illuminated the landscape just perfectly to make the smudges appear translucent; and the motion of the car as it took the curve, making it appear that the ghosts were on the move. "Together," Primeau explained, "they all paint the picture that the 'ghost' is running from this area where they once fought, and into the roadway. And that's simply not the case."

That's how the vast majority of our "caught-on-camera" ghost sightings conclude—with us determining the "spirit" was an artifact on a camera lens, window, or windshield. One story that was a little too gross to green-light involved footage of an alleged sighting of the ghoulish Canadian creature known as The Rake, also spotted through the windshield of a tourist's car. Before committing the requisite resources to produce the story we deduced that the figure's pale, translucent flesh was the result of its entire body being composed of an oddly shaped dropping of bird guano that had, like the Gettysburg ghost, caked onto the windshield. Similarly, as we've seen with highly compressed security camera footage, flaws in the camera and video processor themselves can generate spooky apparitions that materialize, then vanish. That's how we explained a "ghost" of a high school student running onto the field during a football game (it was just a kid moving so fast in low light that his image blurred).

SPIRIT PHOTOGRAPHY AND LORD COMBERMERE'S GHOST

Call me old-fashioned, but I would argue some of the most intriguing, documented ghost sightings happened decades before the invention of the digital camera, back near the turn of the twentieth century when film photography was still in its adolescence and—perhaps not coincidentally—spiritualism was very much in vogue. Mediums and their séances garnered fortune and fame inventing and then perfecting the scam that my buddy Roger tried to run on me. So-called spirit photography purporting to show caught-on-camera ghosts was in its heyday, and fraudsters like England's William Hope could make a living staging convincing fakes with tricks like double exposure, which we now recall as quaint relics from the age when Eastman Kodak dominated the photography industry.

While some of the biggest names from that era, Harry Houdini foremost among them, found the whole business fraudulent; others, like Sir Arthur Conan Doyle, took some spirit photos seriously. Sir Arthur was no dummy, so when we heard about a celebrated image he'd publicly endorsed, our interest was piqued.

The picture in question was taken in 1891 in Cheshire, England. At St. Margaret's Church, a funeral service was underway for the second Lord Combermere; meanwhile, back at his estate, a guest took a photograph of the lord's empty grand library. When the photo was developed it appeared at first to show nothing extraordinary, just a richly furnished room with towering floor-to-ceiling built-in bookshelves. But in the bottom left corner, seated in an ornate chair, is the unmistakable outline of a man who bore a striking resemblance to the recently deceased lord himself—a bald head in profile, and a torso adorned in a formal suit. The legs of the figure are mysteriously missing, which is curious, since Lord Combermere suffered a severe carriage accident that rendered him partly paralyzed and contributed to his death. Sarah Callander Beckett, the current owner of the estate, is sure it was the spirit of the dead and buried lord of the manor: "There was Lord Combermere sitting in his chair, and it really is remarkable. . . . It absolutely is him. I think the spirit was coming home to sit in a place where he would have always sat."

The photo didn't attract much public fascination until Sir Arthur referenced it in a lecture on the topic of spirit photography, later receiving a public rebuke from a Skeptic deeming it a fraud. This prompted Sir Arthur to undertake a rigorous investigation of the photo and its history. In an article he later published in the magazine *Psychic Science*, Conan Doyle eliminated—at least to his satisfaction—the possibilities that the photo was manipulated, or that someone else with a resemblance to Lord Combermere had been seated in the chair while the photo was taken. The only remaining explanation, he claimed, was that the photo truly captured "the semi-materialised simulacrum of the dead man. . . . [The] incident is the best authenticated one of the sort in the history of psychic research."

We came to a different conclusion. While Michael Primeau determined that there was no double exposure trick, he pointed out that the photo did require a very long exposure because early cameras were not very sensitive to light. Any nineteenth-century camera using such long exposure in low light would not pick up every single motion, and indeed, when French photographer Mathieu Stern re-created the Combermere photo in 2018, he was able to duplicate the "missing legs" simply by setting the camera to a long exposure and kicking his legs back and forth as he sat. That led our experts to state that the Combermere photo was an intentional fake. Elementary, Sir Arthur!

THE BARMBY PLACE SHADOW PEOPLE

A more convincing case comes from another bygone era—the age of VHS tape. (I lived through both its dawn and its sunset.) This one also happened in Great Britain, which has been called the most haunted country on earth. It was the summer of 1991 in Barmby Place, in the town of Bradford. Fifteen-year-old Adam Mawson was using a camcorder—for you millennials, that's a handheld video camera people used to make videos before smartphones—to record empty interiors of his house. Adam says he'd been noticing strange phenomena around the property; his video project was an effort to document them. Adam detailed his process for us: "I set up the video camera on a tripod in different rooms around the house where most of the activity was happening and filmed the cassettes setting on long play, as the tapes back then only lasted half an hour on short play."

Like most ghost-hunting endeavors, the vast majority of the footage shows nothing unusual. But after reviewing one recording of an empty room with a chair, Adam noticed something frightening. Out of nowhere, a shadowy figure seems to emerge from the chair. It arises and moves about the room, passing behind the doorframe before circling back, then disappearing through the wall. Moments later a second figure appears from the right and then follows the first figure's path through the wall: "I was scared to death because I thought, 'What the hell is that?' And that's when I showed my parents. And my mum said, 'Oh, yes, I've seen that before. Seen it with my own eyes.'" Adam's family says the paranormal phenomena in their house continued until the time Adam's father became a Jehovah's Witness. They believe the shadows were demonic spirits that were cast out once God entered their home.

The footage ties into the concept of "shadow people," a relatively new category of ghost that has been explored extensively in the work of Heidi Hollis, an occupational therapist and author who has appeared on radio and TV programs as a paranormal expert, including ours. Shadow people appear as dark silhouettes with humanoid shapes and profiles, and they are typically described as negative beings that harass and terrorize people in their bedrooms. Among the shadow people is an individual figure of particular malevolence known as the Hat Man, a famous urban legend who wears a dark coat and a flat-brimmed hat. He is unusually tall and menacing and is often characterized as a demonic figure, if not the devil himself. There have been enough caught-on-camera sightings of shadow people and Hat Man lurking in the background of selfies and home videos to make a decent documentary, which I watched years ago on Netflix.

But what of the shadow people captured on Adam Mawson's camcorder at the Barmby Place? Primeau determined the recording wasn't intentionally manipulated, but we suspected the scene was staged, or that something prosaic could be responsible for the shadows. The most likely possibility was that someone behind the camera, properly lit, was casting the shadows and moving in a rehearsed way to create the effect of the ghost arising from the chair and passing through the wall. That's what I expected Primeau to say, given his skeptical disposition. But he did not: "If the shadow was produced by an operator standing behind the camera, we would expect to see more of that castoff on the regions surrounding the doorway, but it's not produced there. . . . The darker regions being some sort of cast shadow is not really possible." File the Barmby ghost into the annals of the unexplained.

Alexis Brooks firmly believes that spirits can be captured on film, video, and audio recordings. She points to a celebrated study called the Scole experiments, in which two psychic couples in England conducted séances for years and claimed to document sounds and images of spirits. Their research was never peer-reviewed, their methods denounced as unscientific, but the Scole experiments remain a topic of fascination in the spiritualist community. And Brooks thinks advances in technology will yield more proof. "The introduction of digital technology has dramatically accelerated these kinds of phenomena," she says. "From my perspective there seems to be something within the electromagnetic spectrum that acts as a conduit for nonphysical intelligences. Consider the countless reports of flickering lights, radios turning on, or TVs behaving strangely—often right after the passing of a loved one."

But just because we can't explain something doesn't oblige us to stampede toward every exotic theory. And on the show, we've made a point of calling out erroneous interpretations of scientific principles used to make the case for ghosts. Take the concept of the conservation of energy. The theory goes that, as James Joule and others proved in the nineteenth century, energy cannot be created or destroyed; people can't just cease to exist after they die. We must continue on in some manner, even if our physical bodies have become forever inert.

The fatal flaw in that reasoning is that conservation of energy does *not* require energy to stay in the same form. The principle is grounded in the idea of energy *changing* form, and a dead body provides a perfect example of this energy exchange, albeit an unappetizing one: after we die, our bodies begin to decompose. The energy that was previously used for activities like locomotion and consciousness is dissipated out into the environment as gases and food that provide energy to microbes and worms. Energy is *con*served, but it is not *pre*served in one form forever. Our bodies are not closed systems. We are one with the world.

As for the Hat Man? The photos and frame grabs where the Hat Man is observed in the background are usually produced by the specific lighting of the scene, but as we saw with the Barmby ghost footage, they're not all easy to explain. The important detail in most Hat Man accounts, however, is that the encounter takes place in the bedroom, while the experiencer is in one of the intermediate stages between sleep and wakefulness. This is when so-called hypnogogic hallucinations—nonexistent visual or auditory sensations—often occur. It is also when the phenomenon of sleep paralysis takes place, when the brain wakes up before the body does and the experiencer is unable to move. The experience can be terrifying. Another popular explanation correlates Hat Man experience with taking cough medicine. Thus, the currency of the term "Benadryl Hat Man."

POLTERGEISTS

Shadow people and Hat Man are but a subset of the ghosts people report in their homes. A profusion of videos purport to document standard poltergeist activity. (Poltergeists, by the way, are traditionally defined as spirits that make noise and move stuff around, but they aren't necessarily the ghosts of deceased individuals.) Much of this material is not the product of camera artifacting or malfunction, but rather pranks of varying sophistication. Bedcovers seemingly pulling back by themselves (a magician's trick with fishing wire); coffee cups telekinetically sliding across tables (a frequent occurrence after condensation builds on the bottom of the container); peanut butter jars spinning by themselves ad infinitum in a cabinet (until you time the cycles and realize it's gradually slowing down, because someone started spinning the jar on a small ball-bearing stand before closing the cabinet, then reopening it and feigning surprise).

The closest thing we've seen to bona fide, caught-on-camera poltergeist activity happened on October 16, 2021, in the suburbs of Phoenix, Arizona. A security camera in Jason and Tara Doyle's living room was monitoring the couple's two dogs, safely crated in the foreground. The dogs are barking incessantly at some unseen presence or stimulant. Then, at twenty-two seconds into the footage, they suddenly stop in unison, almost as if listening for something. Then suddenly the collar on one of the dogs appears to unlatch itself and the animal either jumps back in fear, or, depending on whom you ask, is thrown back against the cage by some invisible force. Whatever the cause, two strange things clearly happened here: the collar came off and the dog hit the side of the crate. They both struck Jason as anomalous and disturbing: "I pulled up our home security cameras and was like, 'Wow, that's really creepy.' And then I immediately sent the video to Tara, like, 'So take a look at this honey, kind of weird.'"

Our star physicist Prof. Michio Kaku examined the footage and surmised that it was likely the collar had gotten hooked on something, connecting it to one of the latticed wires of the cage; as the dog began to move, the collar detached, further startling the dog, which then flung itself against the side of the crate.

That makes sense, but even after we enhanced the video, blew it up, and slowed it down, we didn't find any evidence of anything connecting the collar to the crate. The footage had been processed multiple times as it was first uploaded to TikTok, then put into the editing software Premiere Pro, so the image is degraded to potentially make something like a string undetectable. But even if one was there, how was it able to completely unlatch the collar, and what was going on beforehand when the dogs just froze? Whether or not one believes dogs and other animals have a "sixth sense" that enables them to detect poltergeists like they can sometimes detect incipient natural disasters or the onset of a hospice patient's death, the incident is a head scratcher.

FAMOUS REINCARNATIONS

If spirits of the dead can inhabit houses, could they not also inhabit other people's bodies and minds? Thirty-one percent of American adults surveyed by the Pew Research Center in 2021 said they believe in reincarnation, and there is academic research to support it. In the late fifties and sixties, Dr. Ian Stevenson of the University of Virginia studied reincarnation cases. He focused on children who claimed to have memories of past lives, in part because kids who hadn't yet learned how to read would have a hard time gathering and memorizing details of someone else's distant past with enough granularity to pull off a viable hoax. He found that in many cases, the young subjects denied even being the child of their present-day biological parents altogether. They insisted that their name was that of the person they'd been before. Of the three thousand cases he compiled, roughly fifteen hundred were what he termed "closed cases," meaning those in which the details of the past life could be independently verified. Even though Stevenson's evidence has been critiqued as anecdotal, that's quite a few, in both absolute and percentage terms.

We spoke to one of the more impressive past-life experiencers, a woman named Barbro Karlén, who was born in Sweden in 1954 and died in 2022. At the age of two, Barbro told us, she explained to her exasperated mother that she hadn't been responding when called by name because Barbro was not her real name. It was actually Anne Frank.

According to Barbro, her parents didn't know much about Frank's story and *The Diary of Anne Frank* was not in wide circulation in Sweden at the time, so it's not clear where she would have acquired salient details of Anne Frank's life. Nevertheless, like Anne, Barbro quickly grew into an avid writer, recording memories of a past life that often came to her in her sleep. "I woke up almost every night screaming and crying and reliving what happened to me in my past life," she told us. "I tried to explain to my mother when she comforted me and she said, it's dreams, it's not real. And I said, 'It is real. Mom, it is really real. It's like two worlds. I live in two worlds at the same time.'"

When the family visited Amsterdam shortly after Barbro turned ten, she says she knew exactly how to get to her prior home. "I said we don't need to call a taxi. I know exactly where we are and we can walk there and I led the way. I said, 'It is going to be there on the other side of the canal.' And sure enough, there it was." Once inside, Barbro says she told her mother there were missing pictures on the wall. Her mother was incredulous, but Barbro insisted they consult a tour guide. "And she said, 'Barbro, you are absolutely right. They have taken down those pictures to put them in frames, but they were there. And Anne Frank did put up those pictures. And how could you know this?' "

It's a compelling story, but the claims go even further. Dr. Walter Semkiw, who took up Dr. Stevenson's mantle after Stevenson died in 2007, says the past life experiencers typically have physical resemblances to their former selves. Stevenson claimed that some of the children he studied even had birthmarks in places where their former selves had suffered severe injuries.

We did side-by-side comparisons of young Barbro Karlén and Anne Frank, and sure, they both looked like smart and innocent teens of European descent, but beyond that I wasn't blown away by the resemblance. On the other hand, who hasn't gawked at those stunning look-alike photos of deceased people from decades, if not centuries past who look like straight up doppelgängers for some of today's biggest celebrities. Google "old photo celebrity reincarnation" right now if you haven't before, and you'll see what I'm talking about—Johnny Depp, Leonardo DiCaprio, Matthew McConaughey—they all had headshots taken back in the nineteenth century when their former selves were living in the age of the daguerreotype.

My favorite by far is an internet-famous side-by-side of Alec Baldwin and Millard Fillmore, the thirteenth president of the United States. Mr. Baldwin has never claimed to be the reincarnation of President Fillmore, though he hasn't publicly denied it either. And as we saw with Barbro Karlén's passion for writing, similar interests pass through lifetimes. Mr. Baldwin has not run for president, but he's known to be passionate about politics and was once rumored to have his eyes on a U.S. Senate seat.

Mr. Baldwin didn't respond to our interview request, but we were hungry to know if there was anything to this. So we reached out to Hoan Ton-That, the co-founder and CEO of Clearview AI, a pioneering facial recognition software company that's used by more than two thousand law enforcement agencies in the United States alone. Mr. Ton-That assured us that his platform's algorithm was impervious to differences that might throw off his competitors—dramatic loss of weight in the face, the growth of a ZZ Top–length beard, and so on.

Clearview AI generates a "distance score" between any two faces. "If this distance score is below 1.0, we put it in a 'matched' category," Mr. Ton-That explained. "Everything above 1.25 is not a match."

To our amazement, Clearview's initial test on the Baldwin/Fillmore photos came back *below* that 1.0 threshold. We were so taken aback we asked Mr. Ton-That to conduct a second test and, as he typically does in high-profile or borderline cases, he brought in a professional facial examiner. The second AI test generated a distance score of 1.04, just barely out of "match" range and into a gray zone they've designated as "similar."

"Barely above the threshold for a match," Mr. Ton-That reported in amazement "So very, very close to the line there. And that's kind of incredible."

Nevertheless, the facial recognition expert found some key differences—the lower earlobe shapes were quite different; and President Fillmore's upper lip was noticeably plumper than Mr. Baldwin's. We concluded that Mr. Baldwin and the former president were different people. Barbro Karlén's story, on the other hand, guided us to a correct but unsatisfying verdict: It's an unsolved mystery. If I'm ever reincarnated, I'll make sure to direct my future self to explain everything.

It may be argued that all of the ghostly and spiritualist phenomena trace back to a basic human trait: the fear of dying. It's deeply terrifying to think it's really all over for us and our loved ones when the reaper inevitably swings his scythe, and that fear makes us vulnerable to both self-delusion and fraud. Still, we need to acknowledge Horowitz's point that the Skeptics may be operating under some basic assumptions about time (that it only moves in one direction) and space (that the brain's object-mediated perception should always form the foundation of empirical knowledge) that may turn out to be prejudices. Even if only a tiny fraction of these reported "ghost stories" are unexplainable, they shouldn't be ignored. "It's not like esoteric or extranormal occurrences are going to be reliably summoned," says Horowitz. "But that doesn't make them any less real."

Chapter 12

CONCLUSION: SUPERHUMANS

A WAFFLE HOUSE RENDEZVOUS

How many confidential sources have I met at Waffle Houses over the years? Enough to know my order before I came within a quarter mile of a menu: the Cheesesteak Melt Hashbrown Bowl and a Diet Coke—can, never fountain—with lemon. As I pulled into the parking lot, a serene feeling of familiarity washed over me. I've been crisscrossing this country for large portions of my professional and personal life, often headed to major cities, just as often to small towns; often with a team, just as often by myself. After thirty-five years, none of it has gotten old—the rental cars, the rest stop snacks, the silent camaraderie shared with a single glance exchanged between fellow motorists at adjacent fuel pumps. I love every bit of it. This land is my land.

As I parked the Dodge Caravan I'd selected from the National Emerald Aisle and hit the door lock button on the key fob, I looked around the parking lot and did a quick inventory as the oceanic roar of the nearby interstate saturated the air: plenty of pickups, some Toyota Camrys, a Jeep. No stereotypical back window gun racks, but an abundance of trailer hitches, mud flaps, and patriotic bumper stickers. Which one belonged to my source? Typically, my Waffle House meet 'n' greets had been with cops, families of murder victims, whistleblowing employees, sometimes criminals. This one was different.

I'd come here, to the outskirts of Fayetteville, North Carolina, to rendezvous with an ex–Delta Force operative. He was part of a tight-knit and tight-lipped group with something secret to tell me, and possibly show me. I'd been instructed to call him Fred, but I had no idea if that was his real name. We were all using aliases, burner phones, and the Signal app to communicate. I wasn't Miguel Sancho from Florida; I was Ben Stencil from Bisbee, Arizona. He was Jonathan Roland, and the leader of his team, whom I'd only meet if this went well, was Sean Weaver.

I once heard Tom Wolfe say that when a journalist meets a potential source, there are only really two points that need to be made convincingly. The first is: you have an important story you need to tell. The second is: *I'm the one you need to tell it to!* Jonathan/Fred needed no convincing on the first point. The second was another matter. Fortunately, our Signal exchange had already evolved from officious to amicable. I'd alerted him and Sean to my pending arrival ten minutes earlier as I was departing the nearby Hampton Inn & Suites.

Ben Stencil: "It's on. I'll be wearing a black baseball hat."

Jonathan Roland: "I'll be in a black hoodie and jeans with a serious look on my face. Like that blue eagle from *The Muppet Show*."

Sean Weaver: "So much black. Like a couple of troubled gothic teens."

Ben Stencil: "OK, I'll bring some eye shadow."

Jonathan/Fred was already seated at a booth as I walked in, eyes to the door, black hoodie as promised. Black beard too, and plenty of tats. Mid-forties, handsome, and fit, he could have passed for a badass cousin of Tom Selleck. By the time my Cheesesteak Melt arrived, we'd broken whatever ice needed breaking and were discussing the plans for the evening. It was 8:00 pm. After this, I'd go back to the hotel and try to sleep for a few hours. At 1:00 am I'd get up and drive out to meet Fred/Jonathan and other members of the group at the property of another combat vet known as "Magic Mike."

What was Mike's magic? I was told he was a "psionic," gifted with the ability to telepathically communicate with UFOs. More than that—he'd trained himself to the point where he could now summon them. And more than *that*—he was now able to control and pilot them. Yes, his powers extended beyond telepathy to telekinesis. Tonight, sometime between the hours of 1 and 6 am, he'd be demonstrating these abilities. In short, I was about to meet a superhuman.

THE END OF LIMITS

What are the limits of human potential? Are they all truly insurmountable, or can some be transcended? The fascination with individuals possessing skills and abilities exceeding those limits has captivated mankind's attention since the dawn of civilization. The ancient Greeks had their demigods, Hercules and Achilles among them, but every culture has its own version of the trope (my idol as a kid was the legendary American railroad folk hero John Henry). Clearly, we are a species that idolizes the exceptional and strives to emulate it.

Now, more than ever, we can. Our species stands at the precipice of multiple breakthroughs that will revolutionize the human body and mind. Gene-editing technologies like CRISPR; brain-computer interfaces (BCIs) like Neuralink; and medical nanotechnology are only a few of the emergent technologies with paradigm-shifting potential. They won't just make sick people healthy; they'll make healthy people superhumans.

We're always eager to investigate documented claims of superhuman abilities on the show for the same reason I've saved this chapter for last: given the accelerating developments in this area, it is the field of unexplained phenomena in which the fewest logical contortions are required to cross over from skepticism to belief; where the incredible is quickly becoming credible; where the anomalous will soon be normal. Indeed, it could only be a matter of months after I complete this book that artificial intelligence will be doing for average thinkers what my 20/20 prescription glasses are doing right now for my crappy eyesight. This brave new near future entails vast possibility, frightening risk, and massive responsibility. "We are as gods," wrote futurist Stewart Brand, "and might as well get good at it."

THE CURIOUS CASE OF THE NORTH KOREAN SUPERSOLDIER

Perhaps some of us have gotten too good at it already. In an early episode we investigated a peculiar photo taken during the extended period of ritual mourning in the Democratic People's Republic of Korea after the 2011 death of Supreme Leader Kim Jong Il. During a three-hour funeral procession through Pyongyang, throngs of civilians and North Korean soldiers were standing in rows dozens deep to pay homage to Kim's casket as it passed by. State-run media released an overhead shot of the crowd, and despite the mandate for conformity, someone stood out, literally. In one of the rows of soldiers a man in an Army uniform towered above his comrades, almost twice as tall as everyone else. The giant was even more remarkable since in North Korea, where famine is frequent, undernourished children typically grow into undersized adults. The average male is about five foot five.

At first, we suspected this photo was part of a lengthy tradition of doctored DPRK propaganda. North Korea is famous for manipulating images to misrepresent itself as a utopian communist paradise, masking the reality of mass starvation with fake images of infinite abundance. The regime has replicated the same image of sheep within a photo of a farm to make it appear less barren and impoverished. Another photo shows identical stacks of bread loaves copied and pasted in the background of a bakery as happy workers go about the day's tasks. Why not sneak an altered image of a supersoldier into the state-produced funeral coverage?

A competing theory was that this hulking man was indeed the product of government-run scientific experimentation—that the North Korean Army had engineered a real supersoldier. The notion is not ridiculous, as genetically engineered supersoldiers could be coming soon to a battlefield near you. In 2020, then director of national intelligence John Ratcliffe wrote in a *Wall Street Journal* op-ed that China was conducting tests to create biologically enhanced soldiers with exceptional physical and cognitive abilities. The warning was reiterated in an April 2025 report by the U.S. National Security Commission on Emerging Biotechnology. "Drone warfare will seem quaint," the report said, "if we are faced with genetically enhanced PLA super-soldiers with fused human and AI."

It is a known fact that China has used CRISPR's "molecular

scissors" to cut and alter human DNA sequences in ways that are forbidden in the West. One scientist tried to use the technology to modify the embryos of twin girls so they couldn't contract HIV. North Korea is China's neighbor and de facto client state, and it has a dedicated bioweapons division within its Army. It is not absurd to speculate that the first lab-grown supersoldier could emerge from the ranks of the North Korean infantry.

What defines a supersoldier, though? Extreme pain tolerance, strength, and stamina perhaps, but not necessarily extreme height. As our military expert Tim McMillan points out, "In a ground combat situation, [a very tall soldier] is a much better target than anyone shorter than you and lower to the terrain." Plus, you can't fit into standard troop transports and bunk beds if you're eight feet tall. The ideal height for a soldier is around six-two to six-four."

So who was the oversized man in the photo? Most likely it was the North Korean basketball player Ri Myung-Hun. Ri is just as tall as the supersoldier in the photo and, as we learned from comparative photo analysis, has the same posture, shoulder slope, and head shape. Why was he in military garb? Well, after the U.S. State Department denied the seven-eight star's request to play in the NBA, North Korea honored Ri with a position in the military. Kim Jong Il was a known basketball fan, though he was not as passionate about the game as his son.

CRISPR-enhanced infantrymen may be just over the horizon, but thankfully North Korea has not taken the lead in that arms race.

CHEF SHARMA'S INVINCIBLE HANDS

"The trick is not to mind it," was G. Gordon Liddy's impressive response when asked how he kept his hand over a candle flame as his flesh burned. Pain tolerance is one thing: feeling pain but ignoring it. But is it possible to not feel the pain to begin with, and therefore have nothing to not mind? That would be a true superpower, and Abhay Sharma might possess it.

Mr. Sharma is a chef at a popular restaurant in Jaipur, India. While his fried fish and shish kabobs draw regular crowds, so do his heat-resistant hands. As Chef Sharma regularly demonstrates, he is somehow able to dip his hands into a vat of boiling cooking oil, with no gloves or mitts to protect his flesh from the scalding liquid, all the while sporting a languid smile. The feat is doubly impressive since cooking oil boils at 572 degrees Fahrenheit. How does he do it?

Neuropathy—nerve damage that often causes numbness—might explain the chef's superhuman ability, but that condition typically impacts fine motor skills. Chef Sharma's are not impaired.

Physicist Michio Kaku believes we're seeing a trick that exploits a phenomenon called the Leidenfrost Effect: "Steam is not a good conductor of heat. If I get a hot skillet and put drops of water on top of it, the water will skitter around because it's floating on a layer of steam. That's the same thing happening here. I think what we did not see is the fact that he probably put his hand in water first to get that layer of water so that when he stuck his hand inside the hot oil, the water turned to steam, and the steam protected him. That's the trick." This is the same technique used by firewalkers. They wet their feet first before stepping out onto the bed of hot coals. As long as they keep moving, the steam generated by the water prevents them from getting burned. (Though at a 2016 Tony Robbins seminar, dozens of attendees were treated for burns after they attempted a coal walk. Perhaps they didn't follow the instructions.)

It's true that Chef Sharma only puts his fingers into the boiling oil for a few seconds at a time, and the flesh on his hand does not indicate he's endured severe burns. But we never see him putting his hand in cold water first, and he's never admitted to doing so. Years of hard work may have calloused his skin to the point that it's become tougher and desensitized, but biologist Floyd Hayes concluded this is a bona fide case of something called acquired pain immunity, in which some bodies can become accustomed to the pain and adapt to it. This has been documented by no less an authority than Charles Darwin, who visited Tierra del Fuego on the southern tip of South America during his famous 1831 voyage. There he noted that the indigenous Yahgan people were able to wear very little clothing despite the ice-cold climate; they even swam regularly in the frigid waters. It is believed that over time they'd evolved higher metabolisms that generated more body heat than the average human.

Another noted case was that of Jewish writer Jack Schwarz, who was captured by the Nazis and transported from his native Holland to the Sachsenhausen concentration camp, where he survived torture and other horrors. He later claimed in his talks and books that he was able to control and regulate the pain inflicted upon him through prayer and meditation. Schwarz would demonstrate his technique by pushing a needle through his arm to the amazement of his audience. He later immigrated to the United States and founded the Aletheia Psycho-Physical Foundation, a New Age healing and spiritual center in Oregon.

We may all soon live in a world without pain, or at least with less of it, thanks to nanoparticle-mediated drug delivery. Recent research in lab rats demonstrated that a specially designed nanoparticle successfully delivered a key pain receptor antagonist, inhibiting the activation of spinal neurons and thus preventing pain transmission. The goal is to develop a safe, non-opioid treatment for chronic pain.

But Chef Sharma's case is cause for even greater optimism. We concluded that there wasn't enough evidence to go with the Leidenfrost Effect explanation, and agreed with Professor Hayes that the chef has attained some measure of acquired pain immunity. The case suggests that such an ability is not a "superhuman" gift, but rather something anyone can achieve. That was Schwarz's lesson from the concentration camp—that the degree to which we are sensitive or numb to physical pain is something we all can control. Perhaps there's a lesson there.

THE SPIDERMAN OF PARIS

Mamadou Gassama was an unlikely hero, if for no other reason than it was in his interest not to attract notice. In 2018, Mamadou immigrated from his native Mali to France without documentation. The government's appetite for deportation ebbs and flows with the election cycles, but it's generally advisable for folks like him to keep a low profile on the streets of Paris.

Nevertheless, on May 26, 2018, Gassama sprang into action when he saw a small child dangling from a fourth-story balcony in the 18th Arrondissement. While a crowd gathered to gawk, Gassama began scaling the outside of the building, launching his body to grab the rails of the tiered balconies until he was able to pull the child to safety before the boy's grip gave way. For his heroism, Gassama was awarded French citizenship and, as the incident made international headlines, duly allotted his fifteen minutes of fame.

Scaling buildings without any safety gear, also known as free solo climbing, has been going on for decades. Frenchman Alain

Robert is known worldwide for his conquests of iconic landmarks and skyscrapers. But this was different. Mamadou has a slim, athletic build, so sure, it's not as amazing as if Dom DeLuise had saved the day like this. But free solo climbing requires extensive training and preparation. Gassama had none. So how did he instantly acquire such an exceptional ability?

"Hysterical strength" is the term often applied to cases where, in life-or-death situations, some people have a momentary surge of extra muscular power. The most common cases involve people lifting vehicles off loved ones pinned underneath after an accident or the collapse of a defective tire jack. One such case is said to have inspired the *Incredible Hulk* comic. These surges are attributed to a rush of adrenaline flowing into the blood, and indeed in interviews, Gassama confirmed that after completing the rescue he was shaking, a typical symptom of an adrenaline rush.

But while it's easy to understand how a mother might risk her life to save her child, we still need to explain why Gassama risked his for a total stranger without hesitation while all the other witnesses on the street did little but watch. Here it was not superhuman strength or agility at play, but a trait sometimes referred to as "superaltruism," which drives certain individuals to make extreme sacrifices for others or a cause they believe in deeply. The instinct is activated most strongly when the emergency involves lives of the most vulnerable, such as children.

The great sociobiologist E. O. Wilson wrote that altruism is an example of social adaptation. A tribe in which individuals—or at least some of them—have a genetic predisposition to sacrifice for others will, over thousands of years, enjoy a reproductive advantage over one in which everyone is only out for themselves. As we saw in the first chapter, Wilson thinks this helps explain the enduring popularity of religion. Perhaps Mamadou's genome was coded for extreme altruism the way others are genetically destined to be extremely tall or extremely smart. In any event, his explanation aligned with Wilson's—he said his faith in God provided both the courage and the strength.

In the end, we said it was a combination of all three—his faith motivated the act of superaltruism; his physique enabled him to initiate the daring climb with no experience, and the shot of adrenaline gave him a boost of hysterical strength to complete it. Heroism, sadly, remains an anomalous phenomenon, but while it may be hard to explain, it's easy to recognize and celebrate.

PSIONICS AND THE FUTURE OF ESP

So, what happened with Fred, Magic Mike, and "psionics" who can summon UFOs through the power of the mind? Over the course of two uncomfortably chilly nights in Mike's backyard outside Fayetteville, I observed the group as they scanned the skies with impressive night vision goggles. They spotted several lights crossing the sky, but they all moved as planes or satellites might. To the crew's credit, they didn't oversell anything they saw those nights, but between sightings, they regaled me with stories of prior close encounters, none of which had been documented convincingly. I kept an open mind, listened respectfully, and thanked them profusely for their military service. I departed North Carolina having successfully laid the groundwork for a professional relationship, but I remained doubtful that Magic Mike or anyone else in this group had been blessed with—or trained to acquire—any kind of superhuman "psionic" ability.

But what do I know? Months later, I'd finally meet the elusive

Sean Weaver and learn that his real name was Jake Barber. He would become one of the Parade of Whistleblowers described in Chapter 3, and the first to come forward about working with the U.S. military retrieving downed UFOs. Like David Grusch and Lue Elizondo before him, Barber told his story with poise and conviction. The "psionic" piece of it was central to his narrative, and it remains so. Barber, Baker, and other respected vets are now part of an enterprise called Skywatcher, which is soliciting investment capital to replicate in the private sector what they claim the government has been doing for decades: summoning, documenting, and communicating with UFOs. Esteemed scientists like Stanford immunologist Dr. Garry Nolan take Barber's claims seriously, so perhaps we all should.

While the integration of psychic ability into the UFO question is relatively new, telepathy or ESP has been the subject of intense popular interest and scholarly research for decades. The field of parapsychology was founded back in the 1930s by J. B. Rhine at no less prestigious a university than Duke. Rhine's lab work centered around subjects guessing shapes printed on cards (now known as Zener cards), and some of the results deviated far enough from what you'd expect from random guessing that they lent credence to the ESP hypothesis. Rhine's results have never been duplicated, and Skeptics have picked apart his methods, but according to author Mitch Horowitz, the science was done "impeccably . . . far surpassing some of the vast but frequently overturned research published in the social sciences."

At Princeton, Prof. Robert Jahn ran PEAR—the Princeton Engineering Anomalies Research lab—from 1979 to 2007. Jahn's work focused on what we'd call telekinesis, the ability of the human mind to influence the output of random number generators. The results were questionable enough that after Jahn retired there was not enough institutional support and private funding to keep PEAR going. But the work is still being pursued by organizations like the Global Consciousness Project. The GCP maintains and monitors a network of random number generators around the world. During periods of peak global emotional intensity, most famously 9/11, the GCP has detected deviations in the randomness, patterns in the numbers that, they claim, would be extremely unlikely to be generated purely by chance. "When a great event synchronizes the feelings of millions of people," the GCP website reads, "the evidence suggests an emerging noosphere of the unifying field of consciousness described by sages in all cultures."

The government has invested in ESP as well. From 1972 to 1995 the DIA's legendary Project Stargate poured millions into studies and applications of "remote viewing" (the preferred Pentagon euphemism for clairvoyance) for intelligence gathering and espionage. The CIA terminated the program after concluding that there was insufficient evidence the program was generating consistent, actionable intelligence of any value. But as I noted earlier, people like Lue Elizondo, who claims to be a remote viewer himself, say that while Stargate may have "officially" shut down, the practice of remote viewing is alive and well within the U.S. military. Mitch Horowitz agrees: "It's a cultural misnomer that Stargate was a bust. Saying so requires a purposeful misreading of the data." Horowitz points out that President Jimmy Carter even acknowledged the program worked in an interview with *GQ*, disclosing that a female remote viewer had helped the CIA locate a downed airplane in Zaire.

The conversation around ESP continues to evolve with every new challenge to the materialist model. As I'm writing in 2025, everybody is talking about *The Telepathy Tapes*, a popular podcast exploring accounts of severely autistic kids, most nonspeaking, whose families have long claimed to have seen them perform telepathic functions. The podcast documents demonstrations with some of these kids, and the results are startling. Dr. Jeff Tarrant, a licensed psychologist, was part of the project team and helped collect its data. He writes in *Psychology Today*: "I have personally observed five nonspeaking autistic individuals consistently achieve near-perfect accuracy on telepathy-based tasks involving randomly selected words and numbers. . . . While preliminary in nature, the remarkable consistency and accuracy observed across multiple individuals strongly suggest that the results cannot be easily explained by chance or conventional mechanisms alone."

Skeptics like our own Mick West point out that psychic powers are of a different order than superhuman strength or pain tolerance. Those involve extreme capabilities in known physical traits or biological function. Psychic powers require us to jettison a purely materialist understanding of the universe, as by definition they defy the basic principles of physics and chemistry.

Or do they? Horowitz returns to the latest research in quantum physics I touched upon earlier. He's especially stimulated by the recent news that Google's quantum chip Willow needed only five minutes to solve a math problem so complicated it would have required today's supercomputers longer than the age of the universe. The results have prompted some, Horowitz included, to suggest that Willow plucked the answer from other dimensions in a vast multiverse.

"The Skeptics may have won culturally," he says, "but they're losing intellectually. Their conviction is we live in a world of chemical compounds, and consciousness is just an epiphenomenon from this squishy machine of the brain. But they are just as susceptible to confirmation bias as the Believers they attack. They just don't admit it.

"Bottom line: you can be a critical Believer, and you can be an ideological Skeptic."

THE LEGEND OF JETPACK MAN

The cockpit audio is so bizarre, it's hard to take seriously.

> **Pilot:** "Tower, American 1997. We just passed a guy in a jetpack."
>
> **Air Traffic Control:** "American 1997, OK. . . . Thank you. Were they off to your left side or right side?"
>
> **Pilot:** "Off the left side, maybe three hundred yards or so, about our altitude."

The sighting is just one of several reported by airline pilots since 2020, who say that upon initiating their final approach to Los Angeles International Airport, they spotted a solitary guy in a jetpack cruising close to their flight path.

On its face it sounds impossible: jetpack technology has been around since the sixties, and though they've evolved considerably in recent years, most models—even those with turbo engines—can only stay aloft for ten minutes max. Plus, it's unheard of to fly one at the same altitude as approaching jetliners—between three thousand and six thousand feet. The prototype of a jetpack developed by New Zealand–based Martin Aircraft is reportedly capable of flying close to three thousand feet, hitting speeds of 46 miles an hour, and can stay aloft for thirty minutes. But it weighs more than 440 pounds without fuel or a pilot; and its configuration looks nothing like what has been spotted over Los Angeles.

Yet the reports kept trickling in, and when a local flight instructor recorded video of her own encounter with "Jetpack Man" three thousand feet above the Palos Verdes peninsula, the story went from aviation chat group rumor to Class A urban legend. Local news stations jumped on the story, and the FAA called in the FBI to investigate.

The instructor's video is peculiar. You can see what appear to be legs dangling below a torso—and at one point a reflection off something metallic, like a backpack. It evokes images of astronauts on spacewalks, but strangely there's no sign of exhaust.

The usual theories emerged, including speculation that it was secret military technology being tested by one of the giant defense contractors. The common flaw in those theories—which pop up frequently—is that, as noted earlier, secret military tech is typically tested at secret military test sites like White Sands Missile Range or Area 51. The whole point is for neither the public nor our enemies to see it, so why would the military repeatedly test an Iron Man–type flying suit near LAX, where it's highly likely to be observed by passing air traffic? Top-secret weapons programs do not engage in such exhibitionism.

The hypothesis I find most magnetic—and sufficiently inspiring to end this little book—involves neither aliens, conspiracies, nor other dimensions. It's the idea that Jetpack Man is an amateur backyard inventor, perhaps a modern-day Howard Hughes manque, who has designed a breakthrough flying technology but is so reclusive he (or she) doesn't want to reveal themself yet. Shy and humble, yet brilliant, driven, and fearless, Jetpack Man toils in his garage working out the kinks on his machine, only occasionally taking it out for test flights along the Southern California coast.

Silly, absurd, fantastic. Yes, the theory is all of the above. It would not be worth a moment's consideration, except for the fact that human beings are notably prone to pursue silly, absurd, and fantastic ideas all the time, even at their own peril. Franz Reichelt, a tailor by trade, spent years slaving away in his Paris apartment designing a "parachute-suit" to help pilots survive crashes in the high-risk years of aviation's infancy. He devoted his life to his invention.

Then he sacrificed it. On February 4, 1912, with an assembled crowd gathered around him, Reichelt jumped from the first deck of the Eiffel Tower to demonstrate his latest model as cameras rolled. The parachute failed to deploy and Reichelt died instantly on impact.

More recently, and less tragically, a gas station owner in Oregon named Kent Couch attached 104 large helium balloons to a lawn chair and flew nearly two hundred miles across the state, drawing international attention and a $4,500 fine from the FAA. And who could forget James Jarrett Miller—aka "the Fan Man"—who flew his powered paraglider into the ring at Ceasar's Palace during the seventh round of the heavyweight title fight between Riddick Bowe and Evander Holyfield in 1993?

I submit that it is the spirit of Jetpack Man that has compelled *both* history's great innovators from the Wright brothers to Steve Jobs; *and* the UFOlogists out in the desert tonight scanning for Tic Tacs with night vision goggles, the Bigfoot hunters getting eaten alive by mosquitoes as they swap batteries in their deep woods trail cams, and the pilgrims flocking to see the latest apparition of the

Virgin Mary, perhaps on a bank window or a barn door. Pascal's God-shaped hole is, in essence, the need to believe that there will always be something better, something bigger, something more to be felt, understood, and achieved, than what our daily experience provides. The search for this "something more" is how a lot of time and effort gets wasted. It is also how progress is made.

And what prodigious progress there has been! My father-in-law, Howard, died in 2013 at the age of ninety-five, not bad for a guy who turned ten before penicillin was discovered. When Howard was born in West Virginia less than 20 percent of this country's population was connected to indoor plumbing. When he died in Chicago, less than 20 percent was *not* connected to the internet. In between, he witnessed the proliferation of the automobile, commercial air travel, and plastics; the dawn of the atomic age, television, the space age, the personal computer, the internet, social media, genomics, and a million other things I can't think of at the moment.

Howard saw much more than an avalanche of new gadgets and gizmos. He saw the world around him getting dramatically better. Despite the perpetual catastrophizing of our news media, things are improving. Extreme poverty and hunger have plummeted while literacy has skyrocketed. Violent death is trending down; life expectancy is trending up. Clean energy is getting cheaper; being a racist, sexist, or homophobic asshole is getting more expensive. Plus, we've figured out quite a bit, though certainly not everything, about the nature of the universe, from distant supernovas to subatomic quarks. And along the way we're cranked out some impressive art, music, and literature. For a species that's only been around for three hundred thousand years—roughly .0002 percent of the age of the universe—we're permitted to take a bow.

Sigmund Freud wrote that humanity has suffered three great humiliations: the Copernican revelation that we do not live in the center of the universe; the Darwinian discovery that we are part of an evolutionary chain that includes all the other animals; and the Freudian insight that the unconscious governs much of our own thinking and decisions. In other words, we hold no place of superiority or mastery in the cosmos, on the Earth, or even in our own minds.

Point taken. But the more we look around, the more justification we have to feel kind of special. Those massive radio telescopes of the Very Large Array keep looking for signs of extraterrestrial life, and while some of the potential technosignatures they've detected look promising, after sixty years of diligent intergalactic searching we've found nothing to dispel the hypothesis that, despite the astronomically small odds that we're alone, the evidence so far indicates that is indeed the case. Regardless of what we may want to believe, any sober assessment of the facts has to accommodate the possibility that *human beings may be the universe's ultimate anomaly*. And even if we choose to accept all the arguments of the UFOlogists and believe another highly evolved intelligent species has traveled here, possibly through other dimensions, to observe and potentially contact us, that means we've accomplished enough to be at least worthy of such an advanced civilization's attention. The spirit of Jetpack Man is the reason why.

What became of Jetpack Man himself? The FBI never identified anyone responsible for the encounters, but in November 2021 it floated the theory that pilots had seen balloons. The day prior to the announcement, the LAPD released video one of its helicopter crews had recorded of a life-sized inflatable Jack Skellington, the main character from *The Nightmare before Christmas*, drifting by the chopper.

But hold on. The figure in the video shot by the flight instructor looks nothing like the Jack Skellington balloon. What's more, Jetpack Man's velocity and horizontal motion documented in the instructor video would require very strong winds if the figure was merely a balloon; far greater than the mild ten knots breezing over Palos Verdes that day, per our meteorologist's research.

You are fully permitted to conclude it was all an elaborate prank, perhaps a variety of different humanoid balloons attached to drones (though you'd still have to explain why the prankster would risk criminal charges flying a drone above the FAA's four-hundred-foot altitude ceiling).

You also have permission to think otherwise. Or to hold more than one opinion at once. Those quantum computing folks invite us, maybe require us, to see the universe through a nonbinary lens. They tell us there are more positions than one and zero, true and false; just as there are more things in heaven and earth than dreamt of in Horatio's philosophy.

Surrendering to the uncertainty, optimistic about the unknown, and perhaps with a bit of a wink, we concluded that Jetpack Man was a human using as-yet-unknown technology. If wonderment can be a religion, consider us faithful practitioners. May Jetpack Man fly on, an Icarus whose wings will never melt. Forever upward. Forever forward. Amen.

ACKNOWLEDGMENTS

I've made enough attempts at publicly thanking people to know that any such effort should always begin with an apology to those who might be left out. Please accept my regrets, and take solace in the fact that you are not alone. I owe you a smoothie.

Since the book would not exist without the television show that inspired it, I should first thank the people who brought that show into existence. They include HISTORY® network's Mike Stiller and Eli Lehrer, and A+E Global Media™'s Rob Sharenow. At A+E Factual Studios, Matt Pearl, Steven Mintz, Steve Ascher, Kristy Sabat, Sharon Scott, and Jhamal Robinson have been loyal champions of both me and the show. It's been an honor to work with them. And, of course, I'd like to give a special shout-out to our host, Tony Harris, who has been a tremendous partner and friend from the moment of our first phone conversation to the wrap of our most recent shoot.

This project would not have been possible without the support and precious input from the team at Atria / Simon & Schuster: my editor Nick Ciani, Abby Mohr, Mark LaFlaur, Alison Hinchcliffe, and Erin Kibbe. Luke Janklow and Claire Dippel at Janklow &

Nesbit are also due immense gratitude for believing in and encouraging an upstart author like me from the start.

The staff of *The Proof Is Out There*® series is too large to name everyone who has come and gone over the years, but I want to give a special thanks to a few people who were there at the show's inception, including Holly Durgan, Ted Kim, Joe Gabriel, and Bob Winters. It is no small feat to create something out of nothing, and they were there to work through that arduous process of trial and error. Others who have been integral to the show's success over the years and also had a direct hand in the book include Marley Jaeger, Brian Prowse-Gany, Ashley George, Chrystal Conley, Genevieve Wong, and Oscar Tubke-Davidson.

Many of the experts featured in the book also merit mention, as over the years they have become both teachers and friends. They include Mark D'Antonio, Tim McMillan, Mick West, Michael Primeau, Matthew Szydagis, Cliff Barackman, Shea Steingass, Rich Hoffman, and MJ Banias.

Finally, a universal hat-tip to all the wild and fascinating explorers and experiencers who have shared their stories and footage with us, knowing that we might disagree with their conclusions. We would be nothing without you. Keep searching, keep pushing, and, by all means . . . KEEP THOSE CAMERAS ROLLING!

INDEX

ABOUT THE AUTHOR

Miguel Sancho is an Emmy Award–winning television producer and author. A veteran of ABC News and CBS News, he is the founder and president of Asymmetric Media, which develops and produces specials and series for clients including A+E Global Media™ and Nexstar. His first book, *More Than You Can Handle*, examined the impact of rare disease diagnoses on families and the breakthrough medicine that is developing new cures. He lives in Florida with his two children, Lydia and Sebastian.